MW00904404

Out
of the
Ashes

My Journey from Tragedy to Redemption

Elizabeth Fahn-Weedor

WESTBOW·
PRESS
A DIVISION OF THOMAS NELSON
& ZONDERVAN

WestBow Press books may be ordered through booksellers or by contacting:

WestBow Press
A Division of Thomas Nelson & Zondervan
1663 Liberty Drive
Bloomington, IN 47403
www.westbowpress.com
1 (866) 928-1240

ISBN: 978-1-4908-4786-3 (sc)
ISBN: 978-1-4908-4787-0 (hc)
ISBN: 978-1-4908-4788-7 (e)

Library of Congress Control Number: 2014915671

Printed in the United States of America.

WestBow Press rev. date: 10/07/2014

CONTENTS

Maps..vii

Foreword xiii

Acknowledgments xvii

About the Author.. xix

Endorsements.. xxi

Dedication..xxiii

Introduction...xxv

PART I: FAMILY 1

Chapter 1:   A Village Childhood................................ 3

Chapter 2:   Ancestor Worship 15

Chapter 3:   Customs and Daily Life in Liberia...................... 21

Chapter 4:   A New Life 29

Chapter 5:   Betrayed By God?.............................. 41

Chapter 6:   The One-Way House 50

Chapter 7:   The Trials of Courtship......................... 58

Chapter 8:   The Naming Ceremony 66

Chapter 9:   A Wedding 75

Chapter 10:   The White Sheet 83

Chapter 11:   The Rain Begins to Fall.......................... 91

Chapter 12:   A Bundle of Joy 101

PART II: WAR 123

Chapter 13: Shackles of the Past 125
Chapter 14: Tubman and Tolbert....................................137
Chapter 15: New Leadership 148
Chapter 16: Samuel Doe, America's New Friend 1980-1989 156
Chapter 17: The Gathering Storm 165
Chapter 18: Anniversary Nightmare................................173
Chapter 19: Rebels on Holy Ground................................180
Chapter 20: By The Creek of Soul Clinic...........................197
Chapter 21: A Journey for Life 213
Chapter 22: The Hiding Place..220
Chapter 23: Marines Aboard Their Ships 229
Chapter 24: Unexpected Journeys 243
Chapter 25: Akouedo Village: Ministry in Exile 259
Chapter 26: A New Country on a New Continent 265

Epilogue 287
Abbreviations and Important Terms 295
For Further Reading...299

MAPS

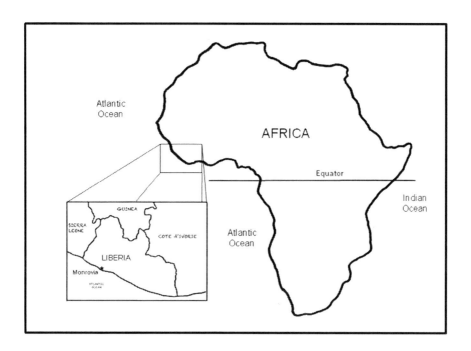

*Liberia and its African neighbors**

* all maps have been hand-drawn by Mr. Gary Baughman

Liberia

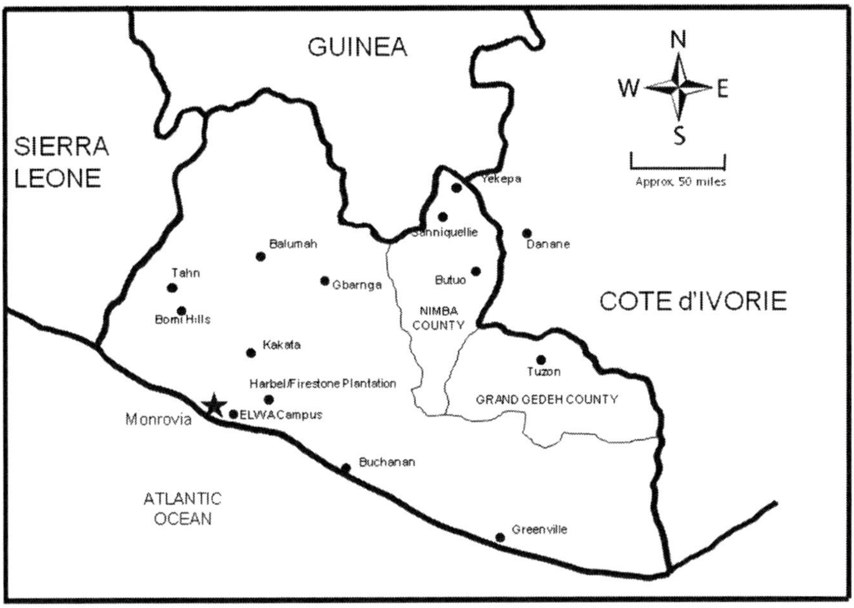

towns and cities mentioned in this book

Monrovia, Liberia

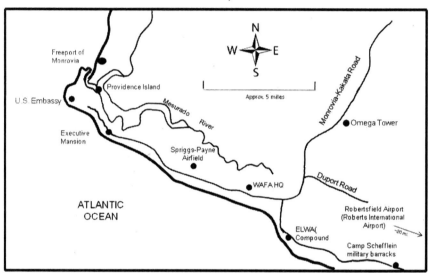

strategic locations in Monrovia that have been mentioned in this book

The "Exodus"

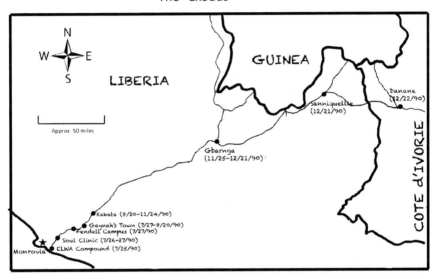

our long journey from the ELWA campus to the Ivory Coast

FOREWORD

When I met Elizabeth "Beth" Fahn-Weedor and Tony Weedor in 1993, I knew nothing about Liberia and little about Africa in general. But Tony was now my student at Denver Seminary. I remember vividly my first talk with him in my office. He said he was from Liberia. Having never heard of the nation, I said, "Did you say Libya?" He then patiently began to tell me his story and the story of his war-ravaged land. I was fascinated and startled as Tony spoke of some of the atrocities of the Civil War and of his family's exile and immigration to America. The Weedors have been my very close friends ever since. Without them, I would likely have never learned of the horrors and hopes of Liberia, a nation founded by freed American slaves. Ironically, most Americans share my initial ignorance of his country. Out of the Ashes will change that.

Over our years of friendship, I picked up bits and pieces, here and there, about Beth and Tony's life in Liberia. I knew that Beth had carried baby Abigail on her back for years while they were fleeing for their lives, and that this had caused her permanent back problems. Tony spoke of being separated from his wife and daughter for a while during the Civil War. But these revelations were never poured out to impress anyone or to solicit sympathy. Moreover, Tony and I usually talked more about philosophy, theology, politics, and missions than we did about his family's time in Liberia. Yet I knew this was an extraordinary story—a story that the world needed to know. So, over a few years I (and I am sure others) encouraged Beth to write a book about her life.

Now, some years later, I am gratified and deeply impressed to read *Out of the Ashes*. This one-of-kind book is, at once, a modestly and honestly written autobiography; a spiritual memoir; a discourse on Liberian culture, politics, and history; and it is a Christian reflection on evil, suffering, and the Christian hope found only through the redemptive work of the Lord Jesus Christ. Beth's story never bogs down into irrelevant personal details. All that she narrates is significant and deeply emotional. This drama was real. Yet along the way, the careful reader will learn a wealth of facts concerning history, Beth's rugged Christian faith, and the ways of God in a world of suffering.

Americans in particular need to listen to the desperate laments of those far from our luxuries and safety, our stable civil government, and our sense of entitlement. American Christians in particular seldom develop a theology of suffering or plumb the depths of Scriptural teaching on living with hope and wisdom "under the sun," when life seems impossible and beyond our ability to withstand its torments. As Solomon wrote long ago:

> I returned and saw under the sun that—
> The race is not to the swift,
> Nor the battle to the strong,
> Nor bread to the wise,
> Nor riches to men of understanding,
> Nor favor to men of skill;
> But time and chance happen to them all.
> For man also does not know his time:
> Like fish taken in a cruel net,
> Like birds caught in a snare,
> So the sons of men are snared in an evil time,
> When it falls suddenly upon them (Ecclesiastes 9:11-12, New King James Version).

This is what Beth Weedor (as well as so many other Liberians) experienced: injustice, cruel and senseless death, and the anguished puzzlement over the meaning of it all. Such is life "under the sun"—that is, life in a fallen world that is still yearning for its full redemption. Yet, because of the achievements of Jesus Christ, the Apostle Paul heartens us with these truthful words of hope:

> I consider that our present sufferings are not worth comparing with the glory that will be revealed in us. For the creation waits in eager expectation for the children of God to be revealed. For the creation was subjected to frustration, not by its own choice, but by the will of the one who subjected it, in hope that the creation itself will be liberated from its bondage to decay and brought into the freedom and glory of the children of God.

We know that the whole creation has been groaning as in the pains of childbirth right up to the present time. Not only so, but we ourselves, who have the first fruits of the Spirit, groan inwardly as we wait eagerly for our adoption to sonship, the redemption of our bodies (Romans 8:18-23).

It is the knowledge of these divinely-revealed truths that kept Beth Weedor and her husband from giving up in the midst of "man's inhumanity to man" as manifested in the Liberian civil war. May this book lead many to embrace the same Jesus Christ that sustained, inspired, and suffered with Beth Weedor. And may God renew and restore the great and deeply wounded nation of Liberia.

Douglas Groothuis is Professor of Philosophy at Denver Seminary and the author of Christian Apologetics *(InterVarsity Press, 2011).*

ACKNOWLEDGMENTS

Thanks to all who encouraged me along the way in fulfilling my dream of writing this book. Thanks, too, to the many who reached out to us during the most difficult times of our lives, especially when we first entered the United States. My grateful thanks are also due to my kindergarten and elementary school teacher, Mr. Philip Nyennetu, who forsook his city life and came to my home village and taught me how to read and write; to Dr. Wes Howard and his beloved wife, Jackie, who made the publishing of this book possible.

A special thanks to Kathy Bergman who spent countless hours editing my manuscript. Thanks to Pastor Jim Walters of Bear Valley Church for reading my manuscript and for your helpful advice. Grateful thanks to Dr. James Keaden at the University of Northern Colorado, Gordon Derber, and Gary and Linda Grauberger, for your many encouragements to me in writing this book.

Huge thanks to Dr. and Mrs. Larry Tiedje, who gave us a shoulder to cry on when we desperately needed one. Your endless support and generosity have helped bring us thus far, and we will forever be grateful! Les and Verla Unruh, Ron and Pauline Sonius, Gary and Karen Mitchell, Jim and Jean Adkins, Elroy and Debbie Thieszen, Allen and Mercedes Green, Dan and Caroline Lamb: thanks for accepting us as your children and for opening up your hearts and homes to us. We appreciate your continued supports and love over the years. Thanks especially to Dad Unruh for leading me to salvation and the saving knowledge of Jesus Christ.

I am thankful to Sylvia and the late Ed Copps from Bear Valley Church who led us from Stapleton airport through the streets of Denver to a fully furnished campus housing apartment at the Denver Seminary, and to the leadership team of Bear Valley Church for making this possible. Thanks to the late Willis Mouttet and his wife, Sue; Roger and Sheryl Shoop; and all our friends at Bear Valley Church. To Dr. Bentley and Sandy Tate, Dr. Phil and Julie Parshall, David and Dr. Vicki Andrea, and Martin and Karen Flaming for your continued ministry support and partnerships with us. Thanks also to Judi Jay, for your inspiring spiritual intervention on behalf of our baby, Abigail. Thanks to Gary Baughman for your wonderful work of editing my book and putting together all the maps needed to give readers a better idea of Liberia's road maps, cities, and its African neighbors. I couldn't have done this without you. My sincere appreciation to Grainne McDonald, for your wonderful work done in putting the finishing touches on this book. My heartfelt thanks goes to my editor, Andrew Needham, who did the heavy lifting of bringing this book to completion, and whose editorial comments and analytical arrangements have helped keep me on track to best share my story.

To all my children, who sacrificially allowed me the time away from you and home to write this book: thanks for your understanding and your tremendous love and support for me. I could not have done it without you. Alieya Leechelle, thanks for tirelessly reading and re-reading my manuscript and for the helpful feedback and suggestions you gave me. To my wonderful husband, Anthony Weedor, for all the sleepless nights I have cost you. Thanks for your loving and forgiving spirit. You are a great team player and have taught me so much. I love you with all my heart!

About the Author

Elizabeth Fahn-Weedor is a speaker and missionary serving with Advancing Native Missions, located in Afton, Virginia. She was born in Liberia into a Muslim family, but became a Christian through the influence of a missionary. Elizabeth attended Denver Seminary and later served for four and a half years in Ethiopia with the missionary organization Serving In Missions (SIM).

Elizabeth is married to Anthony Weedor, with four beautiful children. Because of their dedication and remarkable work in missions, they were awarded the Conway/Maxwell Memorial Missions award at Denver Seminary.

Her first article, "The Changing Face of SIM," was published in the mission's Intercom in issue 158, July–August of 2002. From Elizabeth's professional background, she is now an effective advocate for women who have been victims of sexual harassment and abuse, human trafficking, HIV/AIDS, and female genital mutilation. Elizabeth desires to dedicate her life to speaking for those who are voiceless.

ENDORSEMENTS

Out of the Ashes is a book that will shake, horrify, and inspire you. Elizabeth doesn't have to worry about going to Hell—she's been there and back! She will take you across Africa, strengthen your faith, and remind you of how powerful our God is.

—Jim Walters
Senior Pastor
Bear Valley Church

This is an inspiring book that speaks to all people who find themselves in life's turmoil. It is a page-turner. Elizabeth takes you into the trenches of desperation, human depravity, and unimaginable evil—into the comfort and hope of God.

—Bo Barredo
Co-founder and President, Advancing Native Missions

A spell-binding story of Elizabeth's survival from the evil of human powers, mass murder, and atrocity by those sold into sin. By all means, get this book, and I promise that you will be unable to put it down.

—Jim Means, PhD
Former Chairman of Pastoral Ministry and
Leadership at Denver Seminary

DEDICATION

This book is dedicated in loving memory of my dearest father, Sando Goliah Fahn, who departed this life before the completion of it. Thanks so much, Papay, for your love and the many positive ways you have impacted my life—not to mention your incredible sense of humor that shall remain in the memories of my family forever!

To my baby brother, Philip "Tapla" Siafa Fahn, who left this life in the middle of the civil war. Leaving us at a very young age has left a void in our lives, but your uplifting smile will never be forgotten. To my mother in-law, Gbejoe Manifa Weedor, we miss you so much and you'll forever remain in our hearts.

Also to the thousands of Liberians, friends and family, who lost their lives as the result of the civil war. To the five American nuns and the American missionary couple, Mr. and Mrs. Jackson, who were killed in Liberia. May the seeds you sowed for Christ continue to grow in the lives of the Liberian people you faithfully served.

To my four wonderful children, the most precious gifts from God: Abigail Joy, Alieya Leechelle, Antoinette Pauline, and Anthony Larry "T. J."; and to our son-in-law, Cody Kenneth Mylander, I dedicate this book to you. All of you helped and inspired me to tell my story to the rest of the world.

My dearest grandmother, Maima Kai, you stood courageously against our male-dominated culture to give me an education resulting in who I am today. And to my beloved and wonderful mother, Kpannah Sando Fahn, whose unconditional love for me has shaped my life.

To my darling and loving husband, Anthony Weedor, who is my greatest cheerleader and my soul mate, and who has encouraged me throughout the process of writing this book.

To my Lord Jesus Christ, above all others. I dedicate this book to You. It is Your story as well, not mine alone. Use it and bring glory to Your Name forever.

INTRODUCTION

I arrived into this world on a hot African summer day in 1966. My voice was silent until my grandmother, Maima Kai, who was also the midwife at my birth, slapped my back to clear the fluid from my lungs. Her effort was rewarded with a few loud cries followed by more silence. According to Ma, I laid on the bed with my eyes wide open, looking around curiously as if wondering why anyone would slap such a beautiful baby! I was also a large, chubby baby with bright eyes and lots of black hair, the color of tar. All of the women who attended my birth laughed when they observed my inquisitive nature, and their joyful celebration of my birth resonated throughout our village.

You see, it is the custom of my people to pay careful attention to the details of the birth of every child. Every characteristic is visually and verbally recorded. From these observations, the family predicts the characteristics the child will possess as an adult. Some tribal groups in Liberia believe that the nature of a baby upon arrival from the womb determines its destiny. My entrance into the world appeared to be a very good omen for my future.

I am Elizabeth Fahn-Weedor. I am the second-born daughter of Sando Goliah Fahn, who was the firstborn son of the late clan chief of Tahn, Gola Konneh District, Armah Goliah, Liberia, West Africa. Names are important in Africa. Names identify our family clans and ancestral lines. In Liberia, we are always careful to identify ourselves with our father's clan or tribe. My tribal or given name is

Gbelley Neor. Gbelley is the name given to a surviving twin in my Gola dialect, and Neor means "the woman," a title of power. In the fourth month of my mother's pregnancy with twins, she lost one of the babies but safely carried the other until birth. Tradition holds that the surviving child is powerful and exerts some supernatural power over its twin, which might have been the cause of the other's death. Though I do not have any supernatural power as tradition believed, I was that surviving twin.

When I was in high school, I was given a cross-stitched wall hanging by a woman named Jayne Hutchinson, an American missionary with SIM (Serving In Mission) in my home village of Tahn. The intricate stitches woven so beautifully into its tapestry read: "Trouble is what God uses to mold us for better things." When I married my beloved husband, Anthony Weedor, we hung this wall hanging in our living room to serve as a constant reminder of the ongoing work of sanctification in the Christian life. The process of sanctification does not exempt the Christian from experiencing difficult times but it does provide full assurance that when pain comes knocking on your door, God will not cease to be faithful. We would need this assurance in the years to come.

As a Liberian, whose country had attracted people from all walks of life, and had opened up to the outside world for businesses, I never ever imagined that a violent civil war would tear my country apart in the near future leaving me with a heart-wrenching experience. While some Christians rest in the false security that salvation, once obtained, implies a promise of a life devoid of hardships, nothing could be further from the truth. Yet, there was never a time when God was not present and I can rest assured that this same ever-present God will continue to lead my family and me every step into the future. *Being confident of this, that he who began a good work in you will carry it on to completion until the day of Christ Jesus (Philippians 1:6 TNIV).*

The story that follows is my own personal story of survival during the First Civil War of Liberia, one of the bloodiest civil wars in Africa. It is a story of deliverance, survival and lessons learned—a story that clearly illustrates the providence of God in all things. Not only is this book a spiritual memoir, but it is also a discourse on Liberian politics and history, and on our intriguing and rich culture; and a Christian reflection on evil, suffering, and the divine hope found only through the redemptive work of our Lord Jesus Christ. In my life, though I have experienced both hardship and violence, God's faithfulness and unmerited love have never wavered.

PART I: FAMILY

Chapter 1

A VILLAGE CHILDHOOD

The Gathering Places

My home village of Tahn is located in the northwestern part of Liberia, eighty-five miles from the capital, Monrovia. Tahn lies in the middle of a long stretch of dusty road leading from Bomi Hills to Mano River, two large mining cities that once produced rich iron ore from beneath the soil of my beloved country. Tahn is also known around the world for its large deposits of gold and diamonds. As a result, there is a continuous influx of people from around the world interested in mining the earthly riches of Liberia. Various ethnic groups—Chinese, Lebanese, British, and others—within Liberia and elsewhere in Africa come to our little part of the world to further their own respective quests for financial gain.

Commerce thrives in Tahn, though it may not look that way to western eyes. The main street in Tahn is a dirt road that once was lined with several stores owned by Lebanese businessmen who controlled the majority of businesses in Liberia. Mandingos, a tribe of traders known as the "Jews of West Africa," also had shops on this busy street. They were given this title because of their strong business worldview all over West Africa and their frugal lifestyle. On market days, a visitor to my hometown would also notice many local rural vendors who came into town to sell their produce. Nearly every inch of this road was covered with colorful stalls selling food, produce, fabrics, and various wares.

My family lived with my mother's parents in a home that was located just off the car road, the main street in town. The walls were made of mud plaster, both inside and out, and fortunately, the floor was made of cement rather than dirt, which prevented our clothes and other personal belongings from getting dusty. An outdoor kitchen was built behind our family home where all of our foods were made. Family and friends gathered together in this place to eat meals and to socialize.

This was my childhood home, where my brothers and sisters, cousins, nieces, nephews, and other relatives were born and where we told the stories of our ancestors. This was also the place where my parents and my grandmother buried my umbilical cord. This burial was important because it made a statement of ownership for future generations. It was a way of saying, "This piece of property belongs to my family." Sometimes a coconut, orange, or cola nut tree was planted next to the burial site of the umbilical cord to represent the ownership interests of the family in the future. For as long as that child lived, this tree represented that they were in possession of this particular property.

Next to our home was a blacksmith workshop, which was known in our town as a gathering place for the elders and decision-makers of our community. My father was one of these men. The blacksmith workshop is still important and sacred in our communities, where farming is the primary source of sustenance. The local blacksmith forges the farming tools necessary for our survival. Without his skills, our livelihood would be at stake. This gathering place is so sacred to the people in our village that the men who gather there remove their shoes before they enter. Women are expressly forbidden to come anywhere near the blacksmith workshop.

The close proximity of our house to the blacksmith workshop meant that we could occasionally eavesdrop on conversations between the leaders of the village. They attempted to keep their discussions among themselves, but it was difficult to keep anything private for very long in a small community like ours.

The Story of Our Town

Storytelling is common in our culture, as important stories are passed down orally from one generation to the next. My hometown has its own unique story. My paternal great-grandfather, Zoegoso, and his wife, Zoewah, left their home village of Bomber when they were young along with another family in search of land. After Zoegoso had walked for one-and-a-half hours, he stepped on the land upon which he would build the new village. He cleared the land so he could plant sustaining crops. He then proceeded to burn the land to remove all of the underbrush, but only a tiny portion of the land would burn. So they named the land *Tahn*, which means "small portion".

According to my grandpa Armah Goliah, his family had to shed blood in order for the future residents of Tahn to be a free people in the spirit world. As animists, they believed that the entire area was possessed by spirits called jinn, some of whom were hostile. So my ancestors gathered together and ceremonially offered a sacrifice of a beautiful young virgin girl. They mixed her blood with sand and sprinkled it in the entire area that had been burned and even beyond, as this sacrifice would protect the citizens of Tahn from the curses of bad jinn, or evil spirits, and calamities, such as sickness, bad harvest, and even death.

After the sacrifice had been made and everyone was set to make their living, the medicine man who had performed the sacrifice asked my great-grandfather to pay an immense amount of money for the work to be done for the future town of Tahn. Unable to pay the fee, my great-grandfather pawned his only son, my grandfather Armah Goliah, who was later sold as a slave in Bolah village. This caused the family a lot of sorrow.

Grandpa Goliah remained in Bolah as a slave and married a native of the village, where he had his first child. When his sister, Maima Tangbo, became of age and got married, her husband traveled to Bolah, freed his brother-in-law, and brought him back to Tahn, where he rejoined the rest of his family. After some years, Goliah's daughter who was fully grown with children also came to Tahn in search of her father and the rest of his family. I was old enough to remember their reunion.

Once my ancestors built their first hut and began farming the land, other relatives joined them. Eventually, this small portion of cleared land became a thriving village. As resources around the village began to develop, it became a fully-fledged town and district headquarters for Gola Konneh, the largest district in Grand Cape Mount County.

Even though my great-grandparents are dead and long gone, the citizens of Tahn still respect and honor my father's family because of this heritage. Fahn Baddah, whose family co-founded Tahn and who the young generation thought was the rightful owner of Tahn, always said that my great-grandfather—nobody else—was the actual owner of my hometown. When Grandfather Goliah died during the civil war, the citizens of Tahn would have buried him in the center of the town as a symbol of ownership, but because of the close proximity of the drinking water pumps there, they did not.

My father was "next in line" when authority needed to be exercised in town matters. Because he was the eldest son of his father and the grandson of the original founder of Tahn, he had the responsibility of making every decision in my hometown. Even though the town had government-appointed officials, all decisions had to be approved by my father first. In the case of his death, this ownership and leadership role would have automatically passed down to the eldest of his sons. However, in my family's situation, the leadership role has fallen on my second brother, Ebenezer, also known as Debah, solely because he resides in the country presently and shoulders all responsibilities for both my dad's and my mom's families.

If by chance the eldest child was a daughter, which happened to be the case in my family, she would not easily receive this honor simply because she was a female. Traditionally in Africa, with few exceptions, girls are not allowed to inherit property from their parents, as a female is regarded as the property of a man. When she marries, she becomes the property of her husband and whatever previously belonged to her then belongs to her husband. Thus, in order for a woman's family to safeguard its properties, only sons are allowed to inherit property and leadership responsibilities within a village.

Our culture believes it is the responsibility of the parents to provide for all of their little ones; conversely, when parents can no longer take care of themselves, it is the children's responsibility to care of their parents until they die. There are no such things as nursing homes and senior housing in Liberia.

My grandfather, Armah Goliah, was popular in my village not only for his leadership but also for his marital status. He had three wives who blessed him with many children. My father was the third of his ten children.

My mother, on the other hand, was her parents' only child. Her father, Siafa Gborndiah, commonly known as Siafa Zoebon, migrated with his parents from neighboring Sierra Leone when he was only a young boy. They settled in Tahn where he later married my grandmother, Maima Kai, whom we called Ma Maima. They had four miscarriages and eight babies, all of whom died except for my mother.

Siafa Zoebon was well respected in my home village. He was a quiet man and maintained close ties to his connections in Sierra Leone. As a merchant, he traveled to Sierra Leone frequently in order to bring goods back to Liberia to sell for profit. He made enough money to build several decent homes that he rented out to Lebanese businessmen. He also built the first mosque in Tahn my home village, the worship place for Muslims, and this effort secured respect for him among his Muslim community.

I am the grandchild of my grandfather's third wife, Jenneh Goe. When my grandfather became old, he married a fourth wife called Miata. She was very young and still able to bear children for him. One of their children was named Kemah, who my family gave me when I got married and was expecting my first child. This tradition is common among my people. If I were to die while Kemah lives with my family, my husband would marry Kemah so she could continue to raise our children. In like manner, if my husband were to pass away and leave me childless, I would marry one of his brothers or cousins so that I could bear children who would carry on my husband's family name.

This practice may seem odd to those living in the Western world, but it is not unlike the story of Ruth in the Bible. When Ruth's husband died, his mother, Naomi, desired to return to her homeland. Ruth declared that she would go with Naomi and live with her people. They traveled to Bethlehem, where she met Boaz, who eventually became her kinsman-redeemer, the closest relative in line who had the legal rights to acquire the wife of a deceased relative and all of his inheritance. This way, the name of the deceased would not be cut off among his generation and siblings. Boaz was a close relative to Naomi, and he understood that he should marry Ruth because of this relationship. So this practice goes back to my African tradition.

In Africa, nothing is wasted; everything has a function whether new or re-purposed. What most would consider trash in other parts of the world is precious to people living in Third World countries. For instance, my cradle was a re-crafted tobacco crate given to my mother by a Lebanese businessman in our town.

We also use what nature provides freely for us. To soften my bed, my father cut some palm fronds from a nearby palm tree, which my mother shredded into slivers, and laid them in the sun to dry. This was my makeshift mattress. She covered it with a few pieces of fabric, and this piece of throwaway trash became a luxurious daybed where an infant girl could sleep soundly and securely for hours. This handcrafted cradle kept me safely off of the ground on the farm, protecting me from snakes, scorpions, and many other deadly crawling creatures that lived in my village. For this reason, my mother treasured this simple cradle and her heart rested, knowing that her newborn baby slept peacefully by her side.

Childhood Disease

Measles is a common disease among my people. Throughout Africa it is also a deadly disease, especially among our babies and younger children. I contracted the disease when I was five years old. Every part of my body was completely covered with oozing sores and lesions. There were sores in my eyes, nose, and mouth, as well. Because of the severity of my condition, I was placed in an isolated area in our village to prevent the other children and pregnant women from being exposed to the disease.

The only healthcare worker in my village was a man named Kemukai. In Liberia, we called him a "black bag carrier," which is the equivalent of a nurse's aide or less. Many black bag carriers have little or no formal medical training at all, yet they claim to have these skills so people will believe they have the ability to heal. Kemukai was different. He was honest, and, though he had little training, he helped many people in my village.

Kemukai attempted to treat me with the limited drugs available to him, but one day he gravely pronounced to my parents that nothing could be done for my situation. My parents and my grandmother thought I would not survive but faithfully continued to care for my small, failing body. For two solid weeks, nothing went into my mouth except coconut water. They trimmed my hair very short so that fresh air could circulate around the oozing lesions. According to my mother, I suffered tremendously and often bled from my nose and mouth.

Once again, my grandmother sent for Kemukai, and, after re-examination, he shook his head with a frown. The sores had advanced down my throat, causing a constant flow of blood into my nose and mouth. He gave my mother a liquid medication to drop into my eyes, nose and mouth to ease the pain and gave me some medicine for my stomach as well. He shook his head as he left, leaving my family with no hope of my survival.

It was nothing short of a miracle that my health began to improve and I experienced a complete recovery. Life is not taken for granted in Africa. This was only one of many miracles I would experience in my life, the first of many demonstrations of the providence of God.

Chiggers in My Toes

Ancestry is very important to us and from our very early years we are expected to know both family lineage lines of our parents. For this reason my mother decided that my sister Marie and I visit her family in Juajuwah. Juajuwah is a small village on the border of Liberia and Sierra Leone. Juajuwah means "the end of fear." According to my grandfather, there was a war among several tribal groups in that part of Liberia. People fled their farms and villages in search of a safe place to hide. While in hiding they went without food for days, and many people died of hunger. My family calls this "the time when people could no longer laugh out loud." It is true that no one had the energy to laugh during that difficult time, but this saying also reflected a superstitious fear of falling over dead if one dared to laugh in the face of such adversity.

During that famine and war, it was told that my family went in search of bush yams and other wild fruits to eat. They discovered an abundance of these foods and a large river they never knew existed nearby. As people who had gone without food for weeks or probably for months, they were so filled with excitement and thanksgiving that they—as well as the entire village—decided to relocate to this place. With more than sufficient supply of water and food on hand to help with their farming and the feeding of their cattle, they felt safe and knew they would live well there. As for the war, they took courage in knowing that they would never be caught off guard and unprepared by their enemies due to it being difficult to cross the vast river before getting into their territory to fight them. This was the only entrance to their village. Therefore they were no longer afraid. This was Juajuwah.

As my sister and I traveled to Juajuwah, we were fearful because our family there mostly spoke the Mende language rather than Gola, the language of my father. When we arrived at Juajuwah, we were surprised to discover that it was very small, more like a farm than a village. The entire village was like one large family, mingling together and always attending to the needs of one another. When one person hurt, the entire village hurt. When one person rejoiced, everyone rejoiced.

We stayed with our Uncle Noma and his wife, Auntie Jebeh, and the rest of their family. Every day we feasted on delicious, home-prepared food and fresh juicy fruits straight from the trees. We slept with our great-aunt, Ma Gbessy, in the palaver hut, a large round thatched hut without partitions. She provided hot bath water for us each morning, a very tedious job in most parts of Africa where there is no electricity. Every morning she got up early to light the firewood in the outdoor kitchen and set one large pot on the fire which would heat water for our baths. She was careful to make us get up early in the morning so that no one would see our naked bodies as we bathed.

One week after we arrived in the village, my toes began to itch terribly, especially after bathing in the steaming hot bathwater. I would check my toes but found nothing unusual. When we returned to Tahn, not only did my feet itch but they became very painful even to my own touch, My mother discovered that my feet had been attacked by chiggers which had made a home in my toes. They were starting to reproduce.

Chiggers are tiny bugs that live in the sand. They burrow into the skin and are most commonly found on the feet. Once inside of the body, they suck the blood of their unsuspecting host. Chiggers begin breeding immediately, and if the condition is not remedied quickly, the affected part of the body will begin to rot. They can be extremely painful and are truly disgusting!

Ma instantly began to remove every one of these nasty creatures from my feet. My feet were in so much pain that I was unable to wear shoes for two weeks. Regardless of this unpleasant experience, our stay with my mother's family in Juajuwa was one of my fondest childhood memories. Their communal way of life helped bond them together as a strong family, which made a hugely positive impact on my life. There was no such thing as individualism as it is in the western world. As hard working men and women, they looked after themselves and did not expect the outside world to provide their daily needs. They were poor but very happy and lived a stress-free life.

Cookouts on the Farm

My father was not only a farmer, but a hunter as well. This meant we always had plenty of fresh and dried meat to eat, and we never took this for granted. The men of the village hunted together in a group, and at the end of their trip they brought home bags of both dried and fresh meat to share with the entire village. As a teenager, I looked forward to the day when the hunters returned home with their catch. This was especially true when our father returned home with fresh monkey meat.

On these occasions I was given the opportunity to do my very own cooking which I often shared with a few of my adult family members, especially my dad. When he had eaten my food, he would then say to me, "This is the best cooked food I've had in a long time." Whether his statement was truly sincere, or what most parents would say to bring some joy in their children's lives, I felt great and proud of myself for getting such a wonderful compliment from my dad. With a good supply of meat on hand in our home and abundant rice and vegetables from our farm, my mother made the most delicious meals every day for our family. We felt blessed to have a father who worked as hard as he did to put food on the table which sustained us in a healthy way.

Generally speaking, girls in Liberia do not spend much one-on-one time bonding together with their fathers. This is because our culture has laws and customs which set females apart from our male family members. As a result, daughters rarely spend time with their fathers except when they are requested to be spoken to.

In our family, all of that changed when the monkey meat arrived. It was a special time set aside for our father and his daughters. One morning he would ask, "Who would like to go with me to the farm today?" One of us would respond, "Is there something special at the farm?" If he answered with a smile or laughter, we immediately knew that he had monkey meat waiting for us at the farm.

We could barely contain our excitement when he would say to our mother, "You and your mother should not come to the farm today!" You see, my mother and grandmother hated monkey meat. They could not even stand the smell of it when it was being skinned and roasted. The reason they detested monkey meat so much is because they, as Muslims, they considered it an unclean food like pork. They even refused to touch it. Although my father was also a Muslim, he did not hold as strongly to all of its laws and practices, and he could enjoy eating monkey meat with his children.

When we arrived at the farm, my father would have a huge cookout and all of us children would eat until we could eat no more. His only rule was that no one was allowed to bring any leftovers to town. We were only allowed to eat monkey meat at the farm. It never lasted longer than two days. To this day, I still crave monkey meat soup, steamed with salt and cooked with green plantains in a large pot simmering over an outdoor fire. There is nothing more delicious!

Chapter 2

ANCESTOR WORSHIP

Folk or Popular Islam

Most of my relatives are followers of Islam, except for my siblings and me, who are Christians. My dearest grandmother, Maima Kai, who also became a Christian while in exile in the Ivory Coast, was baptized in Monrovia—very exciting news to us. Growing up in a Muslim family seemed exciting to me as a child, but as I grew, it became more of a duty or chore. Even though my brothers and sisters and I did not go to the mosque to pray, my parents practiced their faith dutifully. In our society, their daily attendance to the laws of Islam automatically classified us, the children, as Muslim, too.

In our communities, there were also many Muslims, African Muslims, who for the most part practiced what is called Folk Islam, and who held strongly to the legalistic teachings and practices of Islam which do not allow women to mingle with men, especially if there was no adult male family member present. Like previous generations of my ancestors, my parents could not read and write. They depended heavily on farming like all others for their sole means of survival. This blended well with our culture and its Folk Islam religious practices, which allows a man to marry or possess many wives. As a result of these multiple wives, he would have many children which would give him more respect and honor within his community and his village.

My family practiced Poplar Islam, commonly called Folk Islam. Folk Islam is a religion of indigenous or tribal practices involving rituals to protect one from the power of witchcraft, demons, curses, the evil eye, and evil spirits; it combines practices of Islam with tribal magical beliefs and makes use of the supposed powers in voodoos such as bird feathers, herbal oils to rub on one's body against evil spirits, and anything that is claimed powerful for man by the witch doctor.

Folk Islam also includes the worship of our family ancestors. So the children in our family often joined our mother's family in a ritual which offered the sacrifice of a goat, sheep, or chicken to our ancestors. Folk Islam teaches that we must perform these sacrifices in order to appease the spirits of our ancestors so that we would be blessed with a fruitful harvest from our farms or so that our ancestors would attend to the needs we confided to them.

My people believed that when our ancestors were happy and pleased with us, they would plead to God on our behalf and God would richly bless us. In addition, most Africans even now always have in the back of their minds a fear of displeasing their ancestors. This fear causes them to take countless precautions to ensure that they do not upset the dead spirits of their ancestors. The blessing of ancestors is also required to secure the births of many children, good fortune, and other items of prayer. My family believed that without the shed blood of an animal, our ancestors would not accept our sacrifices.

After the sacrificial animals were slaughtered and butchered, the younger women gathered at my grandmother's house to prepare the food. We then took all of the food to my grandmother's bedroom where it was kept for a few hours, believing that was when our ancestors ate their shared portion before the food was taken to their graves. We gave an equal portion to each ancestor, starting with the oldest and going down the line to the youngest. Our first sacrifices were at the grave of my great-grandfather. The children sat on the ground, encircling our great-grandfather's grave. The adults stood over us and the food was set in the middle of the circle on top of the grave. The local Imam would say a prayer, followed by a recitation of the names of our ancestors to whom the sacrifice was being offered. Sometimes an Imam could not be found and the prayer was offered by the eldest family member, which was either my great-aunt or my grandmother.

For many years, these sacrifices were made with very little explanation to the children in our family. One day, I finally got the nerve to ask my grandmother why we took food to the grave of our great-grandfather. She told me that humans have no access to God except through our ancestors. This separation is due to the wickedness of man from almost the very beginning of Creation. In the beginning, humankind had complete access to God. One day, God became upset with humankind because of our sin and decided to move far away from us where he could not be reached anymore.

Our ancestors provide a bridge to God, and become our mediators when we offer sacrifices to them. This is why, in Folk Islam, choosing a burial site and attending carefully to the burial procedure and ceremonies are very important. Choosing a good or clean burial site is important because it is where sacrifices would later be taken and made. Also, careful attention has to be paid because good preparation of a burial and the number of people who turn out would indicate both to the living and the dead how good the deceased was which would automatically pave his way to paradise.

These traditional practices, known as Animism, are practiced all over the world. In his book, *Bridges to Islam,* my dear friend and partner in ministry, Dr. Phil Parshall, writes,

> Animistic practices are almost always the remnant from the days before Muslims came to a people and converted them. One would think Islam would have purged such heretical influences from the lives of the new believers. Such is not the case. More often than not, the initial Muslim missionaries were Sufis or at least mystically influenced. They were in favor of accommodation and compromised rather than strictly holding to the letter of Islamic law. This was appreciated by the converts. They could retain much of the old and simply add to it that which seemed good and helpful. Cultural and religious conflict was minimized (Parshall, page 62).

Folk Islam is a blend of Animism and Islam. For instance, when Animist Muslims call on spirits to heal someone, the spirits are expected to tell or show them what kind of herbs to use or what kind of sacrifice to make. Our ancestor spirits also tell us whether God will allow the medicine to work.

Christianity, the faith now given to me by my Lord Jesus Christ, teaches differently than this. God is actually not far away at all, nor do we need the spirits of our ancestors to intercede on our behalf. God has given his beloved people the gift of Jesus Christ, who is our one and only mediator. When Adam sinned, thereby condemning the entire human race to death because of that sin, God did not leave his people without hope. His covenant promise of a Savior in Genesis 3:15 was delivered and fulfilled in the birth of the god-man, Jesus

Christ, whom God sacrificed on our behalf to redeem us from the penalty of our sinful nature.

For God so loved the world that He gave his one and only son, that whoever believes in Him shall not perish but have eternal life. For God did not send His son into the world to condemn the world, but to save the world through him. Whoever believes in him is not condemned, but whoever does not believe stands condemned already because he has not believed in the name of God's one and only Son. Sovereign Lord, as you have promised, you now dismiss your servant in peace. For my eyes have seen your salvation, which you have prepared in the sight of all people, a light for revelation to the Gentiles and for glory to your people Israel (John 3:16-18; Luke 2:29-32). No other sacrifice, no other mediator is necessary. Through Jesus, we have access to our Father.

I remember, at the beginning of each farming year, before my father began to clear the brush from our land, he would go to the imam in our village who often does multiple jobs for people. He would serve as the imam of the Mosque and at the same time be the village "soothsayer" or "sand cutter," as we call them. After this visit, father would offer a sacrifice as protection for the clearing of the land and for the yield the land would produce. One year, my father decided to plant in a large field next to a fairly wide stream. The imam mandated that my father had to make a yearly sacrifice to the jinn that live in the water. While the jinn are part of traditional animist religion in Africa they are also mentioned in the Quran as part of Islamic mythology. They live in a spirit world beyond the visible universe, some of whom are good while others are evil. Without this sacrifice, there was a great risk of drowning and fewer crops would be harvested.

Growing up, we were never allowed to sweep the floors of our home at night because we believed that our ancestors' spirits would visit our homes at night to eat whatever food had fallen to the floor. When they arrived and saw that all of the food had been swept away, they would pass to the next house without leaving their blessings. I was also instructed never to eat any food that fell to the ground because my ancestors needed this food. Even today, everyone who practices Folk Islam knows that when someone's food falls to the ground, our ancestors are telling us that they are hungry for food. Some people have dreams about the dead coming to them in the dark of the night, asking for food. When that happens, now as then, the elders of the family are told and the family immediately offers an animal sacrifice on the grave of that particular deceased family member. In addition, dreams can reveal misfortunes or deaths before they occur. For example, when a person loses a tooth in his dream, it may indicate that he will soon lose a close member of his family.

Another important precaution applies to all people in Folk Islam, especially women, in regard to the care of our hair. At a very young age, girls are instructed not to comb their hair outside in case it drops to the ground. No one is permitted to cut their nails and leave the clippings in a public area without throwing them far away from human eyes. According to an Animist, the hair or nails of a person can be used by others to put a curse on them. In 1985 when I was still at home with my parents, my mother became severely ill with ongoing headaches that caused the middle of her head to sink in to such an extent that one could pour in water as if into a small bowl.

When my grandmother went to a sand-cutter to inquire the cause of her ailment, she was told that someone had used her hair to put a curse on her. My mother used a lot of herbal treatments to be healed from these headaches. Because of these superstitious beliefs, people from an animistic culture live in tremendous fear of the unknown and of each other.

Chapter 3

CUSTOMS AND DAILY LIFE IN LIBERIA

An Arranged Marriage

My mother, Kpannah Sando, was the only surviving child out of twelve. When she was ten years old, Siafa Zoe began to arrange her future marriage to my father, Sando Goliah Fahn, who was the son of a tribal chief. My grandmother, Ma Maima, was opposed to the arrangement from the beginning, but nothing could dissuade my grandfather from implementing his plan, not even his wife's continuous cries and pleading for her daughter's life. She did not like the fact that my father was a lot older than my mother. He was also in a relationship with another woman who had already given birth to his first child, a boy who later died. My grandmother did not want her only child to share a man with another woman who would more than likely mistreat her. This was a common experience for second wives. My grandfather was a quiet man, but he had a mind of his own, and it was made up.

Once the decision had been made, Siafa Zobon finally allowed my father's father, Armah Goliah, to begin making the dowry plan, also known as the paying of bride price which allowed my future father to bring gifts to my mother as she was still young and not yet ready for marriage. The giving of these gifts prepared the way for her future dowry and is a traditional part of the courtship ritual of our people before the marriage ceremony which would legally bind them together as husband and wife. My father also worked on my grandparents' farm, also a traditional way of courtship in our culture.

At the age of sixteen, my mother was given to my father in an elaborate marriage ceremony. She was showered with clothing and household items. Siafa Zobon made a special trip to Sierra Leone and bought the most expensive clothes he could afford for his only daughter.

After my mother wed my father she moved in with his family, as is expected in every traditional African marriage. My mother became a part of a family of eight living in a small, three-bedroom house with other extended family members living there as well. The household always seemed to be in turmoil. Imagine this scenario: three of my mother's sisters-in-law and my mother all had children in the same year, only a month apart. My mother had lost her first baby shortly after its birth. This was her second pregnancy. My mother, who was an introvert, suffered the most by living in such a household in that she found it difficult to speak up for herself. She often allowed her in-laws, especially my dad's sisters, to take advantage of her.

The other women in the home were mean and hateful towards her. Due to limited space in the home, all of the women and their babies slept on mats which were spread on the mud floor with very little space between them. Serious problems developed between my father and his sisters because of their mean spirits towards my mother. These problems were so serious that Siafa Zobon requested the return of his daughter to live under his own roof, which had four bedrooms. My father also came to live in my grandparents' home, which is not a typical scenario for an African man. My grandfather refused to allow his only daughter to continue to be mistreated.

True Love of a Grandmother

I come from what westerners would call a large family. In Africa, there is no such thing as too large of a family. We enjoy being surrounded by many people, and a large family helps to make the huge task of providing for the family seem smaller and more manageable. In addition to the eight children in our family, it was not uncommon for us to take in the children of extended relatives as well. Our home was always full of people and relatives who came to live with us for months or, sometimes, permanently.

Children do not have their own bedrooms in most homes; rather, they are grouped together by gender. When a female visitor came to visit us in our home, she stayed with the girls. When a male visitor came, he would stay with the boys. No matter what the situation or how many people came, there was always room for more.

Living and growing up in the same home with our grandparents was a wonderful privilege, and we considered this to be a blessing. They guided and watched over us during our day to day activities at home. They taught me meaningful and useful stories of life which better prepared me for my own life. Coming from a culture of oral history, the stories of my grandparents' upbringing and the tremendous struggles in their lives always influenced me to make right decisions in my life—and they still do. As a parent myself, their life experiences have greatly helped me in raising my own children. Their unconditional love and compassion for us was incredible. They were always there when we needed them.

My grandmother, Ma Maima (also called Maima Kai), was a very strong, thin lady whose presence was remarkable. Throughout her life, her strong, loving character was evident for all to see. As mentioned, my mother was Ma Maima's only child, and because of this she loved her grandchildren very much. Living in this kind of a communal environment, perhaps you can see the benefit of having our grandparents living with us. Ma Maima, who had attended my birth, had a tremendous impact on my life and staunchly supported the education of the children in our family.

Before the civil war broke out in Liberia in 1989, Ma Maima was the major breadwinner in our family. In fact, when she was young she was chosen as the chief female for the women in our district and village. Her business skill and mind led her to be more successful than other women in our village. By buying and selling diamonds she found herself in a middle class society in our area. Although my father lived at home with us, my dear grandmother was responsible for our care and financial support.

She also made a huge impact on our community because she was a trained professional midwife for the entire district surrounding Tahn. She was selected in our district, Gola Konneh (the largest district in Grand Cape Mount County), to receive professional training as a midwife in Monrovia. She was one of the first medical staff to work at our regional medical clinic when it was newly built by President Tolbert in 1977. Ma Maima served her people so well that at the end of her first year she was honored in the presence of hundreds of people in our home town.

Through her hard work and undiscriminating love for all, Ma Maima won the trust and respect of both men and women in our village. She always went out of her way to assist others, especially strangers. My grandmother was never suspicious of others. It was a great honor and pleasure to see her rewarded this way after she had spent her lifetime serving others. Although she was not a Christian at the time, I still marvel today at her ability to display the gifts of love, mercy and hospitality to everyone.

Standing against Tradition

Ma Maima was a very strong woman who found herself in the wrong place—a male-dominated society. This did not stop her from following her convictions, and she often stood fearlessly in opposition to cultural beliefs and practices imposed on powerless people, especially on women.

In our village, it was considered a waste of precious money and time for girls to pursue higher educational opportunities. When a girl marries, she moves from her family's home to her new husband's home. By doing so, she becomes another man's property and thereby loses the identity of her former biological family and bloodline.

Boys, however, always remain at home and are able to receive the family inheritance. Families encourage their sons to continue their education in order to elevate their social status in the village. Social status means a greater possibility of land ownership, more wives, and more children. In our culture, no matter which gender accomplishes a task, men are always given credit for any accomplishment.

My grandmother understood these prejudices and insisted that my sisters and I go to school and be educated. This did not go over well with the male members in our family, or with the community. Ma Maima did not give up, though, and in the end, Father allowed us to enroll in school. He maintained his manly pride by refusing to supply the funds necessary for school enrollment, uniforms, and books. Ma Maima worked hard to provide the necessary funds and made sure that we finished not only our elementary education in our hometown, but also our high school education, which required us to move to Bomi Hills and Monrovia. This was a huge sacrifice on her part and I am so grateful to God for her.

My sister Marie and I were serious about our education. We were the first two girls to start our education in Tahn and to finish high school. I then began my college education in Monrovia before the Civil War. Next came my two younger sisters, Elydia and Angie, whom we assisted to complete their high school education years later. As the benefits of my education started to show in the positive life choices I have made in my own life like my marriage and my Christian life, people in our community began to recognize that my grandmother's wisdom in sending us girls to school was beneficial to our entire community. This earned my grandmother even more respect in our community. Because of my grandmother's firm stand on the education of women, other girls in my village are now given the opportunity to continue their schooling.

We walked to and from our elementary school every day, carrying our chairs on our heads. If a chair was left at school, it would be stolen immediately. The school building was an old town hall in the middle of Tahn used as a place for meetings and settling disputes among our people. There was no other facility available to be used for school besides this court house. School ended at 2:30 p.m., and as soon as we arrived home my sister and I would join the rest of the family on the farm to do our chores. It was about forty minutes' walk to the farm and another forty minutes back. We did this every day of the week except on Fridays, the Muslim day of prayer. Most Muslims in our village took this day off to attend the mosque for prayer.

On Saturdays and Sundays we would wash the family clothes by hand at a tiny creek next to our farm. This was a tedious process and took many, many laborious hours. After the clothes were washed, we would lay them on low grass by the creek to dry. While the clothes were drying, we returned to the farm and fetched water from the creek, and carried it on our heads in buckets. We then helped our mother with the cooking of our evening meal before heading back to town before the night came. My brothers, Thomas, Debah, Amullah, Musa, and Siafa (who was our baby brother), worked in the field with my father. Although Musa and Siafa were little, they were still helpful in carrying out little tasks.

In a traditional Liberian home, men were not allowed to enter the kitchen to help with housework in any way, shape, or form. Likewise, they did not take care of babies. Household activities were considered the job of a woman.

At the age of seventeen, when I had just started dating the man who would one day become my husband, we visited my hometown together. One morning I was washing my clothes by hand as usual. Tony noticed my hard work, and, in an effort to impress me, he decided to help me with the laundry chores. My father happened to pass through the back of the house and saw Tony washing my clothes. He was completely baffled and stood staring at Tony, shaking his head in disgust. As he walked away, he said in his Kolokua (Liberian English), "He for-nothing man!" To my father, Tony had brought shame to his family and to all of African manhood by washing the clothes of a woman who should be doing that for him.

During the four and a half years that Tony and I dated, if there was any reason for my father to prevent us from getting married, this would have been it. Papay Fahn, as we called my father, could never get past that one incident. As a humorous person, he often reminded Tony about it and had a good laugh at his expense. We always enjoyed his company for his great sense of humor. My father eventually got over the incident the more he got to know Tony and realized that he could not ask for a better son in-law than him.

After all of our chores were done for the day, my siblings and I returned home to face the daunting task of doing our homework. We did not have electricity in our town so everything had to be done by candlelight or lanterns. By eight o'clock in the evening, the entire household was put to bed so that all could rise at half past five the next morning. There were chores to do in the morning before we went to school, including sweeping the front of the house, porch, and hallway; fetching drinking and bathing water from the creek; and lighting firewood to heat water for our baths. Following our baths, we quickly got dressed in our school uniforms and left, most days without breakfast. We ate breakfast only when there were leftovers from the previous night, which we called "cold bowl." These were our daily morning activities.

Chapter 4

A NEW LIFE

Secret Visits to the Christian Church

Almost everyone in my village is a Muslim. There were only a handful of Christians in town when I was growing up, yet everyone looked after one another, both Christian and Muslim alike. Neighbors shared food with each other, and a true, sharing community existed in Tahn. The Muslim Mandingos were the exception. Mandingos did not mingle with other tribal groups, and they certainly would not eat food with us. They were mostly merchants and taxi drivers, but a few of them were also involved with the diamond trade. They also avoided Christians, considering them to be unclean people who could not be trusted. Any food that passed through the hands of a Christian was considered impure and could not be eaten by them.

My family and other families in my village, including Muslims and some of the church-going Christians, treated each other honorably in spite of our different religions. Though my parents were Muslims, they demonstrated one of the commandments I later learned that Christ had called Christians to do: love thy neighbor as thy self. They were also very hospitable to everyone in our village and especially to strangers. Everything in our home or on our farm was made available to all who were in need. My grandmother especially, entertained strangers as though they were angels or within our family circle. She would give up the very clothes on her back in order to meet the needs of others. She often gave up her only meal for the day to serve anyone she found hungry and went without eating herself. Our extended families depended on our household for most of their needs.

The older I got, the more my mind was plagued with this question: "If my grandmother has such great love for everyone, why does she hold to a different set of beliefs than the Christians?" Her life and the lives of my family demonstrated the very command Christ has called Christians to carry out and obey. My parents mourned and rejoiced with everyone in our village no matter what their religious affiliations were. As Mandingo Muslims drew further away from other Muslims in my village, so did other tribal groups, but my grandmother refused to retaliate by doing likewise. As a midwife, she reached out to the Mandingo Muslim community and met their needs even when they were not willing to do the same for others. Although my parents were not and still are not Christians, they are morally upright and outstanding people.

Although I was not a Christian at the time, I had always been told that Christians are people who love one another—and their neighbors. In our public schools in Liberia, we studied the Bible and were frequently reminded of the Ten Commandments and other great and wonderful teachings in it, especially the verses about love.

Armed with this knowledge, I began to look at the lives of the few Christians living in my village, comparing them to the much larger Muslim population. While I did not understand everything about Christianity, I knew that in order to be a Christian, I must accept Jesus into my life and believe that he is the Son of God. I was just like every other person in my village that was without any hope of eternity. I wanted something different in my life than what my parents, grandmother and other family members had. I needed a faith that would give me a better hope for life after death. How I was to accomplish this feat, I did not know.

I continued to wrestle with this question because the unity among the Muslims in our town was spectacular to observe. We looked after the needs of one another, especially in cases of death, marriage, and the birth of a child. I still believe that in some ways the majority of Muslims practice the art of living within their community far better than most Christians do. So making a decision to leave such a communal way of living has to be thought through properly.

I began to secretly attend the local Christian church service on Wednesday and Friday evenings, which was strictly forbidden for a child of Islam. For several weeks neither my parents nor my grandmother knew that I was attending this church.

One Sunday evening I heard my grandmother call to me in a stern voice. From the tone of her voice, I knew something was seriously wrong. I stood before her and she asked,

"Is it true what I have heard?"

I knew immediately that she had heard of my church attendance. Instantly, I wished I could vanish from the face of the earth so that I could avoid the trouble I knew was headed my way. I knew I had to be honest with my grandmother, yet by revealing what I had done, I knew that I would be guilty of disrespecting her authority.

It is very important to respect your elders in Africa. It is considered disrespectful to look an adult in the eye; the gaze of a child is supposed to be focused on the ground when answering an adult. Such body language would not be understood by the Westerner, who might think that when a child will not look you in the eye, he or she is lying. Unable to give my grandmother an explanation for what I had done, I stood there sobbing, my face covered in tears. I was sickened that I had disobeyed and deceived my grandmother, whom I loved so dearly. Surprisingly, after my tears had subsided, she looked me straight in my teary eyes and said,

"I hope you know what you are doing."

Her statement did not give me permission to go to church, but neither did it mean I had to stop. I decided to continue to attend Christian church services until the time that my parents told me to stop. At that time I would have to choose between total excommunication from my family and my entire community. I secretly continued to attend services and even enrolled in Sunday school with three other girls my age. We memorized scripture, sang spiritual songs, played games, and listened to the Word of God, which was taught in a very simple way so that we could understand.

Our little church was taught by the local Christian pastor, James Varney. We also had one missionary family and a few single missionaries who lived in our town. They had chosen to leave their homeland in America to serve the people groups of Liberia. It amazed me that these dedicated men and women of God willingly gave up their own personal comfort in order to fulfill the Great Commission of Christ:

> All authority in heaven and on earth has been given to me. Therefore go and make disciples of all nations, baptizing them in the name of the Father and of the Son and of the Holy Spirit, and teaching them to obey everything I have commanded you. And surely I am with you always to the very end of the age (Matthew 28:19-20).

Most of the children who attended the church in my hometown could not read very well and they had trouble comprehending what they were reading in the Bible. The missionaries went out of their way to help them understand. Some even took on the daunting task of learning our dialect so that they could communicate the gospel to the tribal people who did not speak English. Gradually, I began to understand the differences between Christianity and Islam, eventually coming to understand their differing views of God. I also began to realize that there was something or someone missing in my own life: Jesus Christ.

I continued to attend church services for the next several months, and soon the worship services began to hold a greater meaning for me. As I continued to search for truth, I realized that without Christ I had no hope for eternity. The fear of death and going to hell, which was very real around me, spurred a hunger and thirst for God's Word that I had not previously known.

The sudden death of young people in my village was on the rise and it caused terrible fear among many in my community. The cause of some of these deaths was never determined but most people believed it was due to witchcraft. In one particular month as I still remember, my home village lost more than ten people which caused a major concern within nearby villages, as people began to avoid coming to Tahn. What created more turmoil within me was the fact that all of these dead bodies were buried in close proximity to our house, the only burial site in our village. At night, one had no option but to go outside in pitch darkness to use the latrine. I dreaded this part of my growing years so much.

I discreetly read my Bible as often as I could without stirring up trouble at home. I also decided to play a more active role in my church, and began spending more quality time with other Christians in our town, especially the missionaries who lived among us. Joy Crombi was an elderly single missionary who took a personal interest in me. She began to give me more reading materials to help answer my questions. The number one question for me remained: "If I were to die today, would I go to heaven?"

My Conversion to Christianity

In April, 1981, I felt the Spirit of God convicting me of my sinful nature after I heard a missionary named Les Unruh preached a sermon on the end times, calling me to repentance. Les was the first SIM (Serving In Missions) church-planting missionary to settle in my hometown. He took the interest of the Liberian nationals to heart, which helped him win their love and trust. His message on that Sunday night was very clear and powerful to me. I felt the spirit of God convicting me of my sin and calling me to repentance but I was hesitant to accept Jesus. I was afraid of the potential outcome of a public confession of faith other than Islam. In the middle of this confusion, the Holy Spirit reminded me that now was the time to receive the faith God had given me. Jesus Christ had already made the sacrifice for my sin on the cross through His death which had cleansed my sins away. All I needed to do was to invite and accept him into my life as my personal Savior who had paid the penalty for my sins.

I have always found it difficult to fully explain how the fear of eternity came upon me that evening. I do remember a vivid state of helplessness and a broken heart, so broken that I cried throughout the sermon. As a child born into the faith of Islam, I had been told that Allah was the only way to paradise. For this reason, I knew the consequences of claiming a new faith: I would be ostracized from my family forever. Nonetheless, a calm voice from within my heart reassured me that this was the time to acknowledge Christ as my Savior.

At the end of the sermon, Les Unruh gave an altar call, and I watched three men respond, one of whom was the former district commissioner of my area, one of the most respectable men in Tahn. This created further confusion in my heart, because, according to African tradition, a girl of my age was not allowed to mingle among men, especially older men. With this barrier and the fear of my parents' and grandmother's expected reaction, I stayed in my seat. After a few more seconds, the pounding in my heart was so loud in my ears that I was afraid it would jump right out of my chest.

With sudden clarity, I stood up on trembling feet, begging God to keep me from falling before I could reach the front of the alter, where the three men were still standing. After Les explained the true meaning of becoming a Christian and what such a decision entailed, the four of us acknowledged Christ together as our only hope, our only Redeemer and Savior. A huge sense of relief rushed through me, bringing to my heart a kind of peace I had never experienced before. Only moments ago, I had been afraid of my destiny. Now I had complete assurance that my destiny was a future home with Jesus Christ. The Bible says, that if you confess with your mouth, Jesus is Lord, and believe in your heart that God raise Him from the dead, you will be saved. For it is with your heart that you believe and are justified, and it is with your mouth that you confess and are saved (Romans 10:9-10).

Although this wonderful event was the most amazing experience of my life, I was fearful and troubled over my family's reaction to my news. I knew I needed to tell them but I did not know how to do this without offending them. You see, in a Muslim family, the worst crime a Muslim can commit is to denounce Islam and convert to Christianity. Believing that Jesus Christ is the Son of God is especially scandalous to a Muslim, because it refutes the oneness of Allah and it is the worst sin one can commit in Islam. Nobody can make himself equal with Allah. The consequence of such a crime in the most devout Muslim families is death because such a person is considered as an apostate. To reject Allah means that a person is embracing a heresy, declaring another religion to be higher than the faith of Islam. This act brings shame upon the family name and upon the entire Muslim community in your village.

Most people in the Islamic world, including Africans, tend to live within shame-based cultures. Before we do anything we must ask if our decision will reflect badly or bring shame on ourselves, our family, or our village. Although I was not a practicing Muslim who went to the mosque every day to pray, because my parents practiced Islam and held to the faith, I was also considered to be a Muslim. Considering all of this, how could I tell my family about my conversion to Christianity? I loved my family very much, and I could not stand the thought of losing them overnight. Therefore, I decided to keep the news to myself for the time being.

Meanwhile, I continued to attend church services and began to grow in my faith. I was a new believer in Christ, and I knew my life would never be the same again. I also knew that I would not be able to keep my conversion a secret forever. One day, someone from the church would say something to my family, or perhaps my new life in Christ would speak for itself.

A New Life in Christ

After my conversion, I began to question many things I had done over the course of my life, such as the various Folk Islam rituals and animal sacrifices performed by my family each year. On several occasions, I refused to partake in these activities, and my grandmother asked why. I knew this was the moment I should reveal my new faith to her, but I was afraid to be rejected by my family. I worried about how I would live if I were rejected by them. Who would supply my daily needs? My faith was not strong enough at the time to know that God would supply my needs.

I stood before my grandmother and wept. When she saw my tears and my broken heart, she began to console me. She said,

"I know that you are still young and do not understand what you are doing. Therefore, I am not going to stop you from going to church or from doing what you feel you must do, but I hope in the end you will see the mistakes that you have made."

Only a merciful God, by his providential hand, could have given my heart such a tremendous gift. My love for my grandmother was only strengthened through her compassionate response to me.

Two days later, my father heard about my conversion and was very upset. This surprised me because he rarely got involved in the activities of us children of the family. He called me and asked me if the news he had heard was true. With absolutely no hesitation, I told him of my conversion and desire to attend the Christian church for the rest of my life. In an angry voice I rarely heard, he said,

"I do not want to ever see you in a church building again!"

The harshness in his voice scared me. I quietly walked away, went to my room, and realized that I was not prepared for this kind of pain. I cried myself to sleep that night.

My absence at the church was noticed by my missionary Sunday school teacher Ms. Crombi, who decided to pay me a surprise visit. She asked why I had not come to church, and it greatly touched me to see her concern for me. Her sympathy for my dilemma was obvious, and her concern for me assured me that someone still loved me. She prayed that God would soften the hearts of my parents and take away my own festering pain.

Later that week, I saw Ms. Crombi at a volleyball practice that was being held at the missionary compound. She asked if I would like to do a one-on-one Bible study with her, since I could no longer attend church. Through these studies, I also became better friends with Les Unruh, his wife, Verla, and their family, especially their two daughters, Lori and Michelle. Verla quickly won over my parents when she asked if they would allow me to teach her how to cook some of our traditional dishes. The idea that an American family wanted to learn how to make our African food without refusing it as food that was very foreign to their stomachs was very impressive to them. It gave me the opportunity to spend time with the Unruhs when I would have not have otherwise been able to.

The cooking lessons with this missionary which at times were accompanied with stories of Christian living from her girls, especially Michelle, also helped me to grow in my walk with Christ and made an eternal impact on my life. Over the course of time, my family became friends with the Unruhs, which helped to soften my father's attitude towards my church attendance.

I still refer to Verla and Les as "Mom and Dad" because of the magnificent roles they played in my Christian life and the moral encouragement and support they gave me during the early years of my Christian life. I did not know at the time that my friendship with the Unruhs would one day extend to the United States, and that one of Verla's brothers and his wife, Elroy and Debbie Thiezen, would play a huge role in my family's life during our studies at Denver Seminary.

God continued to work on my father's heart and he finally gave me permission to attend church services once again. No longer did I have to keep my Christian faith a secret from my friends, schoolmates, or the people in my town, but this did not mean that everyone was happy about it. Soon, many people began to make negative comments about me, confronting my parents and grandmother with the shame of my conversion. They wanted me to be punished.

Thankfully, my grandmother ignored these people, mainly because she did not believe I would last very long in the Christian church. While the community wanted my family to send me away, she loved me enough to value my well-being over her social reputation. God, in His sovereign will, used my coming to Christ to bring glory and honor to His name.

Baptized in Christ

The Christian baptism of a Muslim convert is not only a public proclamation to the rest of the people in your home community that you now follow Christ, but it is also a huge step of faith against the cultural practices of Islam within that community. To the Muslim people, it symbolizes the complete disowning of your family, your clan, your village, and, worst of all, the religion into which you were born. To the Muslims in my life, it meant that I would be declaring my attachment to a foreign god.

Regardless, I plunged ahead and signed up for the baptism class to be offered at the annual conference held by my church in January of 1983. After completing the class with eleven other people, we began our journey to the creek where we would be baptized. We sang, with jubilation and joy, words which in my native language, Gola, said, "They are going to be baptized; they are going to be submerged in the water in the name of Jesus." It was a declaration to all around us that we were followers of Christ.

So it was for this reason that I was baptized in a public creek where the women and children of the village did their laundry.

A few of my siblings were in the crowd at the creek. The singing continued as each person was submerged into the creek. At the end of the baptism service, everyone changed into dry clothes and walked back to the church, celebrating as we went.

We were presented to the entire congregation and given baptismal certificates. When I returned home, my parents and grandmother greeted me with smiles on their faces. They had seen and heard what had just happened, yet they smiled! God, in His greatness, had answered my prayers.

Chapter 5

BETRAYED BY GOD?

My Educational Dilemma

A week after I was baptized, it was time for me to return to high school. With the help of my mother, I gathered some food and necessary items and left for Monrovia with my sister. Due to circumstances beyond my family's control, our schooling was abruptly interrupted and we were forced to return home. The break in my education, which I thought would only be for a short time, turned out to be longer than expected. I no longer had a place or somebody to live with in order to continue my education in the city away from my family and village.

I became extremely discouraged because my education was very important to me. But I am not one to sit around feeling sorry for myself. In an effort to take my mind off school, I determined to find ways to serve in my home church, and decided that I would assist Ms. Crombi with the children's Sunday school program. Soon I was busy organizing the children and their activities, but this did not take my mind off my educational dilemma. I worried constantly that I would not be able to graduate from high school. I had good reasons to believe this might happen to me because everyone I knew who had come home on vacation from high school in Monrovia had failed to return the following quarter. Because of the lifestyle of the indigenous people in Liberia's hinterlands, higher education is not given priority. Sustaining life is always at the forefront, and the teenagers were needed to farm the fields or to become wage earners for their family.

I began to pray, asking God to open a way for me to return to school. While I tried to take encouragement from what God had already done in my family in regard to my new faith, many days I secluded myself from my family and wept profusely. Finally, after many weeks had passed, I went to my parents and asked if they had come up with a plan for my return to school. To my surprise, they had decided that I would not be returning to school for the remaining half of the school year.

My very worst fear had become a reality. I was doomed to stay at home without completing my education, just like everyone else in my hometown. My father began to talk of my impending marriage, as I am sure he hoped to marry me off to a man of wealth and influence, hopefully a rice farmer, with whom I would produce many babies. I was soon to become the property of another man, who would be permitted to treat me in any manner he desired. I cried for days and stayed far away from my family and friends. Like the prophet Jeremiah in the Bible, I felt betrayed and rejected by God, so I refused to pray to Him. Obviously, God was not interested in me or my problems.

My desire to be alone did not work for long in our home. Living in a community where people are always around you has its benefits, but it can become a huge liability if one desires privacy. In Africa it is difficult to live in isolation very long. Our lives are like open books to our families and to everyone in town.

A few people in my family began to notice my withdrawal and became concerned about me. Other people in the community began to gossip about me and my family.

"Didn't she say that she followed Jesus? Why can't her Jesus send her back to school? She's just one of those people who have been foolish and misled by those white people. Why don't they help her now? We knew all along that this church business was only for the white people, but our young black people nowadays don't accept what we try to teach them. They deserve what they get!"

Many people went as far as to say I had been brainwashed by the white man about my religion. I have to laugh at this now. My husband, Tony, likes to say to this statement that if they had only known what was in my brain before, they would have been glad that I was brainwashed! But then I began to question God. Why could He not do something to prove Himself? But He was silent.

The village did not only accuse me, but my family as well. They blamed my family for all of the 'bad luck' that was headed my way. My parents had allowed me to convert to Christianity, which meant that I was following a false god. Because of this hideous act, Allah, supposedly, was venting his wrath on me and my family.

When my parents heard these abusive attacks, they began to agree. They believed that Allah was punishing me and that an evil spirit had cursed me. They suggested that I leave the church and never attend any activity associated with it. They told me to go to the local witch doctor, who would tell me what I should do to have my bad luck taken away. Only then would I be able to return to school because the evil forces that were keeping me from obtaining my education would no longer have power over me.

When I heard my own parents speak to me in this way, I exploded in anger and began to cry. I rejected their plans and said,

"I believe that God will make a way for me to return to school, whether it is this year or next year." I informed my family that I would not participate in any more ancestral worship rituals, nor would I go to the witch doctor for help.

This was the first time I had openly opposed the counsel and instruction of my family after my conversion to Christianity. It was a difficult stand to take, but from that time forward, my family knew where I stood in regard to my faith. I felt burdened and my heart was broken. I needed someone to help me, but no one came to my aid. As a young believer, I needed to feel the presence of God in a real, tangible way, but He was nowhere in sight. Perhaps C. S. Lewis was correct when he wrote, in *The Problem of Pain*, "God whispers to us in our pleasures, speaks in our conscience, but shouts in our pains; it is His megaphone to rouse a deaf world." Nevertheless, I continued to hold onto my faith without compromise.

It was only from reading the Bible that I received any encouragement. Through this daily practice I began to understand that God's Word speaks. I desperately wanted to be obedient to His Word and to know His will for my life. I decided I needed someone who was grounded in biblical understanding to be my mentor. Ms. Crombi was no longer at our church, so I decided to ask Ms. Hartwig, a single American missionary woman, to help me study the Bible. Barb immediately dedicated her limited and precious time to me in studying God's word even though she was busy working as a nurse.

Studying the Bible was not the only activity that I did with Barb as she asked if I could join her in administering health care in the surrounding villages in our district. As a nurse, Miss Barb went from village to village with other single missionary women to give vaccines and to teach women about basic healthcare and hygiene. I was honored to go with her on these trips to tiny, remote villages. It was an eye-opening experience to watch Barb go from place to place, walking fearlessly into poverty-stricken homes where she would save precious lives. Her passion for helping others and ministering to extend God's kingdom here on earth has impacted me all my life.

What a lesson it was for me! Being exposed to Barb's heart for ministry and her desire to share the gospel while serving God in a strange country, ignited my passion to serve as a missionary among my own people in Africa today. Looking back, I praise God for bringing such a godly and wonderful Christian woman into my life at just the right time.

Coming of Age

After my fifteenth birthday, my parents and my grandmother told me that I was now old enough to sleep with a man. They warned me that if I decided not to, one day I would become drowsy, fall asleep—and die. According to the tradition of my tribe, once a virgin girl has had her monthly menstruation period but has not had sex, the blood in her body will not flow well to her head. As a result, she could die in her sleep without warning. Most African parents, especially illiterate ones, use this myth to pursue marriages for their daughters at a very young age. This was the first time I had heard this superstition, and I became frightened that I might die.

I decided to speak to Barb about this, and she explained that this was not true. She told me that I was more likely to die from childbirth than from refusing to have sex in this traditional way. Due to the poor healthcare available in my country, especially in the hinterlands, pregnancy was always a risk. I returned home, armed with an arsenal of knowledge about sexual activity and pregnancy, informing my mom and grandmother that I was not ready to have any sexual relationship at such young age. As time went by and they realized that I truly meant what I had told them, they slowly began to back off and to my relief my parents never brought up the subject to me again.

The Sacrificial Lamb

My parents had still not forgotten their previous request that I go to a witch doctor who would help to protect me from my enemy who was about to destroy my life. On one sunny, beautiful Sunday afternoon, I returned home from church only to be confronted by my grandmother, who demanded that the family make an animal sacrifice for my future. My parents and grandmother had visited the witch doctor and he had told them it was essential to make an immediate sacrifice for my protection from the enemy. According to this man, I had a promising future ahead of me but my parents had to fight very hard against the enemy if I wanted any chance of securing this future. I did not know who the enemy was, but my parents were eager to stop him as quickly as possible. In order to do this, it was necessary to appease our ancestor spirits so that they would fight on my behalf.

My parents were instructed to purchase a pure white sheep without any blemish. An imam would recite words of prayer and then would proceed to slaughter the sheep by slitting its throat. He would rub a portion of the sheep's blood on my forehead as protection against the evil eye of my enemy. This was to be done daily on my body for a given period of time to ensure that the enemy would not be able to attack me. After the ritual was completed, we would butcher the sheep, cook it with rice, and distribute it among my family and extended relatives.

I listened respectfully to my grandmother as she described the details of the sacrifice, but I knew in my heart that I would not agree to participate. I told her that if they chose to perform the sacrifice anyway, I would leave the house until they were finished. Even so, a man brought a large sheep to our backyard and tied him to one of our many orange trees. My mother had already collected the food required for the ceremony, and my extended relatives were already assembled to help prepare the meal. My father told me that I was not to leave the house.

Before I became a Christian, the day of a sacrifice was festive and exciting. However, I knew enough Christian scriptures by this time to know that making a sacrifice to an idol, other gods, or anything else for that matter, was wrong in God's eyes. God spoke so strongly in regard to idolatry that I could not ignore it. I remembered Deuteronomy 5:8-10, which said, "You shall not make for yourself an image in the form of anything in heaven above or on earth beneath or in the waters below. You shall not bow down to them or worship them; for I, the Lord your God, am a jealous God, punishing the children for the sin of the parents to the third and fourth generation of those who hate me, but showing love to a thousand generations of those who love me and keep my commandments." I also knew from Hebrews 10:4 that it is impossible for the blood of bulls and goats to take away sins.

However, by the time all of the preparations had been made, I was compelled by my parents to sit and listen for the entire ritual. They had spent a lot of money on my behalf, and I did not want to dishonor or shame my parents, especially in the presence of my neighbors. However, even though I sat down, deep down inside of my heart, I refused to listen. The sacrifice was made, and according to my relieved parents and grandmother, my problems were ended. In their eyes, I had been purified. My filthy body and mind had been cleansed, and Allah would accept me once again.

It was true that I was very disappointed about my situation of not being able to return to school to complete my high school education. However, I knew that killing a sheep would not manipulate or twist God's arm in such a way as to change His will for my life. It was up to God to determine the path my life would take.

Fishing with Miss Barb

My friendship with Barb was growing stronger every day. I often visited her at the mission compound in Tahn, where we would sit together in the shade on handmade benches while we studied our Bibles. I contributed to our friendship by teaching her about our traditional African activities.

On hot summer days in Tahn, the women in my village frequently went fishing. I arranged for Barb to accompany me on one of our fishing trips, but forgot to tell my aunts that I was bringing Barb with me. Fishing is one way that women can provide protein and better meals for their families. It is also one of the social activities that unite women in villages and towns. Barb, who has always seen women with their fishing nets to and from fishing, wanted to see and know how it is done.

When these African women saw this American woman with white skin, blond hair, and blue eyes following them, they became very afraid. They did not like the idea of bringing an American woman, who knew nothing about fishing in our muddy creeks with fishing nets, with us. They were worried that she did not know our bush land and that she would not be able to walk at their pace. My aunts were also especially concerned that she could be bitten by a snake or some other poisonous creature in the bush. However, the fishing went well and Barb was thrilled to experience this part of my culture

As a young girl, I had learned to fish with a net in streams and rivers with other girls and women in our village. My mother was unable to teach me because she was too afraid of water and what might lie beneath its surface. Thankfully, my father supplemented our meals by hunting and we often had enough meat left over to sell to our neighbors. My father loved to hunt, so during the dry season, he went into the tropical jungle with other men from my village for week-long hunting trips. They chose a spot in the forest where they camped, cooked, and dried their game.

By the end of the week, he would return home loaded with plenty of dried and fresh meat. A portion of the meat was then stored in palm oil to help preserve it without spoiling for months. This method of preservation of meat enabled us to still have meat at home while others scrambled for it in the market when the supply was low. During the rainy season which lasted for about six months and prevented my dad and others from hunting and doing much of outdoor activities, the preserved meat would then be consumed over that period of time. My dad also made water fences in rivers and little creeks in nearby areas of our farms every year. He caught a supply of fish, crabs and shrimps from these waters, especially when it rained and the rivers got filled. When it came to farming, my dad was great at it and we had more than enough to feed our large family and other relatives.

Chapter 6

THE ONE-WAY HOUSE

Tony

One day, when I had already become a Christian and was attending high school in Monrovia, I decided to attend a weekly Bible study led by Mrs. Pauline Sonius, one of SIM's missionaries, in Monrovia. The young people who attended the study referred to Mr. and Mrs. Sonius as Papay and Mamay, which means mother and father in Liberian English. The Sonius' had previously served in Sierra Leone for twenty years and later came to Liberia and served for another twenty years. They opened their homes to countless Liberians, both young and old, for the sole purpose of extending God's kingdom. One of those was the man who would later become my husband.

A young man named Anthony "Tony" Weedor was scheduled to speak at the Bible study. Tony had accepted Jesus as his Savior in 1982 at this very Bible study through the leading of Mamay Sonius. Like me, he had come from a Muslim background and had even received training to become an imam. In fact, he was next in line to succeed his uncle as the imam of his village. However, God had a different plan for Tony's life.

I visited this Bible study for the very first time on the Friday Tony spoke. He told us about his ministry in Bomi Hills. I was glued to my seat, listening rapturously to everything he had to say. He was an excellent speaker and used phrases and words from my native dialect, Gola. I chuckled under my breath because his accent sounded funny to me. I realized that no one in the group but me understood Gola or they might have felt the same way I did. I was very impressed that such an obviously smart young man would leave his city life, friends, and family behind in order to preach and spread the gospel in remote places. After his amazing message was over, a large group gathered around Tony to continue talking. I was fascinated and would have liked to join in the conversation, but I did not know any of these people and chose to stand back. I walked out of the room, got into a taxi, and headed back home. I never considered that I would ever see Tony again.

Meeting Tony Again

On a rainy day in May 1984 I left with a few members from our church to go to a weekend conference being held for surrounding villages in a small town called Mecca. Sitting in a four-door pickup truck were a few missionaries and two Liberian nationals. To my great surprise, sitting among them was Tony Weedor! I immediately recognized his round face and huge smile, which compelled me to greet him.

"Hi Anthony," I said through the window.

Tony politely returned my greeting but did not ask for my name. Without another word to him I returned to my own group.

Later that evening, we gathered at the conference center, which was made of several posts planted firmly in the ground and covered with palm branches or fronds to shade us from the hot, tropical sun. Together we ate a meal of rice and sauce. It was served with other foods like cassava, eddoes, plantains, and yams, but nothing satisfies the stomach of a Liberian more than rice. Trust me, we

Liberians love our rice! After the first session, there was a break and my sister and I rehearsed our musical duet, which we would sing on the following day.

Saturday arrived, and our session began with a worship service. We sang many choruses in my tribal language of Gola, songs which were narratives of the Christian faith and Christian living. In Africa, worship is a form of celebration. We sing and dance with enthusiasm, and our services can go on for hours. The loud rhythm of our traditional drums made of goat or sheep skin, and our clapping—the loudest imaginable—formed the rhythmic foundation of our worship. High soprano voices and many dancing feet completed our worship and celebration of God. This is African worship.

After several choruses, my sister and I were called up to sing our duet. Then Anthony gave his testimony, telling the story of how he had become a Christian. Once again, everyone in the crowd was captivated. People were moved to tears as he told of the many struggles he faced before and after becoming a Christian. You see, Tony lost his parents and all of his siblings on the day he converted to Christianity. As far as they were concerned, Tony was dead from the moment he renounced Islam, the religion of his family. People were hungry to hear more.

When Tony finished speaking, out of the corner of my eye I saw him walking directly towards me. He stopped in front of me and asked,

"Are you Elizabeth Fahn?"

I slowly answered that I was but wondered how he knew my name.

He replied, "I've heard a lot about you and I am very pleased to have finally met you." He continued by asking if he could pay me a visit at my home in Tahn at the end of the conference after we left Mecca on Sunday afternoon. I was hesitant, but agreed to the meeting.

That evening, I begged my sister, Marie, to join me when Tony came to visit so I would not have to be alone with him. Thankfully, she agreed. When Tony arrived, we talked about his ministry and his home in Lofa County. Marie left the family room, and a moment of silence fell between us. Slowly, he began to tell me more about his ministry and what he intended to do in the near future. During this conversation, Tony worked very hard to get to know more about me and my family, but I was not willing to share anything about myself with a stranger.

During this short visit, I realized just how gifted Tony really was. I learned he enjoyed memorizing Scripture, which explained how Bible verses flowed so easily from his mouth when he spoke. After he left, I had to admit to myself that I wished we could spend some more time together.

The next morning I was curled up outside on my parents' front porch, reading a book called Her Name is Woman by Gien Karssen. I looked up to see a figure headed my way, carrying a bag on his shoulder and another in his left hand. Upon closer examination, I saw that the man was Tony! I tend to be an introvert, so I immediately considered running into my room to hide. My heart won out as I realized I really did want to talk to him once more.

Tony stepped onto the porch and, with sudden clarity, I realized how handsome he was. He had a natural gap between his two front teeth, which in most African tribes is a symbol of beauty in both sexes. With a big smile on his face, he warmly greeted me and informed me he was leaving for Bomi Hills. He wanted to stop and say good-bye before he left. I soon realized that this meeting was very meaningful for Tony. He easily drew me into conversation, and I found myself wishing I had the ability to be as open with strangers as he was. Soon he stopped a cab and left for Bomi Hills.

One week after his departure, I received an eight-page letter from Tony while still in Tahn. The cab driver who delivered it had strict instructions to hand it to Steve, one of the missionaries at the compound which was on the outskirts of Tahn, about fifteen minutes' walk away. To comply with the instruction given, Steve hand delivered Tony's letter to me at my home. He asked if I knew why Tony might be writing me.

I could not answer Steve's question. According to my upbringing, Tony was still a stranger to me. However, in this letter, he proposed to me! He told me the desires of his heart, going so far as to outline his plans for our future life and ministry together! I decided not to respond to his letter right away so that I would not encourage him further until I had sorted through my thoughts and feelings. I knew he was handsome and highly intelligent, and that he had a heart for the Lord. At the same time, I was not ready to commit the rest of my life to a man who was still a stranger. I decided that time and distance would decide our fate.

Who would have known that one short meeting on my family's front porch would be the beginning of a four and a half year courtship?

God Sent a Rainbow

One morning Jessica, another SIM's single missionary from Monrovia at the time, along with Barb, informed me that they had decided to help me return to school. I was dumbfounded! This news was too good to be true! I could have burst out into loud singing, my joy was that great! Barb asked if I would be ready to travel to Bomi Hills the following day where I would be attending school. Without hesitation I replied with a confident, "Yes!"

The moment I left the mission premises in Tahn, I sang and hopped with joy all the way home. I called my parents and grandmother into the house and told them my good news. They were very excited for me, and in no time they helped me get ready for my departure. As I began to pack my bag, I wondered whether both my parents and grandmother would give credit to God's goodness or to the ancestor to whom the sacrifice had been made.

The next chapter in my life was starting, and despite any ridicule I had suffered for my faith, there is no one who could have accomplished this feat but a mighty God. I had no idea where I would stay once I got to Bomi Hills, but I was confident that God was already working on this situation for me. My parents did not allow me to tell my friends about this good news because they were afraid that I would once again become bewitched by my enemies. This would bring all of my plans to a halt.

The day of my departure dawned, and I was headed to Bomi Hills with Jessica. To my surprise, I discovered that Jessica and Barb—with the help of their missionary colleagues, Hartmut and Friedhilde Stricker—had arranged for me to stay with a couple named James and Mary Konan. Moreover, the Strickers, Barb, and Jessica funded my education and living expenses in Bomi Hills. They had taken care of everything for that school year for me.

I was thankful to my gracious, loving, and heavenly Father for His provisions for me. Surprisingly, when we arrived at the Strickers' home in the SIM compound in Bomi Hills, there was Tony standing at the kitchen sink cutting up vegetables for a meal. This was not a common habit for an African male. I took a deep breath and consoled myself to be strong. Tony came briefly into the living room where I was sitting with Jessica. I could tell he was excited to see me, but I did not strike up a conversation with him. He went back into the kitchen and finished his food preparation. Finally, we sat together for the meal. I must admit that the food was delicious! It made a great impression on me, almost as much as his wide knowledge of Scripture had impressed me at our first meeting!

During the next few days, Tony found a private moment to ask if I had received his letter. He was curious about my possible response. I wanted to inform him how taken aback I was by his letter, considering that I did not even know him. Why would his first request of me be for my hand in marriage? But as I looked into his eyes, I could tell that he was sincere, yet very anxious to know what my response was.

I informed Tony that I needed to pray about our relationship and that I wanted to get to know him better. I was not ready to start a relationship with him. Tony decided that my response was not a negative one, and he continued to pursue me. He visited my home often, always asking if he could help me in any way. My host parents, the Konans, appreciated his company as well. As our friendship grew, I continued to enjoy being with him. Then I began to miss him when he was gone for an extended time on evangelism outreach trips.

Six months later, he again asked if I would respond to his letter. He was leaving soon for Bible College in Yekepa (northeastern Liberia). By this time, I knew I was in love with Tony. I still was not ready to make a commitment, though, because I wanted to complete high school and get a nursing degree from college before I married. To meet my goal we decided we would continue our relationship by writing to each other.

Tony came to Bomi Hills for all of his vacations over the next four years while in college. We had both good and bad times, but with the help of God and our good friend, Hardy Stricker, also referred to as Hartmut who had acted as our matchmaker, we made it through. Hardy, who first worked in my hometown as a single missionary before being transferred to Bomi Hills, knew me from there. He was present in Tahn at the time of my baptism and evidently he saw me grow in my walk with God. When Anthony came to do ministry with him in Bomi, Hardy told him about me and encouraged him to get to know me. When the conference in Mecca was underway, Hardy chose the opportunity to arrange for Tony to attend it, having heard that I would be there as well, making it a perfect time for him to meet me. He was right! I was there and Tony and I met.

Chapter 7

THE TRIALS OF COURTSHIP

Belle Baluma, Here I Come

In our second year of courtship, Tony, Hartmut Stricker, and I visited Tony's village, Balumah, which is located in northeastern Liberia in Lofa County. At the time of our visit, Lofa was one of the largest counties in Liberia and was densely populated, but during the Civil War almost everyone fled to the capital, Monrovia. And at the end of the Civil War part of the county separated from the original region that was referred to as Lofa and formed another county that is now called Gbapolu. I was terrified of going to Lofa County in that it was notorious for animistic worship, voodoos, and black magic. However, I knew that if I were to marry Tony, I needed to see his home village and know more about his family.

We drove for an entire day and spent the night in a tiny, uninviting village shack as we still had not arrived in Balumah. In Liberia, once you drive outside of Monrovia, you are at the mercy of anyone who chooses to show you kindness, especially for lodging. There are no hotels or guesthouses in the hinterlands. Thankfully, our host was hospitable.

The next morning we left and drove for many more hours on narrow, dusty roads riddled with potholes and bridges made out of logs. The bridges were so shaky that we held our breath while we crossed them. Then the road ended, and so did any semblance of civilization. From that point, we had to walk, a real test of my love for Tony. We walked through thick, dense forests on dirt trails for six to seven more hours with our luggage balanced carefully on our heads before arriving in Fasama.

Fasama is where Tony's mother was born. Tony's relatives who lived there welcomed us, and his aunt provided delicious food for us. With gratitude in our hearts, we thanked Tony's family, said our goodbyes and continued our journey to Balumah. Such kindness is a typical example of African hospitality. A traveler or guest is never sent away without being fed first.

Forty-five minutes later we arrived in Baluma, and I was exhausted. Tony had jokingly told me that Baluma was "the most beautiful city in Liberia." Of course, almost every African thinks his or her home village is the most beautiful of all villages! In reality it is never the case, and so it was with Baluma. It was smaller and more distant from larger towns than I had thought. Tony's family was shocked to see us, because there had been no way to inform them of our trip. They quickly prepared a meal for us to eat, and because it was late we retired to bed.

The next day Tony, Hardy and I joined his family on their rice farm for the day. It was a thirty minute walk from town. Throughout the day, I had the opportunity to learn more about Tony and his family through my conversations with them. Tony came from a family of five children, two girls and three boys. As the third child, Tony did not spend much of his childhood years at home. In order to attend school, it was necessary for him to live away from home because when he reached school age there was no educational facility in his home village. As in most African villages where there were no schools, parents sent their children to live with other relatives where there were schools so that they would have the opportunity to get their education. If the school was only at an elementary level, they would then be sent to another town or city to complete their high school education. For those of us who came from the hinterland, gaining a higher education was a great sacrifice for everyone; and for the children it required lots of hard work away from our families and loved ones.

When Tony was thirteen, he was sent to the home of a relative who lived in Number 7, one of the divisions of the Firestone plantation located outside of Monrovia. He stayed there for only a year and was then sent back to Baluma. While in Baluma, his uncle brought him to Bomi Hills to live with him while he attended school. Due to the hardships he faced in his uncle's home, he decided to move to Monrovia where he remained and completed his high school education.

Tony's oldest sister, Ma Janga, had already left her parents' home to live in her husband's village. His older brother, Austin, had married and brought his wife, Bendu, home to Baluma to live with his family and take care of his aging mother. In most African cultures, when a son gets married, he brings his wife to the home of his parents and becomes the leader in the family. The daughter-in-law assumes the role of preparing food and caring for the entire household. Her mother-in-law would be available to make major decisions, to help care for the grandchildren, or to settle disputes among the members of her immediate family. Bendu was a hard-working woman and a tremendous help to Tony's family.

On my second day in Baluma, I received my first test of womanhood from my future mother-in-law, Gbejoe. Early in the morning Gbejoe asked me to go to the creek and fetch some drinking water for the house. I knew she had a hidden motive, but I wanted to impress Tony's family, so I immediately picked up the bucket and headed for the creek. This was not as easy as it might seem.

Every African tribe has its own dialect, and I did not understand the dialect spoken in Tony's village. I was like Ruth in the Bible, who went to Boaz's farm, gleaning grain in his field among total strangers. When the servants in the field spotted Ruth, they began to talk and whisper about her behind her back.

As I walked to the creek with the other women in the village, I could not understand exactly what they said to each other. I knew they were wondering about my identity, but I decided not to worry about it. I hurried to fulfill Gbejoe's request. I wanted to show her that my mother had raised me properly. My mother, who was a hard-working woman, had taught me everything I needed to know in our culture, so I knew I would be able to handle anything Tony's mother asked me to do.

Less than ten minutes after I had returned from the creek, Tony's mother called me to the kitchen. A decapitated chicken was lying on the floor. She pointed to it and said something in her dialect, which of course I could not understand. However, I could tell that her statement was drenched in sarcasm and ridicule. The other two women in the kitchen chuckled at my expense. Anger crept through my veins, and it took all of my will power to resist the urge to react. Instead, I called Tony to interpret for me and discovered that she wanted me to prepare a meal for the family using the dead chicken.

My mother had warned me that I would someday be tested in this way by my future mother-in-law which is typical behavior for most mothers-in-law in Africa. This memory gave me a renewed sense of courage and strength. I was ready to prove to Tony's mother and the other women in that kitchen that I was not a lazy city girl from Monrovia. I immediately changed into more casual and comfortable clothes and took charge of the kitchen. I set a pot of water on the firewood to boil and then put the chicken in the boiling water to make it easier to remove its feathers. I removed the feathers and then butchered the chicken into bite-sized pieces. It is said in Africa that a woman who does not know how to cut up a whole chicken does not know how to cook. Therefore, she cannot make a good wife.

Tony's mother also asked me to prepare a special sauce of cassava leaves well known to my tribal group, Gola. That was music to my ears. I put my heart and soul into preparing that meal. To my future mother-in-law's surprise, the food was more than delicious! It was well-seasoned and properly cut-up. The rice was cooked just right. If there had been any doubt in her mind about my ability to cook, her first bite squashed it. Tony's brother, Austin, thanked me profusely for the meal, and it appeared that I had passed my test.

Another Test of a Different Kind

Three days after that meal, I woke up early in the morning with a sharp pain in my neck. In just a few hours, the entire left side of my neck, including my chin, was swollen. As the day progressed, I grew fearful as it became harder and harder to breathe. I developed a high temperature and began to feel intense pain throughout my body. By evening, Tony was very concerned about me, but he did not want to appear weak in front of me. The night was unbearable, and no change in position brought physical relief. Tony and Hartmut knew by now that my problem was serious and needed immediately medical attention. I thought to myself: if only my mother was here; she would know what to do.

It was decided that Hartmut and I would go back to Bomi Hills while Tony stayed with his parents for a few more days. The morning of our departure, Tony's family gave us a live goat to take back with us as a way of thanking us for our visit. Our trip back to Bomi Hills took another day and a half's journey which I thought would never end. When we arrived at Hartmut's house, his wife, Friedhilde, made chicken noodle soup and gave me some pain-relief and fever-reducing medication. I slept through the day for the first time since my ailment.

The next morning, I went to see the doctor, who informed me that there was an abscess on my neck that might need to be surgically drained. I was discouraged and decided to go home before having such an invasive procedure done without the help of my mother. On that same day I left for my home town of Tahn. When I stepped out of the taxi, my mother jumped off of the stool on the front porch and ran to me. She grasped my hand and supported me with her own body, guiding me to the house. I lay down on a mat and began to tell her about my trip to Tony's village, reliving each test I had been asked to perform.

I told her about my illness and the pain I had been experiencing. I watched as fear crept into her eyes. I soon fell asleep, and when I awakened I saw my grandmother, my mother, and a few other relatives in the middle of a serious discussion. My family had called for the help of our local witch doctor. Folk Islam teaches that nothing happens without a cause, whether it is illness, famine, family misfortune, or even a sick animal. The question is never what caused the problem but who caused it. The intent of my parents was clear; they wanted to know how to divert the illness or misfortune back on the person who caused it in the first place. They also wanted the witch doctor to give me protection from any future attack.

The witch doctor began to perform ceremonies, and told my parents that my ailment was caused by a female member of Tony's family—someone with whom he was very close to. He said this woman did not want us to get married, and that had I stayed any longer in the village, it would have been bad for me. He told my family that they must act quickly. Angered and fearful, they began to use every herbal remedy that they knew. On the first day alone, I consumed more medicine than I had used over the entire course of my life. Some smelled so bad I could not bring them to my mouth without gagging. They rubbed some medicines on my swollen neck, which actually felt good to me. However, I continued to feel tired and unable to do anything for myself.

That same night, my sister Marie went into labor with her first child. My grandmother needed to attend to the birth, so she had to leave our home and go next door to our second house that she had built for us children, where my sister resided. My mother had a difficult time going back and forth between the two homes, torn between caring for me and spending some time with my sister. When I woke up the next morning, I discovered that I had become an aunt. It was Christmas morning.

None of the treatments I had been given were helping, so my mother and grandmother went out to hunt for additional treatments.

While they were gone, my friend Barb and her colleague happened to see me sitting on my front porch as they were walking to church that morning. They had not known beforehand that I was home from Bomi and ill with a swollen neck. They were shocked and sad to see me in so much pain. When the church service was over and they on their way back to their compound, Barb promised to return to town later on that same day with some antibiotics for me.

When my family returned from their long hours of searching for other alternatives, they brought a man with them who was an elementary school teacher, originally from Sierra Leone. He asked me a few questions and felt my neck. By then, I had already taken two doses of antibiotics and a couple of pain killers provided by Barb. This man made some herbs for me to drink and to rub on my neck. I began to pray that if this man's herbs were not going to be effective that he would not get the glory or praise for healing me. I wanted God to receive all the glory for the healing power that would take place in my body, nobody else. Three days later, between the antibiotics and the herbs, I was able to eat and drink, though not completely healed from my ailment. The swelling on my neck decreased substantially. Barb returned a few days later and encouraged me to take the rest of my antibiotics even if I did feel that I was better.

Chapter 8

THE NAMING CEREMONY

Life and Death

On New Year's Day, we held the naming ceremony for my sister's baby. It was a day of festivity for our family and a few of our town members, as well. Baby-naming ceremonies are still carried out in many parts of the world since days of old, especially among Muslims, but also among some Christians as well. When a baby is born, the child is kept inside for six days. On the seventh day, the parents officially name the child. Boys are circumcised on that day in most parts of Africa. However, within a Muslim community, circumcision is not performed until the baby boy is over one year old. Educated families often choose to have it done in the hospital before they are discharged.

When a child is named after a living relative, that relative takes the baby outside in the presence of everyone gathered and reveals his or her name. An elder of the family then offers a word of blessing and protection for the baby. If the child is named after a family member who is deceased, one of the parents or the grandparents takes the baby outside and reveals the name.

Ben was named in the presence of all of us. Marie and her husband, who were also members of my church, asked Pastor Varney, our pastor, to offer a word of blessing over the child.

Everyone present ate food prepared specifically for this time of celebration. This was a Christian naming ceremony.

Soon after the ceremony, a soccer match started as part of our New Year's celebration. My young Uncle Sirleaf was the goalie, and my Uncle Sylvester was the team's president. During the second half of the match, Sirleaf was kicked in the stomach by a player on the opposing team, hard enough that he had to be carried off of the field. He developed a high fever and was in excruciating pain. My family tried to care for him throughout the night, but they soon realized they could not help him. He was driven to Bomi Hills and immediately taken into surgery. After they had opened up my uncle's stomach on the operating table, the surgeon realized that it was too late to save him.

Sirleaf died that day. One week after God delivered a precious child to earth this joyous celebration was tainted by the death of my uncle. African tradition says that news like this is to be kept a secret from women and children, so some of us did not know immediately of his death. We were told that the hospital needed some mats and bed sheets for my uncle's hospital room, but the truth was that they needed the mats and sheets to wrap his body to transport it back home.

It was a great shock to my entire family to see the body of my uncle in the back of a pick-up truck. When the truck approached our home, it was decorated with palm thatch branches, which indicates that a body is being transported. So we knew right away that something unspeakable had happened: Sirleaf was dead, and we grieved his untimely death. They carried my Uncle Sirleaf's body out of the truck and laid it gently on our front porch.

In no time at all, the majority of the townspeople had gathered in our yard to share in our sorrow, joining in our wails and cries. Staring at my uncle's lifeless body, I could only think of revenge for his death. The story circulating around town was that his injury had been pre-planned. How I wished for justice to be rendered, but this was not to be.

A few weeks after my uncle's death, I finally began to see significant improvement in my physical condition. I wondered whether the antibiotics had cured me or whether the herbal treatment performed by the witch doctor had accomplished my healing. I came to the conclusion that it must be the antibiotics, but I could never say this in the presence of my parents. To doubt the work of the witch doctor would have been disrespectful to my parents and everyone living in my town who heard the news.

Reunion with Tony

Tony finally made it back to Bomi Hills after spending two additional weeks with his family. While in Baluma, there was no communication between us because of its remoteness from everything. My family was not pleased that Tony had not returned to Bomi with me considering how ill I was. However, he could not have visited his village for such a short time and immediately taken off with me without spending some personal time with his mother.

Tony's relationship with his family, especially his mother, at this point in time was beginning to soften or look somewhat better than after his first few years of becoming a Christian. Though they believed he had betrayed them and their community by changing his faith, a mother's love for her child is always there even though sometimes under strain. Tony's relationship with his mom, although at times up-and-down, was improving as time went by. At the end of Tony's additional two-week visit in Balumah, he immediately came to my home in Tahn. When he saw me, he could not believe how the initial pain I suffered at his family's home had turned into a major health problem. He felt guilty for not coming back with me during my illness. Tony spent four days with me in my home town then returned to Bomi Hills. After my complete recovery, I returned to Bomi Hills and spent two more weeks with Tony before he departed for the African Bible College to complete his last semester of school. Our only communication would now be by mail. By this time, we had become very close, and we knew that we loved each other.

Another Mystery Illness

A few months later, I had the opportunity to again travel with Tony along with a missionary friend named Renate, who was from Germany, to visit Tony's family. Renate's ministry focused on translating the Bible into my native dialect of Gola. The journey took less time on this occasion because logging companies in the area had extended the road all the way to Tony's village.

The day after our arrival, Tony decided to tell his family about our plans for marriage. He asked his mother if she would come back with us to my hometown to meet my family. In Africa, this is the most respectable way for the groom's parents to make arrangements for their son's marriage. On the morning of our departure, Tony's mother woke up with a severe stomachache and vomiting. We learned that the night before she had swallowed some herbs in order to cause her stomach irritation, so that she would not have to come with us to meet my family.

I struggled with her action. Nothing could have justified what she had done to me, her future daughter-in-law. I felt completely rejected. I managed to gather the courage to thank Tony's family for allowing me to visit, and we left for Bomi Hills and then continued to my home.

My family was excited to see me and anxiously waited for news about my visit to Tony's family. At this point, I was beginning to question our engagement because of his mother's unwillingness to meet my family. Because my mother was treated poorly by her in-laws, I had made a promise to myself that I would not marry a man whose parents did not love me. I prayed to God that I would not have to deal with such hatred in my own marriage. After my father heard everything I had to say, he became very upset. He said that if Tony's mother did not meet them before the wedding, he would not allow the marriage to take place. My father was not the kind of person to speak decisively very often, but when he did, it was the final word.

I left home to return to Bomi Hills so I could say goodbye to Tony before he left for college once again. I told Tony about my parents' reaction to the treatment I had received at his home, emphasizing that if Tony did not convince his mother to meet my parents, he would be standing at the altar alone. Tony thought I was joking at first, but he later saw the seriousness of the situation and was greatly upset. He contacted his uncle, Tommy Davies, in Bomi Hills, who then reached out to his sister, Tony's mother, informing her how important it was that she met my family. We still did not hear anything from her.

We spent the rest of our time together making our wedding plans. By this time, neither of us liked to be separated from the other.

Graduation and the Marriage Proposal

My graduation day finally arrived. My sister Marie also graduated on the same day. Together, we were making history in our village, being recognized as women who had completed high school when most women in our village had not. I was more than overjoyed when Tony told me he would be coming to Bomi Hills to celebrate with me. My parents and other family members were also coming to celebrate this important day with me. In most parts of Africa, nobody gets an invitation to a graduation, wedding, or funeral. As long as they know the person having the celebration or anyone related to that person - everyone just comes.

On the morning of my graduation, I awoke with a heavy heart. I had expected Tony to arrive the previous day, but he was nowhere to be seen. By two o'clock in the afternoon, Tony still had not arrived. This was a history-making day, as my sister and I were the first generation in our family to graduate from high school. My grandmother could not hold back her tears as she watched my sister and me walk forward to receive our diplomas. This was extremely significant for me, having both parents who could not read and write. It was a time of great rejoicing for my family, and from dusk until midnight we feasted and danced in glorious celebration.

A little after midnight, after everyone was asleep, I heard a quiet knock on the door. There was Tony, standing with a bag in his hand under the one, lone light bulb that hung in front of the apartment complex. I fell into his arms, and he began to tell me of his struggle to get to my graduation using Liberia's inadequate public transportation. There was nothing to forgive.

We traveled to my family's home so that Tony could meet privately with my father to inform him of his intention to marry me. My father said he would gather our entire family in order to receive their approval. When the family was assembled, Tony declared his intentions about our relationship, and my parents accepted the request. However, they reminded Tony that they must meet his parents before any other plans could be made. Our culture's tradition says that Tony could not represent himself in the arrangement of marriage; he must bring a representative to speak for him.

Tony agreed to my father's terms. He had no choice but to comply because a woman cannot give herself in marriage to a man without her father's blessing. This was to protect my honor and the honor of my family as well.

Tony's Graduation

In the meantime, Tony had successfully met the requirements for his degree in Biblical Studies with an emphasis on broadcasting. The African Bible College is located in Yekepa, in the northeastern part of Liberia, bordering Guinea and the Ivory Coast. It is one of the nicest locations in Liberia, shielded by a mountain that is over 14,000 feet high. The campus was severely damaged during the civil war but was later rebuilt by Samaritan Purse, Franklin Graham's organization. It is well cared for, and it looks very much like a college located in the Western world.

I traveled with Tony's spiritual parents, Ron and Pauline Sonius, and a few of his close friends to attend his graduation. No one from Tony's family came to rejoice with him over this important milestone in his life, but Tony's spirit was not quenched. I am always amazed at Tony's bright spirit, which is uniquely crafted by the hand of God to handle these kinds of situations with such grace and dignity.

This was not a surprise to Tony because his relationship with his family was strained on account of his conversion to Christianity. For Tony to achieve his educational goal was a miracle written into Tony's life by the providential hand of God. My mind could not shake the thought that it was the unconditional love of God for Tony that had provided for this miracle. Tony had grown up in a Muslim family and was being groomed to be the imam of his village. The open rejection by his family would have been more than most people could have borne. Yet with no financial means of his own, he was able to accomplish this goal with dedicated hard work and the assistance of friends and other Christians, especially Ron and Pauline, who led him to Christ.

Before Tony enrolled in Bible College, he had been so hungry for the Word of God that he had mingled each day with other Christians to try to understand salvation and the Christian life. He struggled with unanswered questions and then decided to participate in a Navigator Bible Study in Monrovia. The leader, Chuck Brood, took Tony under his wing and encouraged Tony to memorize Scripture. Ironically, Tony's Islamic background, which included the daily practice of reciting the Koran, prepared him to memorize and hold tight to biblical scriptures. The more he read his Bible, the more he desired to become educated in biblical theology. His spiritual parents helped to support his goal to attend Bible College by introducing Tony to the Strickers who allocated a paying ministry job for him in Bomi that helped cover some of his college tuition and personal expenses while in college. Tony was able to enroll in the African Bible College, where he was granted a work scholarship.

I dressed for Tony's graduation in a stylish navy blue dress that I had made specifically for the ceremony. Every detail of my appearance was perfect, and I felt prepared for the occasion. Tony was excited to see me, and we both enjoyed spending some special time together for those few days, having been away from each other for a while. One of his college professors, Mrs. Barbara Lentz, came to me during my visit to the campus and said,

"God has given you a fine, godly young man. He has been a joy to have in my class, and I have enjoyed watching him grow."

Her words reminded me that I could not ask for anything more in my life; God had given me the desire of my heart. Mrs. Lentz's statement reaffirmed my decision to marry Tony.

Looking back at all of the hardships that Tony had to face to achieve his dream of obtaining a college degree, I can do nothing but give God the glory and praise for what He has done in our lives.

Chapter 9

A WEDDING

Wedding Preparations

In June, 1988, Tony finally returned to Monrovia after his graduation, and we began to prepare for our wedding. We officially sent out our wedding invitations to friends in Monrovia and Bomi Hills, though as is the custom people would still show up without any, especially friends and family from my home town. Tony began searching for a home for us in Monrovia. He was also busy attending various orientation sessions for his upcoming job with SIM, the mission organization through which many important people had entered into our lives. However, we were once again reminded that our wedding could not take place without a representative from Tony's family agreeing to attend our wedding.

When Tony received a letter from his mother stating her refusal to attend our wedding, I knew we were in serious trouble. My father was a man of his word. No wedding would take place unless he first met Tony's family.

We also found out that Tony's eldest sister, Ma Janga, who according to African tradition is his second mother, had also decided not to come. Her reasoning for not coming was she could not close her shop for the time that would be required to come to my home for our wedding. With all of these problems popping up at the last minute, I felt as if Tony's family was trying to sabotage my wedding. My family had already announced our upcoming wedding to everyone we knew, and were expecting Tony's family to show up in good faith. I wrote Tony and suggested that if his mother would not attend, he should ask his Uncle Tommy and Aunt Satta, whom I loved so dearly, to attend. They could represent his mother to my father and the rest of my family. Without any hesitation, Tony informed his Uncle Tommy about the situation. Uncle Tommy then contacted his sister. His mother's refusal to come to our wedding, I later learned, was mainly because I was not from the same tribal group as Tony and did not come from the same village. In the end, she did come but only as the result of her brother Tommy's persistent requests for her to meet with my family. He constantly pointed out to her how terrible her son would feel if she were not there to support him.

A wedding was a big event for small villages like Tahn. In particular, my wedding was anticipated by everyone in town because it would be completely different from our normal cultural wedding practices. As a Christian wedding, it differed in that it took place in the church and not at home. The ceremony focused mainly on Tony and me as a couple and not on the entire families and extended relatives. There were vows being made between us both in the presence of our Christian brothers and sisters, and mainly before God that would be taken seriously. Also, it was the first and biggest of its kind in my home village – a wedding which combined our Christian beliefs and traditions with some of our cultural traditions too. Many of my family members had already contributed the livestock we needed for our wedding celebration. Many others were contributing other food for our festivities. Everyone in my family and community showed up to give their support for my wedding, even though I was no longer a part of the Muslim community.

Plans had already been made to have our wedding cake delivered from Monrovia to Tahn, an eighty-five mile trip. My wedding dress and the bridesmaids' dresses, long white African gowns, were already being made. My bridesmaids' heads would be wrapped with the same material as their dresses: a traditional fabric similar to that worn by Muslims all over Western Africa. The men would wear beautifully-embroidered turbans to match the fronts of their shirts. Everyone would wear traditional handmade sandals. By doing these things, we hoped to honor and respect our Muslim families. Our wedding would not be extravagant or expensive, but I was certain that it would be the most wonderful day of my life. Most of all, we prayed that our wedding would give glory to God.

The Setting of the Bride's Price

It was difficult, but we did our very best to honor our families without compromising our Christian faith. This required Tony to pay a dowry for my hand in marriage. The payment was made in a traditional African Muslim marriage style. On the first of July, my parents and other extended family members negotiated the price of the bride with Tony's mother and extended family. This dowry payment is one of the most important parts of a traditional marriage. Anything can be bartered: money, jewelry, cows, sheep, or hand-woven materials.

In older days, the paying of a dowry was a symbolic act of "belonging," but as time passed, it became a symbol of status. In East Africa, for example, the more cattle a man gives for the dowry of his intended bride, the greater the honor for her family. Dowries are given for different categories: virgins, unmarried women who are not virgins, widows, and divorced women. The bride price for a virgin is the highest price offered, and most men will pay as much as they are asked because it brings honor to the future bride's family as well as the family of the groom. This also states how he desires to be treated and known by the community or village.

When my family presented the bride's price to Tony's family, it was outrageously high. I was not allowed to make any objections, even though I felt that I should speak up and defend Tony. To do so would have disrespected my own family, so I tried very hard to keep my mouth shut. Tony's family went off into a corner to discuss the price. Commonly referred to as the "hanging of heads," this conversation often ends up in a huge fight among family members. While we waited for their response, there was a festive atmosphere in our home. Family and community members were celebrating with us, enjoying food, and joking with each other.

When Tony's family returned, they tried to lighten the atmosphere with a few jokes, and Tony's uncle eventually presented the amount requested by my family. My father thanked Tony's family and presented the money to the rest of our family. The bartering for my hand in marriage was not done, however. My mother's educated second cousin, Uncle Harris, interrupted my father and said that the dowry price was not enough. Tony's uncle took their group outside for another time of head hanging. When they returned, they added additional money to the amount that had already been given to my father. Another family member spoke up and demanded that Tony's family should pay even more because of the great training and education my family had provided for me, not to mention that it was rare to find a girl of my age in my area who was still a virgin. Right there, I wanted to shout a loud 'Amen'. Though I was in sympathy with Tony for the outrageously large price that my family was requesting from him and his family, he needed to know how lucky he was to have me as his wife!

For the second time, Tony's family added more money to the bride price. The haggling continued until my grandfather, old man Goliah, who was the oldest person in the room, interrupted everyone.

"Stop this money matter," he ordered. "The paying of the dowry for this woman will never end, and as long as Tony shall remain married to her, he will continue to pay us her dowry. So let us give him his wife and be done with it, because as far as we are concerned, our daughter is priceless!"

My heart beamed with pride at my grandfather's words, yet I would not risk showing my excitement in order not to disrespect him or my family. While the men continued to talk, my mother and grandmother brought in a huge trunk filled with my departure gifts. Among them were bedspreads, table cloths, and African suits that had been made for me.

There were also dishes, pots and pans, pot holders, silverware, kitchen knives, a mortar and pestle (used for grinding spices), and a little stool commonly used in the kitchen by African women. In a typical African kitchen, the lady of the home is expected to sit on a short stool while a younger girl stays by her side to hand her what she needs. My family gave me all of these items to show Tony's family the depth of their love for me. The bride price had been paid, and at last I could be given to Tony and his family in marriage, though this would involve yet another ceremony. My father's oldest sister held my hand and set me on the lap of Tony's aunt, at which time I was officially presented to everyone who had gathered in my parents' home as witnesses. This was also a formal presentation to Tony. I was now his wife. Tony was asked to take me from the lap of his aunt and take me away as his wife.

To our families, we were married, and they expected us to sleep together from that day forward. However, we waited until the next day, July 2, for our Christian ceremony before we consummated our marriage. While we wanted to please and honor our families, we also wanted to make a public proclamation to our Christian friends by having a wedding ceremony in our church. At this time we were not sure that our families would feel free to come to our church wedding since they were Muslims. We had formally received the traditional blessing of our families; now we desired to be married within our covenant family at church.

I woke up early to the crowing of the rooster. That rooster always made it his business to come to my window every morning at that same hour to noisily announce the breaking of a new day. I awoke with a new sense of peace in my heart, a kind of joy I could not explain. However, throughout this whole process, I still was not looking forward to leaving my family to start a new home of our own. It seemed like such a huge commitment. I prayed that we would not have children too soon after our marriage. There was so much we wanted to do together as husband and wife.

I heard the Islamic call to prayer from the local mosque and knew my parents would be getting out of bed soon. Tony would not be allowed to see me until we arrived at church for the ceremony. Likewise, I was not allowed to be seen in public until I was dressed and ready for my wedding. To this day, I do not understand the reason behind this western custom, but I know that though traditions are different around the world, within each culture, they serve as a source of comfort and familiarity.

Around noon, I heard Tony's voice in our living room, followed by the voices of some my family members, who reminded him that he was not to enter my bedroom. He questioned my family about the sense of this, knowing that we would be married soon, but the women in my family did not give in. I remained in my room, laughing with a few of my friends about Tony's dilemma. Tony left the house, but secretly waited until everyone had left the living room and then walked to my bedroom window on the side of the house. He called me to the window and commented,

"No one can ever stop me from seeing you." Tony had not come for any specific reason but only to see me.

We finally made it to the church's yard, which stood in a large open field, waiting to be ushered in. Up to this time we were not sure if our families would feel comfortable to come to our church wedding ceremony since they were Muslims. As we waited in the car, I took a quick glance at the audience and was amazed to see that the church was completely filled with people, so full, in fact, that many stood by the windows and at both front and back doors. Among them were also many curious Muslims standing outside of the church building. They wanted to see how a Christian wedding is performed, but they were not supposed to go inside a Christian church. To our pleasant surprise, both sets of parents and almost all of my Muslim family members showed up at the church. What a joy this brought to our eyes and our hearts!

When both bridal parties had lined up, waiting for my arrival, a long strip of white fabric was rolled out down the aisle of the sanctuary. An archway decorated with beautiful local flowers curved overhead between the lines of bridesmaids and groomsmen providing a stunning entrance for us, the happy couple. There were also two banana trees planted in buckets on either side, their long leaves pointing gracefully in the air. It was a lovely sight! My cousin, Fred Cooke, walked me down the aisle, and my pastor, Rev. James Varney, performed our marriage excellently. His wife, Mary Varney, sang two traditional Gola church songs, accompanied by African sambas, drums, sasa, and the clapping of hands. Tony and I were pronounced husband and wife. His spiritual father, Papay Sonius, challenged us with a few words and then prayed for us. The ceremony ended with a beautiful rendition of "To God Be the Glory," which was sung by one of Tony's college professors, Mrs. Ruth Bliss.

The Gift Wrapped in Banana Leaves

While organizers were putting the final touches on the reception, we left for a short drive. As we drove back towards the reception hall, we could not believe the number of people that were lining the paths to the hall. According to tradition, we would not send anyone away from our reception. Liberians always make more than enough food to accommodate unknown guests. And so did my family for my wedding. They made enough food to have fed half of the town's people. We got out of the car and stood in a receiving line where we received innumerable handshakes and hugs. Finally, Tony and I, along with our wedding parties, made it to the bridal table, where we were served with the food made for our special day.

After everyone had finished eating, Tony's college friend Sampson Nyantee (nicknamed Babee) presented us with a gift on behalf of their entire college class. The present was wrapped in several layers of dried banana leaves. Each time a banana leaf was removed, one of Tony's friends told a funny story, and everyone laughed a great deal. This show of affection for us is still something we value and treasure.

Chapter 10

THE WHITE SHEET

Giving Honor

After we said farewell to our guests, we headed for the SIM mission compound where we spent our wedding night. This way we could have privacy, away from the eyes of the many relatives who would have loved to be with us at all times. We stayed at the mission compound for four days and with my grandmother for two additional nights before returning to Monrovia. Our stay at my grandmother's house was in compliance with a request from my family. Traditionally, in a Muslim marriage, when a virgin gets married, the aunts and grandmother of the bride enter the couple's room very early in the morning after the wedding night in order to fetch the white bed sheet that had been laid on the couple's bed. By this time in the morning, the groom has had enough time to prove his manhood, and the white sheet provides evidence of the young woman's virginity.

While the sheet is being taken from the marriage bed, a group of traditional singers and dancers stand by the door, as well as a man with a gun. If the white sheet comes out of the bedroom with blood on it, the bride was actually a virgin. The gun is fired three times, dancing commences, and the group goes to the home of the bride's parents where the sheet is revealed to everyone. However, if the sheet is as white as the day before, the bride has lost her virginity prior to the wedding. This could instigate an automatic divorce, bringing great humiliation for the bride's family.

My family wanted us to honor this tradition in order to prove my virginity to our entire community. I did not object, but Tony did. He refused to subject me to such a cultural practice for something that should remain private between us. So, in order to show respect to my family and prove that we had not compromised our sexual purity before our marriage, we gave them the results of my premarital exam, which had been done by an American missionary OB/GYN doctor at the ELWA (Eternal Love Winning Africa) hospital. The irony of this could not escape us as we remembered that my family members were the very people who had told me that I needed to have sex or else I would lose my mind and die. After all was said and done, we believe that God was honored in our wedding ceremony. To God be the glory, forever!

An African Marriage

As an African woman who was born and raised there, I have seen the countless hardships that women go through in caring for their husbands and children, not to mention their hard labor in farming the land to meet their daily needs as well as being able to put food on the table for their family. Growing up, I had a difficult time imagining myself living such a life. I prayed that God would make my life different so that I would not suffer like my mother, aunts, grandmother, cousins and other women in Africa with such endless jobs.

When Tony and I decided to get married, the first thing I did was to have an honest talk with him. Our conversation consisted of what we both expected in our marriage and how best we could complement each other so that we would have these wishes met.

Most of all, in order to help make our marriage to work we needed to have Christ be the center of it, that by living a Christ-like life we would glorify His name. In our marriage, Tony and I have always believed in open and honest communication with each other, equal partnership, respect, love, appreciation and forgiveness. Doing work or tasks around our home is never my job alone as is expected in our African traditional marriages. These and many other things we do I believe make our marriage different from most African marriages.

In David Lamb's book, The Africans, he states that "[t] *he* African woman produces seventy percent of the food grown on the Continent, according to the United Nations. She works longer and harder and has more responsibilities than her husband. She is the economic backbone of the rural community, the maker of family decisions, the initiator of social change, the harvester of crops. She is the hub around which the spokes of society turn" (Lamb, page 38).

Most Africans, especially illiterate ones, go into marriage solely for the purpose of bearing numerous children for their respective families. In the case where a child or children are not born within that union, the blame will always be cast on the woman. It is her fault that she cannot get pregnant. The husband will then marry another woman, often a virgin, who will bear him his children. Most of these marriages, as in other parts of the world, are arranged long before the betrothed even meet for the first time.

Growing up in my hometown, I saw the tremendous sacrifices and countless responsibilities of the women in my communities. Women were responsible for cooking, cleaning, and the raising of children, which included caring for them when they were ill. They were constantly on the run, tending to the needs of their children and husbands, as well as other family members to the extent that they often neglected their own needs. For example, my mother did everything for our entire household every day without taking thirty minutes of rest for herself. Each day, after she had made the main meal, she would share all of the food among us and eat nothing herself. While everyone ate, she sat among us surrounded by empty pots and a huge dish pan to clean.

In Africa, the outdoor markets are mostly run by women, who also do the plowing of the fields. Girls are expected to engage in hard labor more than boys. As a young child and even in my early teens, I hated going to the farm where so many of these chores needed to be done so much so that one day I foolishly decided to run away from my mother to the other side of town. While crossing the dusty road, I fell flat on my face and stomach and could barely raise my body from the ground. My parents, my older sister Marie and my neighbors were standing around laughing at me. When I finally rose to my feet, I had no choice but to pick up my load and set it up on my aching head. The farm work still needed to be done, this time with a broken body. Marie and my mother enjoy telling this story about me to this day, especially to my children.

In the old days, the role of an African man was clearly distinguished from that of a woman. According to my grandfather, men seldom stayed in the village with their families; they were constantly warring with enemy tribes or with other villages, especially during rainy seasons. During the dry seasons, they were busy with farming and hunting, which were their primary means of survival. Today, men in our village stay closer to home while their women slowly kill themselves through endless labor. Women toil and labor while middle-aged and elderly men find their way to the entrance of the village to sit under shady palm trees. There they drink homemade beer, palm wine, or cane juice (as we call it in Liberia); smoke pipes or lick their snuff. A grinned tobacco that is consumed by placing it on the tongue for some time. And discuss problems pertaining to the village. This cultural practice goes all the way back to Old Testament times when men would sit at the city gate and discuss the matters of the city: her husband is respected at the gates, where he takes his seat among the elders of the land (Proverbs 31:23).

Later in our lives we served in Ethiopia as missionaries. My husband wanted to be culturally sensitive to the Ethiopian people and thus affiliated himself with the men of the village by doing this very thing—sitting at the entrance of the village and visiting with the other men. We did not have electricity in this village during the day, except for three hours of light at night when we ran a generator before bedtime. One day, Tony left the house, as other African men would do, without telling me where he was going. This act of manliness was unusual for my husband, and it never occurred to me that he would be sitting at the city gate with other men.

I had desperately needed Tony's help on that particular day and finally, frustrated, I prepared our family dinner. I looked out the window and saw Tony walking as fast as he could towards our home. The moment he entered the house and saw the look on my face, which he usually describes as my "Tahn look," he immediately apologized. I asked him about his whereabouts and he said,

"I was sitting at the city's gate solving the problems of the city."

I could not hold back my laughter and said, "The next time you decide to sit at the city's gate with the village elders, it is there you will have your evening meal, which in no way, shape, or form shall come from this home or be cooked by these hands of mine."

We both laughed, and it soon became a fun memory of our time in that secluded, remote Ethiopian village. According to David Lamb, "in Kenya, women represent only 10 percent of the University enrollment, 16 percent of the labor force and 6 percent of the job holders earning more than $375 a year. Their illiteracy rate-70 percent-is doubled that for men. With few exceptions, women in Africa inherit nothing from their fathers and can be divorced by their husbands without any settlement" (Lamb, page 38).

As an African, I have seen this occur many times in my own country of Liberia, especially among my illiterate fellow citizens. In most cases, these men take everything their wives ever earned, down to the children who in almost every case always go to their fathers and then send the woman back to her family empty handed. After all, a woman has no ownership of property or children in her marriage except when the man willingly chooses to share a few of his possessions with her.

When it comes to sex, women are to be available at all times because it is their duty to comply with the wishes of their husbands, no matter how they might feel. In most cases, women are considered nothing more than baby-making machines, completely owned by their men. Sadly, even if a wife satisfies her husband in bed and enslaves herself completely to him by meeting his physical needs, it is still possible and, indeed, likely for him to have affairs with other women. In fact, this behavior is expected. While a woman works tirelessly to support her family, it is not unusual for her husband to use almost all of his earnings on extramarital affairs.

The African View of Life

Africans often wonder why Westerners are always in a hurry or get perturbed so easily. For example, if someone has an appointment and shows up fifteen minutes late, the Westerner becomes rattled and upset that the African is rude and disrespectful of the Westerner's time. On the other hand, the African knows that the person will be there waiting even if they are fifteen minutes late—and understands that it is the fellowship that matters the most, not the time.

In Africa, we do not live by the clock as Westerners do. For this reason, some Africans say, "The Westerners have the clock, but we have the time." If circumstances do not go according to plan, Africans will not become distressed. They know and believe that there is always another day - another day for paying bills, for making appointments or performing any task. Africans know that to seek medical care means that he will have to make an hour's journey on foot to the medical facility, where he will stand in line for another hour or more. By the time he is about to be seen by the nurse or doctor, he might be told that he cannot be treated until the next day. He then arrives the following day, only to go through the same procedure. In Africa, nothing is ever certain; you live one day at a time, each and every day.

In Africa, we believe that life will still go on despite any interruptions. Here in the West, entire days will be ruined when something unexpected happens. Westerners find our way of life difficult to comprehend and accept. Africans, on the other hand, view interruptions in life as situations which help to build lasting relationships and character. For example, my husband was asked by a church in the USA to do a cultural orientation for missionaries who were going to leave for Africa. The schedule for this orientation was given to him months ahead of time. As the time drew near, the organization reminded Tony of his commitment. However, instead of showing up on time, Tony chose to be thirty minutes late to the meeting. Everyone was impatiently waiting, and when Tony finally arrived he gave a big smile to the group. Before he began to speak, the first thing he did was to remove his watch from his wrist and lay it on the pulpit. He then began to discuss the African's view of time.

Tony explained that in Africa, people are more valued than schedules. Most western missionaries do not realize that constantly looking down at their wrist watches in the presence of their African guests indicates to them that you have had enough of their visit, therefore they need to leave. As a result, the African will conclude that Westerners must not love people very much, as the Africans do. This ended the first cultural lesson for these future missionaries. Africans, in most cases, keep deep secrets to themselves and do not share them easily with others, especially confidences about their families or themselves. Trust takes time to build with an African. If such a trust is broken, personal information will never be shared again with that person. Because Africans treasure friendships, they would often allow themselves to be hurt by a friend and others they truly respect in order not to offend or ruin the relationship.

There is another trait that is usual among Africans. According to Lamb, Africans will often follow anyone who calls himself a leader and will accept his authority without researching the person. I believe this particular trait is the result of colonialism. I have heard some horrifying stories about colonial masters who mistreated African nationals. The natives were expected to carry out any task without any questions or comments, and when they did object their masters often beat or severely punished them, sometimes to death. Today, this kind of leadership acceptance is still typical in almost every African country: the people are not allowed to question a leader's authority and to do so might mean that your body would be found the next day, lying lifeless in the streets.

Chapter 11

THE RAIN BEGINS TO FALL

Honeymoon?

On July 8, 1988, Tony and I packed up all of our wedding presents and the food that my family had given to us, and headed to Monrovia, where a nice three-bedroom apartment was waiting for us. We had given a down-payment to our friend, Sulia, for our first two months' rent. As a newly wedded young couple, we were excited and ready to move into our own home and start our lives together. One of my plans before my marriage was to have a place of my own and not carry on our tradition as expected of every African married woman: that is, moving into the home of my in-laws with my husband and living with them. But to my surprise, this plan or goal was far from being met.

The apartment we had engaged in Monrovia had been rented out to another family unknown to Tony and me. It was occupied by the time we arrived. This surprising news met us as we pulled into the driveway of the apartment, and the guard refused to open the gate for us. The truck driver, wanting to return to Bomi with other passengers awaiting his arrival, became impatient as Tony spoke with the guard of the apartment. Without any sympathy from him, he compelled us to unload all of our belongings in the pouring rain with no place to go with them. Tony paid the driver and asked the guard to watch our possessions while we inquired about the apartment.

Our most prized possessions, including a brand new queen-sized bed, a mattress and a dresser purchased with money I had earned working at missionaries' homes while in school, sat on the ground and soaked in the rain. As we unloaded our remaining wedding cake and other food items, I refrained from breaking down into tears as the rain soaked through my clothing. I had vowed to be with this man through thick and thin therefore, I had to remain strong and go on.

We met with Sulia and found out that the landlord, after faithfully promising Tony and Sulia the apartment, had given it to someone who had offered more money—an American missionary. Being eighty miles away from Monrovia, Sulia was unable to relay this disappointing news to us. To make matters worse, Sulia was not able to stay and help us find a solution to our dilemma because he had to pick up his wife from the airport, who was returning from the United States with their newborn baby. Thankfully, he decided to take us to his family's home for the night.

At this point, I could no longer hold myself together. I was on the verge of collapsing from anger, sorrow, and regret. I had only been married for six days and had not been on a honeymoon, nor did I even have a place of my own to sleep. I was angry with my husband and with Sulia for what was happening to me. Tony recognized my state of despair and immense disappointment and immediately told me to stay in Sulia's apartment while they tried to get our things out of the rain. Some of our possessions were taken to Sulia's apartment and the rest taken to the home of Edward, a young man I had dated before meeting Tony.

This was an awkward situation, to say the least. My break-up with Edward had left hard feelings between him and me, and included

Tony. A few national leaders of ELWA and a top leader of Campus Crusade, Liberia, had become involved. One of these leaders had gone as far as to try to have our German friend, Hartmut Stricker "Hardy," deported by the Liberian government, though he was not involved. They claimed that as a missionary Hardy had no business getting involved in the intimate relationships of Liberians, especially by splitting two people up whose minds were set for marriage. A true Christian leader, they believed, does not behave in such manner, therefore he should not be allowed to stay and work in the country.

In most parts of Africa, national leaders will often use their positions or power to manipulate the law of the land in such way as that against foreigners. After all, they know which buttons to press and how to get wheels turning. These leaders went as far as mentioning to me that Edward had been awarded a scholarship to travel to the United States and I would be given the opportunity to travel with him if we did settle our disputes. They used this as a way of enticing me to continue to date Edward. Any young girl of my age would have jumped in the air to reach for such an opportunity for a promising future, but I would have none of it. My mind was made up. My break up with Edward was solely due to him not being committed to our relationship. He was in a serious relationship with another girl far above my age while dating me. When I found out and asked him about it, he denied it. But as time went by, the truth was revealed and from then on I did not trust Edward. I told him that everything was over and we should go our separate ways.

Edward still wanted us to get back together so he got those leaders involved, hoping that they would say the magic words to me. To rely on him at this particularly tough time in my life added insult to my injury. Thankfully, Edward assisted us by taking in our personal belongings when we desperately needed his help. Both

Tony and I had no relatives close by to whom we could have taken our personal belongings. As in other parts of Africa, there were no public storages available to at least rent for a while. It was night time and with the downpour of rain, it would have been difficult to get any assistance from anybody. Among Sulia's friends, Edward's home was the closest to him and as his good friend and former college mate, he knew Edward would assist him regardless of what had transpired between him and me.

I was exhausted and broken with sorrow in my heart. This was not how I had expected to start off my married life. The last time Tony and I had eaten was in Bomi so I was hungry and filthy from being in the rain, but I no longer had the strength to pick up a spoon and feed myself. Not even the delicious food I had brought with me from my sister. All I wanted was to take a hot bath or shower and crawl into a nice, comfy bed for the night and let sleep take away the sorrow and pain of the day. The condition of the room in which we were to spend the night was not pleasant.

All I could think of was the warm home and loving family I had left in Tahn. In a moment I began to wonder if this was how marriage was, difficult and unforgiving. Tony fell asleep immediately but I tossed all through the night, unable to sleep. I wondered how anyone could sleep with the heavy snoring noises that Tony was making, and I fell deeper into self-pity. I should have been tightly wrapped in Tony's arms, comforted and protected in this strange home. Instead, I lay flat on my back with tears streaming down my face as the continual hum of countless mosquitoes filled the stuffy air in the room.

I barely slept that night, and then was awakened early the next morning by someone stamping loudly outside the door. We were so eager to get out of that house that we left without having breakfast and went to the ELWA campus, where Tony was to begin his ministry career. We met my brother-in-law, Benjamin, and told him of our housing dilemma. Ben immediately offered his home to us. It was heartbreaking to accept the fact that we would have to move into their home, especially when their family was such a large one, but we had no choice. Although his house was unfinished, his generosity and care meant so much to us and we were grateful he was willing to share his home.

When we arrived at Ben's home later that afternoon, we were given a room that had no door, nor an actual window. There was a thin rope strung above the doorway with a piece of fabric hung to keep curious eyes away. The window was partially covered with colonnade bricks and was sealed with a large cardboard box to keep away flies, mosquitoes, and the cool night breeze. The walls and floor were not plastered and there were no ceilings. In the middle of the room there was a full-sized bed with a thin, sponge mattress.

I have always been a private person, and I do not adapt to changes very well. I had a very hard time adapting to this new lifestyle, especially given everything I had imagined that my marriage might become. I desperately wanted a small space to call my own for the first few weeks of my marriage.

In addition to this hardship, I soon became the cook for Benjamin's large household. This lasted for two weeks until some friends stopped by and encouraged us to seek other accommodations. With their help, we finally found a studio apartment style room to rent in a house hosting two other families with children, a communal kitchen to be used by all three of us women, and the homeowner. It was nothing fancy, but we at least had a room that was private and a sitting place to accommodate our guests. The best thing about our home was that it was close to the ELWA campus. Tony was able to come home daily for lunch, which meant I could spend precious time with him during the day.

This was helpful for me in that I had not made any friends in the neighborhood who would keep me company, but as time went by Tony and I became accustomed to our married life and began to build friendships with others.

An Inexplicable Surprise

It was not long before my daily routine activities started to become mundane and boring. Marriage was not the constant adventure I had hoped it would be, and I became a restless housewife. I spoke to Tony about my boredom, and it did not take much persuasion for Tony to agree that I should begin to attend college. Before I had graduated from high school in December 1988, I had sat and passed the TNIMA nursing school examination in Monrovia. This was before my marriage and my excitement to return to school to acquire a nursing degree had not been quenched, and I could not wait to get started.

The nursing school was under the umbrella of the JFK Hospital, which was the largest government-owned hospital in the country. Because it was the only one of its kind in Liberia, there was a long waiting list for student enrollment. Even some of the brightest students did not stand a chance to enroll if they did not use bribery to entice school officials. Yet, by God's provision, without doing anything illegal, I made the enrollment list for the following year based solely on my entrance exam score.

Meanwhile, I had graduated from high school and was now married. Shortly before my college classes were to begin in August of 1988, Tony and I visited the nursing school and met with a few administrators. As our tour came to a conclusion, the dean of students told us that all first and second year nursing students were expected to live in the dormitory. The information instantly caused an eerie kind of silence to settle in between Tony and me. I knew Tony would never agree to this kind of living arrangement. Thoughts raged through my head regarding any possible loophole for my problem. No solution was to be found.

For a week, silence and frustration settled between us like a thick fog. Finally, I gathered enough courage to ask Tony about his thoughts regarding our situation. Tony did not hesitate and said,

"There is no way that I can be a single married man. Will you put your education and career before your marriage?" I was devastated, but convicted by his words.

Obviously, this was not the answer I was longing to hear. I had expected God to convince my husband about the importance of furthering my education. Surely a nursing degree was a goal worthy of a few compromises! The more I prayed, the greater my conviction became and I understood that separating from my husband for such an extended period of time was not the right thing to do. Still, I continued to hope that God might have another plan for me, and I forged ahead with great determination to enjoy my marriage and my new, sweet husband. I decided to tell Tony that I would forego nursing school for now and ask him if it would be possible to become a day student at one of the nearby colleges. The request met Tony's approval for my education. He agreed that I return to school, and soon.

A month passed and a sudden sickness swept over me. Every morning, I suffered non-stop nausea with flu-like symptoms. I decided to visit the ELWA clinic where Tony worked, faithfully preparing Bible study materials as an outreach to Muslim patients. The clinic was the best in the area, where most expatriates in Liberia came to seek medical help. After some tests, I was diagnosed with malaria. I underwent the required treatment for a few days and felt a little better. Still, a lingering sick feeling remained in my stomach, especially in the morning hours.

By the end of the month, my morning sickness had increased greatly. Unable to bear the constant nausea I went in for a pregnancy test. The result of the test came back positive. Tony and I were in shock, but I took the news harder than he did. I cried for weeks, greatly disappointed that I would not be able to further my education. I should have received this news with excitement and jubilation, but there was no celebration in my heart.

Tony became more caring and loving, trying his hardest to console me. I began to rely on him as my sole source of comfort. Every morning a hot bath was waiting for me in the bathroom (there was no indoor plumbing in our home so bath water had to be heated and carried inside). By the time I was finished with my bath, breakfast was waiting for me on the table. As Tony left for work each morning, he told me not to bother making lunch for him, encouraging me to stay in bed until he returned home. For the next two weeks he attended to my every little need, all the while carrying his own work load.

I finally began to recover from the malaria and managed to take over a few of the household chores. One morning, I woke with a heart-wrenching feeling of homesickness for my family. Tony noticed my quiet demeanor at breakfast and probed me for more information.

I said to him, "All I want is to go home and be with my mother for a while."

To compromise with me, he agreed that I go to Bomi instead of Tahn where the road was not dusty and rough. Tony did not want me to travel on such a rough road as the Tahn road for fear of losing our baby through miscarriage. He graciously told me to pack my bag, and I left for Bomi to stay with my sister Marie and Aunty Mary instead, where the road was much smoother.

My days spent in Bomi with friends and family were refreshing and relaxing. I was able to take my mind off my future plans and enjoy the good old days with family. All of my friends were excited to see me and could not wait to hear about my new life as a married woman; not that I had anything wonderful to tell them, considering what I had been through! On Friday afternoon, when I woke from a nap, my sister Marie came into the room and informed me that my husband had just arrived. I did not believe her at first, but as I stepped out of the bedroom I saw Tony beaming from ear to ear.

He approached me with loving, open arms and said, "Do you think I would let you stay here without me for one whole week?"

I smiled with happiness; we were both so pleased to see each other again. Tony stayed in Bomi with me until the following Sunday, and we both returned to Monrovia.

After I returned to our home, I began to make plans for the coming of our bundle of joy. I believe God used my days away from home to give me peace within to accept the role He had placed me in as a wife and soon to be a mother; a life He was entrusting to my husband and me. Soon, I told Tony that I wanted a bigger house, and he wasted no time in finding one. By the end of my second trimester we moved into a three-bedroom house and prepared for the arrival of our new little one. I was finally ready to accept God's precious gift to us, and with all of my heart to love and nurture our precious child, God's wonderful gift of life. I am convinced that my new attitude was formed because of Tony's many long prayers for me and his true commitment of love and support for me, even in the hard times.

While we were waiting for our baby to arrive, I took a few classes at Monrovia Bible College, which was located on the Carver Mission compound in Paynesville, a stone's throw from us. My hope was to be able to transfer my credit hours to another college at a later date.

Most women have cravings during their pregnancies, and I was no different. I craved crabs and ate them almost every day. One day, my girlfriend (who was also pregnant) and I went to the beach to catch crabs that had washed up on the shore. We not only caught many crabs but had a grand time running through the surf and kicking up sand. When we returned home, our husbands laughed when they saw our huge, sand-covered stomachs. We made a large pot of pepper soup with rice and had a feast with our crabs. We continued our crab hunts until it was time for us to deliver our babies.

Chapter 12

A BUNDLE OF JOY

Abigail

On Sunday, May 22, 1989, I woke up from my sleep feeling some discomfort in my lower stomach, so I decided not to go to church with Tony that morning. With the help of my little Aunt Kemah, who had been given to me by my family right after our marriage to help me around my home, I cooked a meal of rice and cassava leaves. Unable to eat just then, I lay down for a nap and waited until Tony returned home from church. We ate our meal together and later had a large, juicy pineapple that he had brought home for dessert. As I took a bite of that scrumptious pineapple, I felt a sharp, stabbing pain in my lower back, but the pain went away as quickly as it had come. An hour later I felt another pain. I was in labor.

I began to pace back and forth in our bedroom. Soon the pain became unbearable. I asked Tony to go for help, and he called Pauline Sonius and asked her to come over to our home. Mamay and Papay Sonius arrived with Carol Kejr, a registered nurse, and I was whisked away to the hospital. Men were not allowed to be in the delivery room, so Carol stayed by my side and coached me through the delivery. At 11:49 in the morning, I gave birth to the most beautiful, bouncy baby girl I had ever seen. She weighed 6 lbs. and 12 ounces and was a long baby with lots of hair.

With my beloved husband now at my side, the nurse placed our precious baby into my arms, and I soon forgot the pain I had endured. My thoughts focused solely on this wonderful work of God, who had knitted such a tender and special little life together for us. I marveled further that God had entrusted this beautiful baby into our care. The joy on Tony's face could not be mistaken as he cradled his baby tightly in his strong, yet tender arms. He thanked me for carrying such a wonderful and beautiful baby for him, and he offered a thankful prayer to God for both the baby and for me.

After two days, we were discharged from the hospital and arrived home to find that Tony had carefully prepared everything for us. Once again, Tony offered a word of prayer and praise to God. We dedicated our baby to God on that day. As new and inexperienced Christian parents, we asked for divine wisdom and guidance so that we might raise our child in a godly way.

On this same day we named our baby Abigail, which means "my father's joy." There was no doubt that Abigail truly was Tony's joy. He made a promise on that day to love all of his children unconditionally, just as Christ had first loved him. He understood the feeling of being rejected and unloved by one's parents and vowed never to subject his own children to such a burden and pain.

My Sister's Visit

When Abigail was first born she was a colicky baby. She cried a lot during and after eating in her first few weeks of life. I did all I could but could not get her to stop. I even began to watch and change what I ate, like collard greens, cabbage, pineapples which I love, spicy hot food, and a few other suspect foods but nothing helped. I soon became too tired from the weariness of being unable to help her. Coupled with her colicky cry was the difficulty I had in producing enough breast milk to satisfy her. That problem was quickly taken care of by eating roasted, or what we called 'parched', sesame seeds for about a week. I also drank hot Ovaltine chocolate drink a few minutes before breast feeding. Yet, Abigail's hysterical cries continued. I was plagued with her cry until one of my neighbors, who was skilled in child-rearing, came over and shared some mothering techniques with me.

She cautioned me not to pick Abigail up every time she cried because when she got accustomed to being held until she slept, it would become a difficult habit to break. All I needed to do was to put her in her crib until she fell asleep, and if not, I should let her cry for a while and she would fall asleep on her own. Frankly speaking, as a first time mom who was very afraid of causing any harm to my baby, I did not want to listen to her advice. I also feared that if I lay her in her crib while awake, she might choke on her saliva and pass out. But as Abigail continued to cry, I decided to give it a try.

For the next few weeks, I was careful to be sure that Abigail had a dry diaper and was not hungry before placing her in the crib. The first night, Abigail cried for almost fifteen minutes after I had laid her down. Out of fear, I ran to the crib and picked her up. Immediately, she quieted. Her abrupt stop from crying affirmed what my neighbor had said to me. I changed her diaper and fed her for the second time, once again placing her in the crib. After ten minutes of crying, Abigail finally fell asleep for five hours. A few days later she began to sleep through the night. From then on, Abigail became a happy and smiley baby full of life and every teenager in our neighborhood enjoyed holding and playing with her.

Traditionally, when a woman gives birth in Liberia, her mother, mother-in-law, or close female relative comes to stay with her as a caregiver. This could be as long as six months to a year. According to our tradition, a woman who has just given birth is not supposed to lift any heavy weight, scream, or braid her hair. She is not allowed to sit up for too long so that she will not be plagued with back pain. So, four days after I gave birth to Abigail, my sister Marie came to Monrovia and stayed with us for a month.

Sis Marie took charge of everything. The first thing she did was to pierce Abigail's ears. My eyes filled with tears as I watched my precious baby who was only a few days old feel the pain of the piercing, but tradition requires that a baby girl's ears must be pierced right after birth or within a few weeks of birth. There was no numbing administered and Marie used an unused sewing needle to poke holes in Abigail's tender, young skin. Every morning I took a hot bath and was able to relax. Marie made special meals of beef, chicken, and fish, which are believed to replenish the blood lost by the birth mother. At night, she made sure that I covered my head with a scarf to keep me from catching a cold.

In Liberia, we have an unpleasant custom of tying our stomachs right after giving birth. My grandmother used this technique in her midwifery practice. A strip of cloth or scarf is wrapped tightly around the stomach every day for about six months. An ace band or belly band is also perfect to be used. This painful act is supposed to prevent a sagging stomach and stretch marks. It is also intended to help the uterus re-position itself quickly. After I came to America and had my other three children, I continued this practice, carefully binding my stomach in the tradition of my grandmother and it really helped.

In the Hospital Again

The night I returned home from the hospital, I had difficulty breathing. The next morning, my face, hands, and feet were swollen.

By noon, I had a severe headache and pain in the back of my neck. Tony decided to tell my friend Barb Hartwig, a missionary nurse, about my symptoms, because he had to leave Monrovia to preach in Gaynah's Town, a small village outside of the city.

It was a hot Sunday morning, and the air outside was muggy and humid. Less than thirty minutes after Tony left, Barb came over to take my blood pressure. She immediately left and returned with another missionary friend, Ruth Clark, who was also a registered nurse. They calmly told me to get dressed so they could take me to the hospital. They instructed my sister to stay home with the baby.

When we arrived at the hospital I was ushered into the emergency room and immediately given medicine without explanation. The doctor took my blood pressure and checked my vitals, and still I had no understanding of my condition. I stopped Barb as she rushed past me and demanded that she tell me what was wrong with me. In a calm, soft voice, Barb said,

"Just relax, Elizabeth, you will be fine. Try not to worry."

I tried to take her advice, but the fear of unanswered questions raged through my mind.

After five more hours in the hospital, Barb took me to her home where I was given more medication and monitored by her regularly. After Barb had attended to my needs and helped get my blood pressure under control, she finally told me that my blood pressure had gone up to 140/120. She had not wanted to tell me earlier so that I would not drive my pressure even higher with my worry.

Tony returned that evening and immediately came to Barb's house to check on me. Barb reassured him that I would be alright and informed him about the nature of my condition, but I could see his anxious eyes examining me. Finally, she gave me the okay to go home. She instructed me to go on a strict, salt-free diet and gave me medication to control my blood pressure.

Pneumonia

Two weeks later, after a wonderful dinner outing at the ELWA campus, Abigail began to cry more than normal. She had difficulty breathing and was not nursing very well as a result. My inexperience as a new mother gave me no understanding or skills with which to handle this dilemma. Tony and I had done all we knew to try to comfort her, but she continued to cry every moment she was awake. Soon her fever began to rise so high that we decided to take her to the ELWA hospital, where she was immediately admitted. Abigail had pneumonia.

During her first few days in the hospital, Tony and I experienced the most difficult, painful and challenging experience of our lives. Though it has been twenty-two years since her illness, I still find it difficult to share this story. The joy of experiencing the greatness of God's creation displayed before your very eyes through the birth of your first child, followed by watching that same child experience such great suffering and pain, was more than we thought we could bear.

Tony and I wondered why God would allow our innocent baby to go through such hardship and pain in this early stage of her life. We prayed for a miracle to heal her little life but there was no answer to our prayer. We asked all of the "why" questions that any loving parent would ask, and all we received from God was silence. Tony and I cried for days and also fasted for a couple of days in prayer for Abigail.

In order to determine the kind of pneumonia that Abigail had contracted it was necessary for a blood culture to be obtained. When the nurse came to draw my baby's blood, she found it difficult to find a vein in either of Abigail's tiny hands and arms. As a result they had to shave one side of her head to draw the blood from a larger vein and to run an IV, as well. The process was very painful for me to watch.

Abigail became dehydrated because she could not eat well. Her breathing became shallow, and her condition continued to deteriorate. The doctor finally decided to put Abigail on oxygen to assist her breathing. He also ordered an incision to be made above her right ribs, where he would insert a tube to drain the fluid which had accumulated in her tiny lungs. My heart was overcome with grief. Each look at her little frame caused my anxiety to grow, and my tears flowed freely. My questions to God flowed freely as well. Why was God allowing our baby girl to go through such pain? The more we prayed for healing, the more silence we endured.

Our family still did not know that Abigail had been admitted to the hospital, so Tony sent a message to my family informing them of Abigail's ailment. By the third day, we were still waiting for the results of the blood culture so that the doctors would know which antibiotic would be effective against the bacteria plaguing my little daughter. My parents soon arrived, along with my grandmother, and their comfort was priceless to me. With the help of a good missionary friend of mine who also served with SIM Liberia, Mary Decker, she soon made a schedule to enable members of the missionary wives community at the ELWA campus to take turns caring for Abigail in the hospital. This allowed Tony and me to find some much-needed physical rest. She also contacted members of her church, Bethlehem Baptist Church in Minnesota, who started a prayer chain for Abigail's healing.

On the fourth day of Abigail's hospitalization, we received the results of the blood culture and it was determined that her pneumonia was caused by a staphylococcus bacterium. My heart continued to grieve as I watched her tiny diaphragm move slowly up and down as her lungs struggled to breathe beneath the oxygen mask. My mother was now in tears and began to inquire about the treatment Abigail was receiving, because her condition did not seem to be improving. Tony and I tried to explain that the treatment had not been administered yet and that Keflex, a strong antibiotic, would soon be given to Abigail.

On the fifth day, Abigail's condition took a turn for the worse. She was gasping for air for minutes at a time. The doctor soon arrived and asked everyone in the room to leave, including Tony and me. After thirty minutes of examining our Abigail, he ushered Tony and me back in the room and said that Abigail was not responding to the antibiotics and that her body was weakening. He was concerned that Abigail's condition was declining rapidly and that she might not survive through the night.

Tony and I immediately began to cry, realizing that our precious baby might soon be taken from us. Before long, several of our missionary friends showed up at our side and tried to console our aching hearts. Meanwhile, when my grandmother and mother heard the news, they asked us to remove our daughter from all of the machines that were attached to her tiny body so that we could take her home. They believed that we needed to take our daughter to a native herbalist or sorcerer. They believed that the herbalist would have a good chance of healing Abigail.

After Tony and I talked about this, we told our family that we would keep Abigail at the hospital. My family stood against this decision, talking directly to me in my native Gola language and stating emphatically that Abigail's illness would not be cured by drugs, but only by country herbs. Twice, they tried to convince us, but we refused to give in.

In the midst of this, we got a call from Judi Jay, a British missionary with SIM, who had been praying for Abigail. As she rocked her baby to sleep that evening, the Lord revealed to her that the prayers for Abigail had been heard and answered. She asked that we call on the elders of the church to pray over her and anoint her with oil. Soon Abigail's room was filled with the elders from the International Church of Monrovia, the parent church of our home church, Monrovia Evangelical Church. They read scripture, prayed, and anointed Abigail.

By this time Tony and I were completely worn out, mentally and physically, for we had not had a good night's sleep since our daughter had been admitted into the hospital. We did not want to leave our baby's bedside, but our friends, especially Michelle Sonius, my spiritual sister, banded together and demanded that we get some rest while they stood by our daughter's side on our behalf. I reached towards my daughter and put my pinky finger into her small hand. She gripped my finger without letting go. A torrent of sobs erupted from my very soul, and I was filled with grief and sorrow as we left her side.

Lord, Take Her Home

Tony and I left the hospital room of our sick daughter and went to Michelle's house on the ELWA campus. The memory of my precious little one holding my finger possessed me as Tony took my hand into his own. Together, we lifted the life of our baby up to the Father in prayer, asking Him to take the life of our child if that was indeed His will. We did not want to see her suffer anymore. That was the most difficult prayer of our lives.

Though we had prayed for her survival and would continue to do so, we also knew that we must give to God what was already His. Only God knew what was best for our baby. Even though my pain and grief felt like the hand of God's wrath upon my heart, deep-down I knew that He was and is a merciful and just God. I also knew that mankind does not always understand the ways of God.

Job best described my anguish when he said, the arrows of the Almighty are in me, my spirit drinks in their poison; God's terrors are marshaled against me (Job 6:4). Though these words expressed my feelings at the time, I later realized that God shows His love to us even in suffering.

Dr. James Means put it well as he mourned the death of his loving wife, Norma:

"No matter what I think at the time, the trials I face are due directly to His love for me. I appreciate what Charles Spurgeon said," 'into the central heat of the fire doth the Lord cast His saints, and mark you this, He casts them there because they are His own beloved and dearly loved people.' "If I cannot accept this profound truth, I can never stand unvanquished in grief or sing like Paul and Silas in the prison in Philippi. If I cannot submit to the superior wisdom of God's ordination, then I can never grasp the purposes of pain, even the privileges of it. God is concerned with making me strong; God is not concerned with making me comfortable. We may think that these are strange ways for God to show His love, but God knows what best promotes His objectives. The darkness of this hour and the loneliness of this grief testify to the symphony of God's love for me. It is the symphony written in a minor key, but beautiful nonetheless" (Means, page 23).

In the midst of the difficult time of our baby's ailment, I was encouraged by 2 Corinthians 5:8, which says, We are confident, I say, and would prefer to be away from the body and at home with the Lord.

I continued to question why God would allow my baby to suffer. I would have preferred that she be in a better place where there was no pain and sickness than to continue to suffer so terribly. Like the Psalmist, I questioned God: But I cry to you for help, O Lord; in the morning my prayer comes before you. Why, O Lord, do you reject me and hide your face from me (Psalm 88: 13-14)?

I knew in my heart that my prayers might not be answered in the way I desired during those tough times but Tony and I also knew that we would be reunited with our baby one day in our eternal home, our future glory. There we would rejoice and celebrate together a faith that the prophet Habakkuk professed during his own time of trials:

Though the fig tree does not bud and there are no grapes on the vine, though the olive crop fails and the fields produce no food, though there are no sheep in the pen and no cattle in the stalls, yet I will rejoice in the Lord, I will be joyful in God my Savior (Habakkuk 3: 17-18).

After our heart-wrenching prayer, I lay within my husband's comforting arms, shedding even more tears before I finally fell asleep. We were awakened by the sound of the telephone in the living room. Hesitating at first to pick it up in case it was bad news, Tony finally jumped out of bed, ran to the living room, and grabbed the phone. He returned to tell me that I needed to go to the hospital to feed Abigail.

With uncontrollable tears streaming down my face, I told Tony, "I know that my baby has passed away and this is their way of asking us to go and say our final farewells to her."

Tony replied, "Beth, don't think this way. I don't think they would lie to us. Let's go and see for ourselves."

Tony's loving rebuke allowed me to slowly take control of my grief, and we left for the hospital. As we entered Abigail's room, the atmosphere was quite different than it had been the previous evening. I could hardly believe my eyes! The two long oxygen tubes that had been attached to her tiny little nose were no longer there. Her lips that were covered with what looked like white, soapy foam from not being able to swallow or breathe on her own was all dried and gone. The color of her lips had also returned to normal. She no longer struggled to breathe.

All I could say was, "Glory to God in the highest, for He is truly the mighty healer and the King of Kings!" God had, in His perfect timing, performed that miracle in the midst of our own failing hope, regardless of our own desires or strength. Our little baby, who once could not suckle, was hungry and wanted to feed. When I began to breast-feed her she cried, realizing that there was no milk coming. With no formula available, as it is common in most African hospitals, a volunteer wet-nurse was sought within the hospital.

A Mandingo woman, who also had a sick child on the ward, volunteered to breast-feed Abigail that night. In Liberia, Mandingos are normally frowned upon and are considered to be foreigners. Most Liberians despised them, just as in the same way the Mandingos despised Liberians. Most Liberians believe that Mandingos came to our country to exploit our natural resources, especially our diamonds. What most Liberians do not realize is that the Mandingos were among the very first ethnic groups in our country. Mandingos were in Liberia before the first freed slaves from America arrived. They are Muslims but other Liberians will not associate with them.

That Mandingo woman did not care about our religious background nor hers either; she immediately offered to help our daughter without any hesitation. It did not bother me that a Mandingo woman was feeding my child; God's gracious provision of nourishment for our daughter was a blessing of immense measure.

The next day Judi Jay, who had asked for prayer for Abigail, asked me to breast-feed her son who was a little older than Abigail so that it would help my milk to increase; while she came to the hospital routinely to feed Abigail, I went over to her house to feed her son as well. In no time our daughter's vital signs grew stronger.

The doctor ordered some blood work in order to ascertain whether Abigail was out of the woods yet.

My family arrived, and they were shocked when they entered the room and saw Abigail's improvement. My mother asked about the medicine that had been given to Abigail, and I decided to give her an answer in addition to the antibiotics that our daughter had received. I explained to her about prayer, in a Christian sense. You see, in Islam, it is believed that God is great and man is sinful so he cannot reach to God except through the prayers of our ancestors. I was able to explain to my family that in Christianity, Jesus Christ has given us direct access to our Father, the Almighty God, who is able to answer us, be it yes or no. She could not help but respond: "Your God is great!"

The doctor returned with Abigail's blood work and told us that our daughter also had malaria and was anemic. She needed immediate treatment for this, including a blood transfusion. Though Tony had the same blood type as Abigail, he was unable to donate his own blood as he was suffering from malaria at the time. Although I was a universal donor, I was not in a strong enough condition to donate blood to my baby, having just given birth and having been faced with such huge stress because of her illness. Again, we sought a volunteer to help our daughter, and our dear friend Michelle volunteered to help. Meanwhile, another friend volunteered to breast-feed our little girl. Later, the wife of Abigail's main surgeon, Dr. Nancy Wood, a British doctor working at the ELWA hospital, brought in some formula she had purchased for her. Another doctor who truly ministered to both Tony and me during this tough time was Dr. Verma Troko, a Liberian doctor who worked at the ELWA hospital.

Through various means, I was able to increase my milk supply and resumed breastfeeding. I marveled at the generosity and the true love of the many people who had come to our aid and the fact that my daughter had been able to live off of Mandingo milk, British milk, and Liberian milk. Besides, she now carried American blood in her little Liberian body. Our loving friends from all over the world had come to our aid during this time of need.

The next morning, Dr. Wood, the main surgeon who headed the team of five doctors that had been treating Abigail, discovered that she had accumulated some more fluid in her lungs. He then scheduled her once again for surgery to remove the fluid. Abigail spent another two days in the hospital and was then discharged. The meaning of Abigail's name—'my father's joy'—took on a whole new meaning for us as we finally brought our daughter home from the hospital.

As Abigail grew and heard the story of her ailment, she decided to take on the middle name of Joy, in gratitude for all that the Lord had done for her. I marvel at how God used Abigail's healing in the life of my family. My mother has a saying, "It is God who gave you back her life." Even today, she has not forgotten the greatness of God because of this event. Though my mother is still a Muslim, she often encourages us to pray to our God because of what she has seen Him do for our daughter with her own eyes. Such praise cannot be given to a witch doctor or a herbalist. Such praise belongs to God, the Most High, alone. We may not know all of the answers about Abigail's healing, but we know this: God chose to be merciful to our precious little baby for His glory, not our own.

After we came home from the hospital, our friends and neighbors continued to speak about Abigail's miraculous recovery. A missionary lady once said something to me that has remained in my heart to this day:

"As Christians, when we are given something from God, He expects us to hold that which He has given loosely, not so tightly that it stands in our way of our love and devotion to Him." God had allowed us to be brought to a very low point in our lives in order to teach us a life-long lesson, and no one except God himself could have helped us rise from there. C. S. Lewis puts it best for me: "God, who foresaw your tribulation, has specially armed you to go through it, not without pain, but without stain" (C.S. Lewis).

At the end of our baby girl's ailment and our own struggles in dealing with it, I realized with confidence that God alone should and would receive the glory and honor for her recovery. On May 22, 1990, Abigail celebrated her first birthday. It was a huge, significant milestone in her life because we had not expected her to live to see that day. Our close friends, those who were greatly touched by her story of survival, brought gifts to commemorate her birthday. What a mighty God we serve!

Front row, from left to right: Antoinette, Ma Maima, and T.J.
Back row, from left to right: Me, Papay,
Ma Kpannah, Abigail, and Alieya

From left to right: Papay, Ma Maima, Angie,
Debah, Elydia, Ma Kpannah, and me

Alieya with my father

My dad, mother, and grandmother

My dad, Sando Goliah Fahn (Papay)

Front row, from left to right: Antoinette, me, Alieya, Abigail
Back row, from left to right: T.J., Tony, Cody

Book cover photograph by Rob Hawthorne

PART II: WAR

Chapter 13

SHACKLES OF THE PAST

House of Slaves

While Tony and I were beginning our new life together and facing our own struggles, all around us unrest and violence were spreading throughout Liberia. To fully understand the history of Liberia and the tragic Civil War which took place in Africa's oldest nation, one must first understand the underlying issues that fueled the conflict in the first place: that is, firstly, the Transatlantic-slave trade or the West African slave trade, which transported millions of Africans across the ocean to the New world as slaves, and secondly the return of free slaves to Africa, mainly to Liberia, in the early nineteenth century.

These settlers or colonists who were set down on the coast of Liberia took full control of the country and enslaved the indigenous Liberians in their own land. The subjugation of the native population by the new arrivals was to sow the seeds of anger and desperation which resulted in the bitter Civil War that was to tear the country apart, a Civil War that Tony and I and our baby along with countless others were to endure in the coming days.

A mere three kilometers off the sunny Senegalese coast of West Africa, a weather-faded structure called the House of Slaves stands proudly on the shores of Gorée Island. Dutch colonial slave masters built it in 1776 and from the windows of this dilapidated building, one may gaze far across the Atlantic Ocean towards lands unknown to those living in ancient Africa. It was here on Gorée Island that Arab slave traders bargained over the worth of African lives with European traders. Captured Africans spent their last days in their homeland painfully chained to the walls of underground cubicles, waiting to be transported to Europe and the Americas.

In the House of Slaves, there was a chamber called the weighing room, where slave traders assessed the qualities of future slaves to determine an appropriate market value. They judged men according to muscle mass, women by their breast size. Children were appraised by the condition of their teeth. An ideal candidate, the "perfect" slave, weighed at least 140 pounds. Those who weighed less were fattened like livestock until they reached the proper weight. Sickly captives plagued with ailments like pneumonia or tuberculosis were separated from the rest of the slaves and thrown into the Atlantic Ocean to be eaten by creatures of the sea. The bottom line was profit, but hatred is often as strong as currency. Two centuries later, the Nazis would use a similar selection process to determine who would live and who would die in their infamous death camps.

Buyers placed their captives on ships bound for an unknown land filled with uncertainties. Some captives would experience unimaginable cruelties upon arrival at their new home while others, mercifully, would be treated humanely. One out of every seven died at sea. Those who attempted to run away were punished with anklets embedded with spikes, which were fastened on their feet to prevent future escape attempts. If a slave was verbally defiant, traders would put a metal ring around his mouth, pull his lips through the ring, and drive a spike through them to prevent him from speaking.

At least ten million African slaves, perhaps more, were transported from West Africa to the Americas and West Indies between the 16th and 19th centuries. A large percentage of these slaves landed in the West Indies, Brazil, and Argentina to work the rich farmlands. A smaller percentage ended up in North America, many to be used for the same agricultural purpose. In those days, not unlike today, African tribes and villages fought among themselves for power and wealth, and wealth was measured in human lives. The power and prosperity of a tribal chief corresponded to how many prisoners his warriors captured. As his own personal wealth and influence grew, he became famous and respected as a chieftain. When the first Arabs came to Africa in the 7th century, many from Medina, they traded tobacco, gin, soap, and iron farm tools for ivory, animal skins, timbers, and slaves. As they purchased these slaves and took them to Arab countries, it is believed that many of the male slaves were later castrated and sent into the army while others were hired to work in private homes as eunuchs. This inhumane treatment was carried out to prevent the reproduction of the black race in Arabia.

Portuguese traders also came across the area in West Africa which they named the "Grain Coast" because of its flourishing and abundant spices, which is present day Liberia. Among the many spices were the Aframomum Melegueta peppers found on the coast of Cape Mount County to Cape Palmas in Maryland County. When the Portuguese traders found out that the Europeans loved these spices, they soon began to trade with the indigenous people for these peppers and their trade soon extended to India in response to a huge demand. Africans soon secured a new source of income. Tragically, the pepper trade quickly turned into slave trade and different routes into the African bush were discovered by these slave traders, bypassing the Grain Coast. These areas would later be known as the Gambia, Angola, Nigeria, and the Senegal Rivers. In no time, these Portuguese, French, Danish, Spanish,

Dutch, English, Americans and Swedish slave traders had booming businesses across the Oceans.

According to my grandfather, who told me many war stories from our ancestors, a village chief took great pride in selling his native enemies to a faraway village or another land, where the likelihood of their return was minimal. As a result of these slavery practices, many tribes in Africa, particularly in Ghana, initiated the widespread ritual of physically marking their children at birth with tribal markings. They believed that by marking their children, they made future identification possible in case children were sold into slavery in other villages in Africa or around the world. This became a widespread tradition in almost every part of Africa. One never knew when a miracle might occur, and a child displaying the markings of his tribe might return home.

Liberia, a Nation of Freed Slaves

The African slave trade across the Atlantic reached its pinnacle around 1790 with as many as 70,000 slaves taken just to the Americas that year. At the same time, Quakers living in America were repeatedly petitioning Congress to recognize the wickedness of the slave trade and end its practice. With that force, it appeared there was another force opposing it. The United States abolished its international slave trade in 1807, though slavery within the country persisted almost sixty years longer.

By 1820 there were over 240,000 freed African-American slaves living in America. Most of them lacked the necessary skills to lift themselves out of poverty. They lived under strict laws that hindered any hope of future opportunity for their families. Many people of African descent who were living in America began to unite in an effort to fight against racism and slavery and to protect their personal interests and future endeavors.

The debates about the status of freed slaves in America continued furiously over the next few years. Some Americans feared that the continuing presence of blacks would be detrimental to the future of America. Some abolitionists believed that freed slaves would be happier and more independent if they were sent back to Africa, where they would not face discrimination as they had in America. Some former slaves saw resettlement in Africa as an opportunity to own land away from the tyranny of slavery; others hoped to become missionaries, explorers, or agents against political colonialism.

With momentum gathering, Thomas Jefferson, who was president of the United States of America at the time when Great Britain abolished slavery in 1807, condemned the "Violations of human rights which have been so long continued on the unoffending inhabitants of Africa," and urged Congress to end the trafficking of slaves in the same year. This statement certainly seems ambiguous to me now, knowing that it came from a president who at one time employed and sold slaves (Thomas, 551).

As a founding father of the United States, Jefferson also wrote,

"Among the Romans emancipation required but one effort. The slave, when made free, might mix with, without staining the blood of his master. But with us a second is necessary, unknown to history. When freed, he is to be removed beyond the reach of mixture" (Sirleaf, page 3).

Jefferson didn't take into consideration the lives of the people that would be dumped into the unknown, who were more like strangers on their own continent. All he and the others wanted were to rid them from their society, so he warned that the continued presence of blacks in America was a threat to the young nation he had helped founded.

Henry Clay, the Speaker of the House of Representatives, also known as the "Star of the West," presided over the first meeting of the American Colonization Society and asked in his opening remarks:

"Can there be a nobler cause, than that which, whilst it proposed to rid our country of a useless and pernicious, if not dangerous portion of its population, contemplates the spreading of the arts of civilized life, and the possible redemption from ignorance and barbarism of a benighted quarter of the globe" (Thomas, Huge; The Slave trade).

Clay's words in later generations might be considered as ethnic cleansing, but God in His sovereignty used his words to bring about changed lives and civilization to an entire nation. However, not without many years of struggles and enslavement of the natives of the land did the change occur. Once again, history reveals evidence of the unpredictable and fallen nature of the heart of man. Even with this effort by Jefferson and Clay to rid America of the black race and slaves, it would take many more years and a Civil War before the end of slavery would be achieved in America.

These heated debates continued over the next few years in America. Some Americans feared—like Jefferson—that the continuing presence of blacks would be detrimental to the future of America. Some abolitionists believed that freed slaves would be happier and more independent if they were sent back to Africa, where they would not face discrimination as they had in America. Some white Christians, who supported the dignity of all men, supported the relocation of slaves to Africa with the hope that they would reach out to unreached people groups there with Christianity. In later years, this mindset helped to spread Christianity across Africa. I am a beneficiary of this mission. Sadly, the first missionaries who came to Liberian shores saw my people as savages and headhunters. Therefore, one of the aims of their missions was to bring the "light" to the "dark continent" of Africa.

With various factions brewing up different ideas to solve this burgeoning dilemma, the American Colonization Society (ACS) was founded in 1816, by a group of white men who were considered the early nineteenth-century movers and shakers: Representative Robert Wright of Maryland, Francis Scott Key of New Hampshire, Senator Daniel Webster, some prominent members of the clergy, law professors and some business men. Among them were also Congressmen John Randolph of Virginia and Bushrod Washington, who served as the Society's first president, forty-four years before Lincoln's Emancipation Proclamation. Later, a major part of the city of Monrovia was named in honor of Washington, Bushrod Island.

The ACS immediately began to raise funds to establish the first colony of freed American slaves in Africa. This effort was initially the white man's idea in order to get rid of freed blacks from their midst. The idea was later embraced by the freed black community in Philadelphia, the largest such community by far, and by one of America's most influential and rich black men, the sail manufacturer, James Forten, along with other leaders of freed black slaves, Coker and Allen. The majority of the freed blacks refused to accept the idea at first because it sounded to them like kidnapping. However, Coker and the ACS were able to attract a small number of the freed blacks to the idea later, while hundreds of thousands refused to do likewise.

Soon, the "Back to Africa" movement began. In January 1820, eighty-six former slaves boarded the Elizabeth and set sail for Africa. Many of these were women and children from Virginia, New York, and Philadelphia. Three ACS members accompanied the group. Six weeks after settling on Sherbro Island, now a part of Sierra Leone, a quarter of the ship's travelers and all three ACS agents had died from malaria and other diseases common on the island. The remaining survivors fled across the strait to the town of Freetown.

Having lost their first expedition leaders to diseases, the society decided to send Dr. Eli Ayers in search of a more suitable land for the future settlers. With the assistance of President James Monroe and Captain Robert Stockton, who commanded the expedition, Dr. Ayers bargained with African tribal chiefs for a piece of land called Cape Mesurado. Because of a previous failed attempt to secure this particular piece of land, Capt. Stockton decided to point a pistol at the head of the local African leader, King Peter, who realized that selling the land was preferable to losing his head. The pointing of the gun at King Peter's head was the first act of violence by the settlers against the natives who had no understanding of handing over ownership of their land through such a process. This proved to be just the beginning of trouble for the settlers and the natives. The Americans secured the land with a payment of goods including gunpowder, beads, tobacco casks, nails, shoes, rum, umbrellas, beef casks and soap, amounting to a total of $300.00 in value. Capt. Stockton also promised King Peter that the settlers would not interfere with his tribes and would have nothing to do with the slave trade.

With a new land secured for future immigrants, the next band of settlers landed at Cape Mesurado in 1822. They named the new settlement Christopolis, "The City of Christ." In 1824, it was renamed Monrovia in honor of President James Monroe, the fifth president of the United States, who was also a member of the ACS. The land, which was only a colony, continued to be ruled by white governors from America, who represented the interests of the ACS. It was not a sovereign nation at the time, nor did it have a fixed government, so the United States government refused to recognize its existence for a good fifteen years later.

The settlers faced continual political threats from other nations, especially Britain, which was in the habit of invading the coastline of Africa on occasion, including what would become Liberia. The colony finally declared its independence in 1847 and became the Republic of Liberia. Britain was the first country to recognize Liberia as a sovereign nation, the United States refusing to do so until after the American Civil War.

The region was already home to sixteen ethnic or tribal groups, though the newcomers may not have recognized the differences among them. We natives can discern a person's tribal origins by differences in skin color, physical appearance, or traditional skin markings on the face, teeth, or body. The Gola, Kissi, Mandingo, Via, Gbandi, Kpelle, Loma, Mende, Gio, and Mano tribes lived in the north of present-day Liberia. The Bassa, Dey, Grebo, Kru, Belle (also known as the Kuwaa), and Krahn were in the south and east.

Liberia, the New Republic

The influence of American culture in the new country was obvious. For instance, the Liberian flag is red, white, and blue, similar to the United States flag except for the number of stars and stripes it contains. The Liberian flag has eleven stripes instead of thirteen, representing the eleven signers of the Declaration of Independence. The star in the dark blue upper left corner of our flag symbolizes the fact that Liberia is the first independent republic on the continent of Africa. Even the wording of the Liberian Constitution, which was drafted by a Harvard law professor, contains phrases which might sound familiar to Americans:

"We, the people of the Commonwealth of Liberia, in Africa, acknowledging with devout gratitude, the goodness of God...do, in order to secure these blessings for ourselves and our posterity, and to establish justice, insure domestic peace, and promote the general welfare, hereby solemnly associate and constitute ourselves a Free, Sovereign and Independent State by the name of the Republic of Liberia, and to ordain and establish this Constitution for the government of the same."

When you look at a map of Liberia today, you will see that many coastal cities are named after influential Americans or American cities: Buchanan (after President James Buchanan), Monrovia (after President James Monroe), Greenville, Harper, Robertsport and many more.

The settlers from America referred to themselves as Americo-Liberians. In many ways, they considered themselves superior to the native African population. They brought American culture, traditions, and language with them and openly rejected the ways and culture of the indigenous Liberians. They chose English as their preferred language, rather than adopting any of the indigenous tribal languages, and they retained American ideologies such as the concept of privately owned property. This idea clashed with the natives' understanding that all property belonged to the community; in other words, communal sharing of property was the normative ideal for the native Liberian. The African communal co-operative system of sharing assured that every community member had shelter, sufficient food, clothing and other resources for life for them and their families.

Following the colonial practices of the French, British, and others, the Americo-Liberian regime controlled the entire coastal area and carefully stayed away from the hinterlands, the rural inland areas where most of the indigenous people resided. The

Americo-Liberians neglected the indigenous people and their issues. The indigenous peoples received little or no aid or development from the government, except for roads that were built for the exportation of iron ore, rubber, and timber to coastal cities. The sales of these resources mainly benefited the three percent of Americo-Liberians who ran the country. They built the best schools for their own children, and there were no schools for indigenous children.

In many ways, the new settlers considered themselves superior to the native African population, which caused the indigenous people to scoff at the newcomers, whose ways conflicted with their own. They wore expensive clothing as an outward sign to the natives of their Christian faith and civilization. In the end, the indigenous people had no choice but to adapt to the foreign culture, food, dress, art, and architecture of the Americo-Liberians. Americo-Liberian settlers made up ninety-three percent of the ruling power of the new colony, but the natives outnumbered the settlers fifty to one. However, it was no surprise that they maintained control of political, social, economic, and religious organizations. The natives were forced to obey the law of their land but denied the rights to become citizens of the colony. Due to this ill treatment, the natives became strangers in their land, their birthplace.

In order to maintain control and prosperity in their settlement, Americo-Liberians hired indigenous men to work on their farms. Many were forced into cheap labor and even sold into slavery. The daily wage for an indigenous Liberian who worked on farms owned by settlers was twenty-five cents. A monthly wage was one to two dollars. They were treated poorly by their Americo-Liberian masters by being pressed into hard labor, while others were beaten to death. Orders often included directives to shoot and kill indigenous people who trespassed on the properties of Americo-Liberians.

Eventually, Americo-Liberian settlers moved inland from their coastal enclaves into the hinterland of Liberia. They tried to maintain separation from the natives and elevate themselves at the expense of others. They even gave the men and women they hired American names. In their estimation, tribal names were too difficult to pronounce. When I was in high school, Americo-Liberian children who were my age group would still make fun of tribal names. To them, these names sounded strange and funny.

I personally believe that if the Americo-Liberians had attempted to treat indigenous Liberians as valuable and equal, the pages of our history books would have been written very differently. Sadly and surprisingly, the Americo-Liberians considered themselves superior to the indigenous people due mostly to their lighter skin color and hair texture as a result of interracial marriages in the United States. Even their religious beliefs became a means of oppressing the natives. As slaves in America, the settlers relied on Christianity to help them endure and survive their many hardships, but when they came to Liberia, they used the same Christianity to enslave and oppress the indigenous people of the land.

As freed slaves who were oppressed for their entire lives and who had no rights in America, they returned to Africa on a quest for freedom. Having found it, they used their freedom and newly gained power to take away the freedom of the rightful owners of the land.

Chapter 14

TUBMAN AND TOLBERT

Masonry in Liberia

The inner conflict in Liberia simmered for the next one hundred and thirty years, at times threatening to boil over. By the 1920s the Americo-Liberian abuse of Liberia's tribal peoples had gained international attention. The League of Nations charged the Liberian ruling class with abusive labor practices, including the "patronage system," in which able-bodied tribal Liberians were forced to carry Liberian officials in hammocks while others carried their loads or suitcases on their heads. Americo-Liberians also went into villages during planting and harvesting times and collected both men and women to do unpaid labor on roads and other public projects. At times, government officials instructed Liberian soldiers to raid tribal villages at night and collect laborers for cocoa plantations.

Bowing to American pressure, the Liberian president and vice president resigned in 1930, and William Vacanarat Shadrich Tubman became president. Though his own family had come from America as freed slaves, his love for the tribal people gave him a political power base in the hinterland. His father, William Tubman, was a strong member of the Masons.

Masonry in Liberia was a prestigious and influential form of secret society for the settlers. Important political decisions were first made in the Masonic temple before disclosing them to the general public. The power of the Masons basically ran the country of Liberia. The settlers made it their business to build a Masonic Temple within every settlement, though not as elaborate as the one in Monrovia. The largest of them all was built in Monrovia on Snapper Hill; with its majestic size it is still visible to the eyes of all, visitors and citizens alike. At first Masonry was only for Americo-Liberians and all indigenous people were excluded from being members. They believed that Masonry was based on brotherly love – but among its members only. However, the ceremonial practices which they brought with them from the United States became very dangerous to tribal Liberians. At a certain time of the year the Masons would kill a vast number of people around the country, sending an alarming fear amongst its citizens. During their annual celebrations of this tradition, it was common for corpses of children to be found in the streets of many counties with body parts harvested.

These ritualistic killings were carried out by elite government officials who were also members of the Mason in Liberia in order to retain their governmental positions during the country's elections. As time went by, the few indigenous Liberians who served in government and were wards of Americo-Liberians or had strong connections with this elite group of people, also became members of the Masons. Masonry has a culture of its own in Liberia.

The Masonic Temple in Monrovia, which was badly damaged during the Civil War, has been renovated by President Sirleaf's regime and is now in frequent use. The number of cars that can be seen daily around the premises of the Masonic Temple is evidence that this practice or tradition is still alive and well in Liberia. Membership in the Masons can greatly contribute to one acquiring a better position in the Liberian government.

Tubman's National Unification and Open Door Policies in Liberia

As newly elected President, Tubman pushed for a policy of "National Unification" immediately upon taking office. Native tribal groups had representatives in the government for the first time, the terms "Americo-Liberian" and "the natives" were banned, and the government focused on making education available to all Liberians. "We are all Liberians," said Tubman, though Americo-Liberians still held most of the power. Through this policy, President Tubman wanted to integrate the indigenous peoples and the settlers into a common people. His focus was mainly on the hinterland, and to have this policy implemented, he appointed natives into leadership positions.

Although indigenous Liberians were now represented in Tubman's administration, they continued to be greatly oppressed by his leadership. They were still unrepresented and without power and privilege in the Monrovia ruling class, unlike Americo-Liberians. All opportunities and wealth that came into the country from its fast growing economy went only into the pockets and bank accounts of these special people. Tubman and his top associates lived in the most luxurious homes and governed from fabulous public buildings in Monrovia. They travelled the world in the finest clothes during their vacations overseas. Nevertheless, a large number of the Liberian population, especially those living in the hinterland, remained in the worst living conditions one could imagine, without any hope. His Unification Policy survived as a symbol, but not as an agenda that actually worked.

Tubman's Open Door policy helped introduce Liberia to the rest of the world. He led the way for business people from all walks of life to take interest in the many opportunities which Liberia provided as a country. As written in our constitution, no white person can be granted citizenship in Liberia, so to compensate, Tubman gave long term leases to foreigners at very low tax rates. As a result, elite Americo-Liberians who had access to land and properties began to make use of them by leasing them to foreign corporations. These many incentives helped bring more businesses into the country. Meanwhile, other Americo-Liberian elites began to confiscate lands that had been owned by past generations of indigenous Liberians as long as they could remember. Similar land grabs also took place in my home area where hundreds of acres of land were taken by several government officials.

It is estimated that under the Tubman and Tolbert administrations, the purchasing and stealing of land constituted one of the largest "land grabs" in the history of Africa. However, Americo-Liberian land grabs were nothing compared to the land seizures by white farmers in South Africa, Zimbabwe, and Kenya during colonialism. Unlike these countries, the land grabs in Liberia were perpetrated by people of the same skin color as the indigenous Liberians. While many had a lighter skin color, it was the same black race!

My husband and I usually tell Westerners that the worst prejudice that one can experience is "black on black," in that they can be fearless and cruel to one another and there is no recourse. An excellent current example is Zimbabwe and the ill treatment that President Mugabe is imposing on his own people. Other examples are the bloody Civil Wars that continue to occur on our continent of Africa, where the lives of hundreds of thousands of people are being destroyed by their own people, although not without the involvement of superpower countries.

When the Firestone Tire and Rubber Company, which is an American Company, heard of the Open Door policy and the opportunity it presented, they swiftly jumped on board and came to Liberia in 1926. The company received nearly a million acres of land for little or nothing from the Liberian government, along with a one percent tax on the rubber that would be exported. Firestone natural latex rubber was the only rubber available to America and her Allies during World War II. They used the rubber to build tires for their war planes, anti-aircraft guns, jeeps, and other important military equipment.

"For the next eighty years," writes Ellen Johnson-Sirleaf, "Firestone amassed huge profits and had a strong and decisive say in Liberian politics. The Mount Barclay site—renamed Harbel for Firestone founder Harvey Firestone and his wife, Ida Belle—grew into a town as large as nearly any other in Liberia. Those tappers worked in what an international workers' rights group called, as late as 2006, a 'gulag of misery,' according to a story in the Philadelphia Inquirer. That group, the International Labor Rights Fund in Washington, D. C., has filed a federal lawsuit against Firestone alleging that the company overworks and underpays its workers while exposing them to hazardous chemicals, inadequate safety measures and harsh living conditions" (Sirleaf, page 46).

Firestone Plantation was accused of environmental and labor abuses, along with employing child labor. The majority of these children did not attend school due to the lack of educational facilities, and the tremendous needs required of them as children to assist their parents to meet their fourteen-hour daily work shifts. And even as this book is being written, Firestone still has ownership of the land which was renewed by our interim government during the Civil War until 2025. Originally, the land was given to Firestone for ninety-nine years at the price of six cents per acre, making it the largest rubber producing plantation in the world at the time.

In my opinion, Firestone returned little or nothing to the country in terms of permanent development, unless one counts the American parboiled rice which Firestone introduced to the Liberian population causing a terrible dependency, as I shall explain. Firestone is now part of Bridgestone, a Japanese company known in most parts of the world. Yet, there have been no beneficial changes or differences in the operation of Firestone in Liberia since Bridgestone bought the company.

In order for Firestone to appease the Liberian government and its employees on the plantation as they continued to pay them low wages, they began the tradition of supplying their workers with imported rice from the U.S. Consequently, with this "help" from the U.S., most Liberians living in coastal areas stopped the production of rice on their farms and immersed themselves fully in producing rubber. As a result, the employment numbers for the Firestone plantation company increased dramatically. Liberians asked themselves, why endure hard and tedious rice farming when you can readily get enough supply of rice to feed your family every month? This fall in the numbers of those involved in rice farming would later lead the country to the beginning of its downfall. Whether this action by Firestone was intentionally carried out to reduce local rice production in Liberia, I do not know. However, I do know that it worked in Firestone's interest; they got more employees for their company for little expenditure.

During his administration, President Tubman also extended the right to vote to owners of any hut upon which taxes had been paid. He also extended that same right to women for the first time in the country's history. One of Tubman's outstanding achievements was the co-founding of the Organization of African Unity, and as one of the founding fathers in 1963, he gained international recognition for his contribution.

President Tolbert's Agenda for Total Involvement

When Tubman died in office in 1971, he was succeeded by his Vice President William R. Tolbert, who had served with him for twenty-one years. According to Dr. William Ardill, in his book Where Elephants Fight: "President Tolbert presented his economic theory called" "humanistic capitalism." His idea combined the best of capitalistic free enterprise and the African extended family system of sharing of wealth. The rich were to share their wealth with the poor. The extended family sharing continued but the rich never shared with the poor. Some said Tolbert "developed under development." Illiteracy was around eighty-five percent." (Ardill, Page 46).

Tolbert, with all of his great intentions for Liberia, was surrounded by people who did not fully accept his ideas of economic change and development. And surprisingly, these people were primarily his family. As the old saying goes, "Your own family can be your worst enemy." And so it was with Tolbert and his family. One of those pitted against his leadership style was his brother Frank Tolbert. Frank accused Tolbert of being too lenient on the natives. For this reason, he opposed most of the President's policies which in turn caused others to go against the ruling party as well. Again, as the saying goes in Liberia, "If your own house doesn't sell you, the streets will not buy you."

Tolbert also had ambitious plans for the improvement of Liberia. When Tolbert began his effort to eradicate ignorance, poverty and disease, his primary focus was on the citizens in the hinterland. One of his big ideas was "From Mat to Mattress," a campaign to help alleviate the Liberian population from poverty to a better quality of life. Literally, it would remove the Liberian people from sleeping on floors to sleeping on beds with comfortable mattresses once they become self-sufficient. The fact is that sleeping on mattresses was very foreign to most Liberians, especially those in the hinterlands. So to help implement this idea, Tolbert provided the Liberian people with low-income housing in the city of Monrovia at reasonable rates. His vision for "his" Liberia was geared toward change; a change that would have freed Liberia from the dependency that had been created by the United States in the form of handouts.

These handouts were largely given to Liberia annually as aid during past regimes. But President Tolbert was a die-hard pragmatist, who wanted the "total involvement" of every single Liberian in making our country self-reliant. As a result of his philosophy, he made some drastic decisions in establishing relationships with countries such as Cuba, the Soviet Union, China, and other countries. These moves were the first of their kind in our country's history by any of its Presidents; clearly this did not please the U.S. government.

To the United States, these changes were not good for its geo-political grip on her step-child, Liberia. The U.S. did not want to see Liberia have any ties with these Socialist or Communist countries. As a result, there was immense pressure from the United States government for Liberia to cut every tie with these countries' leaders; but Tolbert responded very slowly to the request.

President Tolbert also implemented the building of new schools and clinics, where such development had never previously taken place. My village of Tahn was one of those fortunate places that benefited from his development and educational plan. In 1977, the Tolbert government built a six-room clinic in Tahn. It was a great success and saved many lives in throughout the district. It provided much needed medical help to hundreds of people who would not have received it elsewhere.

The Rice Riot in Monrovia

Unfortunately, Tolbert allowed corruption to spread widely within his administration. The gap between the rich and poor continued to expand and became so vast that even the illiterate Liberians could not accept it any longer. The trouble really began when the Ministry of Agriculture proposed increasing the price of a one hundred pound bag of rice from twenty-two dollars to twenty-seven dollars. Rice is the staple food of the Liberian people, so this increase was not something that the population welcomed!

The reason for the increase was simply to encourage the Liberian people to create more rice farms in the country. It would discourage farmers from leaving their farmlands and coming to the city in search of jobs, which was already taking place in large numbers. As more of the country's land had been transferred and leased to foreign companies in search of natural resources, people had stopped farming and had become dependent on imported rice.

On the morning of April 14, 1979, two thousand students rallied to protest the price increase. By the end of the day the rally had grown to ten thousand. When the police ordered the crowd to disperse and used tear gas, the demonstrators began to loot shops and destroy government property. More police reinforcements came in to help clear the streets, and President Tolbert ordered the police to shoot into the crowd and disperse them by any means. He also called on troops from neighboring Guinea to enter Monrovia and help keep the peace which really aggravated the Liberian population.

The political unrest in my country continued and Tolbert's government began to go downhill really fast. April 11, 1980 was The One Hundredth Anniversary of the Liberian Baptist Education and Missionary Convention. Tolbert and his leaders had planned a week of events and activities for the conference, which began

145

with a concert at the Centennial Pavilion on that Friday evening. Dr. Tolbert was not only the nation's president but he was also the President of the Liberian Baptist Missionary and Educational Convention. As an ordained Baptist minister, Tolbert used his role as an international peacemaker and mediator for other African leaders. If he had stepped down from his presidency as planned, he could have played a role as an international leader, which would have ensured his legacy in history as a leader who cared for the welfare of all Liberians.

In 1979, the Organization of African Unity summit was hosted in Liberia for the sole purpose of re-establishing Liberia's leadership role. As head of the Organization at the time, Tolbert wanted to generate economic growth, which usually follows after the hosting of the summit in any country. In preparation for this summit, President Tolbert spent "an arm and a leg" (as we usually say in Liberia) in order to make a spectacular impression on the rest of Africa. The Unity Conference Center, where the summit was held, is said to have cost 33 million dollars. The Hotel Africa located outside of Monrovia in Virginia, Liberia, was also built for the OAU summit. Fifty-one villas were built to house the heads of states who attended the Conference, along with an enormous swimming pool built in the shape of the map of Africa. These structures cost an additional 36 million dollars. It is believed by most Liberians that President Tolbert robbed the nation's bank mainly to make a name for himself.

The summit, although turning out to be a great success, failed to bring much economic benefit to the country. Rather, it left a tremendous deficit in the Liberian economy. In the end, the total cost of the entire Conference was 101 million dollars.

As president, Tolbert made many economic and social promises which he failed to keep. He was deaf to things happening around him, and for some strange reason, he was clueless as to the instability and troubling events in the country he governed. Tolbert misled himself by believing that the Liberian people greatly loved and respected him, not realizing that he had bitter enemies and that his policies were becoming very unpopular among the common people.

Chapter 15

NEW LEADERSHIP

President Tolbert's Assassination

It was in the early morning hours at 1:00 in the morning, April 12, 1980, when heavy shooting began at the Executive Mansion. In no time at all the perpetrators were able to scale the Mansion's Iron Gate and overpowered President Tolbert's soldiers. They broke down Tolbert's bedroom door and found him lying in bed, despite all of the high security there. Tolbert was shot in the head and his body dismembered in his own bedroom by an army officer named Harrison Pennue, who had managed to enter the Mansion and reach the eighth-floor bullet-proofed residential apartments, leaving his wife Victoria begging for her life. She was undressed, leaving her only in her underwear as she walked through the streets to her prison cell.

Most Liberians believed that Master Sergeant Samuel Doe, who was to become a significant person in future events, was not among this group of killers led by Pennue who spilled the blood of President Tolbert and twenty-six others who were believed to have been his security personnel. It was believed that Samuel Doe hid himself behind some bushes in the Executive Mansion grounds while the seventeen soldiers got rid of President Tolbert and his government. Meanwhile, it was widely speculated that five foreign figures dressed in military uniforms which were different from those of the Liberian military were seen on the grounds of the Executive Mansion early that morning. Not only were their uniforms different, but among them were two white foreign soldiers.

Immediately after the assassination of President Tolbert, one of these foreign soldiers approached a group of five Liberian soldiers who happened to have been around the Mansion at those early morning hours. One of these five was Samuel Doe who had the highest rank among the group as a Master Sergeant. And little did Doe know that he was at the right place, at the right time, and that the leadership position of an entire nation was to fall right into his lap. Doe became known as one of the coup leaders of the second Republic.

Many Liberians and others around the world wondered how the killing of President Tolbert could have happened on the eighth floor of a presidential building like the Executive Mansion of Liberia, which was guarded by soldiers. And where was America, who had this tiny country of Liberia, especially the capital, Monrovia, in her palm, and the Executive Mansion at her fingertips? How could they not have seen these sixteen soldiers and Doe, a Master Sergeant, on the grounds of the Executive Mansion, and better yet, how could they not have heard of the coup plot before it even took place? Besides, it has still never been determined why Tolbert spent the night at the Executive Mansion on that evening of April 11, the first night of the convention, rather than at his Bentol village, which he usually did over weekends.

The information which was widely disseminated throughout the country was that President Tolbert was just too exhausted to have traveled to his farm home in Bentol after such a long evening. But how could he have been easily convinced to do so? Nobody knew. As Liberians, we may never know the answers to all of these questions.

But one thing we do know is that the U. S. Embassy, which stands on a peninsula known as Mamba Point, and is also located on the very top of a hill that overlooks the seaport of Monrovia, has the capability to see, and hear in advance all political unrests that take place in my country.

Samuel Doe knew nothing of how to lead the country's military. He, along with two staff sergeants, four sergeants, eight corporals, and two privates, took charge of our entire country, having no idea whatsoever as to where they were headed with it. On the morning of April 12, 1980, ELBC, the Liberian local radio station, proclaimed that "The armed forces of Liberia have taken control of the country in order to bring to an end the 'Rampant Corruption' that is within the Tolbert government." This unexpected announcement was a total shock to the entire nation and brought chills to the country's population, except perhaps to Tolbert's opposition parties. Throughout the entire day there were constant announcements made about the "People's Redemption Council" (PRC) government which was now in place and headed by Samuel Doe.

Another question that still remains unanswered concerns the statue of the "unknown soldier" that was erected soon after Doe came into power. As the story goes, some Liberians believed that the statue was in memory of one of the five foreign soldiers who were present on the grounds of the Executive Mansion on the morning of April 12, 1980 coup, but lost his life during the assassination of President Tolbert.

Samuel Doe, who came to power through gruesome bloodshed, was a twenty-eight-year-old man from the ethnic Krahn tribe of Grand Gedeh County. His father was a former army private and a temporary school teacher. Doe was born in Tuzon, a small village in Grand Gedeh County. It is believed that he worked his way through night school and into the tenth grade at Marcus Garvey High School (while others still hold to the rumor that he was a sixth grade dropout).

Grand Gedeh County is one of the largest counties in Liberia, yet it has remained one of the least developed areas in the country. The Krahns, who make up only five percent of the country's population, were never exposed to civilization at an early stage, and thus there are only a few educated people among them.

It is also believed that Doe spent some time in my home area of Tahn and Lofa Bridge, working in diamond fields. As most African leaders would do, Doe enlisted in his government most of his Krahn friends with whom he had worked in diamond fields in villages around the Tahn areas. Many of these individuals had little or no education but soon became top government officials in Doe's regime. Even after he came into power, Doe and his buddies constantly harassed the locals in these areas and illegally confiscated their wealth (diamonds and gold) from them.

By the morning of April 13, 1980, the streets of Monrovia were filled with low-ranking soldiers, most of whom were from the Krahn tribe of Samuel Doe. The situation in the capital of Monrovia became chaotic. Several tribal groups chose the opportunity to dance throughout the streets of Monrovia to celebrate that they had overthrown one hundred and thirty-three years of corrupt Americo-Liberian regimes. They also chanted slogans and sang songs against Tolbert and his fellow Americo-Liberians saying: "Native Woman born soldier, Congo woman born rouge!" They referred to the Americo-Liberians of past regimes as 'rouge', while referring to the children of native women as soldiers who had redeemed them from their many years of oppression.

On this same day, Doe pronounced himself as the head of the State of Liberia and then named his fifteen cabinet members, most of whom were soldiers. Also, without much of a surprise to most Liberians, he named Gabriel Baccus Matthews as his new foreign minister. Baccus, who in the past years had become a major thorn in the flesh to President Tolbert and also a strong opposition leader to his government, was now at the front of the ruling administration of Doe.

Shocking News

The news of the coup reached my village by way of the radio and I was to hear of it while going about my usual chores with my family in my small village. On the morning of the coup, April 12, 1980 I was awakened by a knock on our bedroom door and heard my mom saying that we needed to go to the creek to wash clothes. Living up-country (that is, the rural part of the country, about eighty miles from Monrovia), there are certain things that must be done at a certain time of the day or else you will get the short end of everything. Those included getting fresh and clean drinking water from the creek, washing clothes at the creek, visiting a medical facility, and so on. If I did not do the wash early in the morning, I would have to do it in dirty water and deal with a crowd of other women all struggling for a place to do their washing.

I was still drunk with sleep, but slowly managed to get out of bed and get myself ready for my morning chores with my mom. While we were at the creek and almost done with our washing, a man traveling from town to his farm delivered the horrific news of what had happened in Monrovia. A bloody military coup had taken place in Africa's oldest republic. The few of us who were at the creek were shocked! The adults among us could not believe what they had just heard. Since we were all women, the bearer of this tragic news advised us to hurriedly pack up our belongings and leave for town immediately. Meanwhile, as a good gesture, he volunteered to stay with us as we gathered our clothes to leave the creek. My mom, along with the other women, was now frantically rinsing her clothes and picking up whatever belonged to her in order to leave as quickly as we could. In less than ten minutes my mom and I were on our way to town.

Upon our arrival, the effect of the coup was obvious everywhere in our peaceful little town. People were in disbelief. There was hardly any movement to be seen anywhere, especially on our side of town. On normal days people came from every part of town to catch taxis going westbound to Mano River or northeast to Bomi or Monrovia. But this day traffic was slow. Out of concern and fear, men from the town had begun to crowd along the only car road so that they could get better information from the few people who were coming and going through town. At about noon, a flood of military supplies and soldiers began to arrive. Army trucks, security vehicles, and soldiers came from Mano River and drove through the village at break-neck speed.

Residents of my hometown gathered around shortwave radios— some so old that I wondered how any sound could come out of them—and were glued to the BBC hourly news updates on Liberia. In most parts of Africa at that time there were no reliable newspapers, so radio was the only source of information. And because of the high illiteracy rate and the remoteness of other parts of the country, radio in fact was the "king of media" for many people.

After we had listened to the radio for some hours, a taxi-load of Tahn's residents was dropped off in front of my parents' house bringing news from Monrovia. They told us about soldiers running wild in the streets of Monrovia, looting, raping, and killing innocent civilians. This news suddenly stirred up the listeners, and the majority of them left for their homes. The few of us who remained were still holding onto some hope that the report was false. As the adult men listened and talked about what they were hearing on the radio, more army trucks sped by on the dusty, pothole-filled road, leaving the village residents covered in brown dust and despair. Liberia had never experienced a coup before; the news of these brutalities was nerve-racking and unsettling for everyone. By late evening, the news of the coup was announced in all the sixteen local dialects of Liberia. President Tolbert had become the only serving leader of the OAU who was assassinated as President of his nation.

Looking Evil in the Eye

On April 22, President Doe held a brief press conference and invited reporters from around the world to join him on the beach at the Barclay Training Center. To me, this was the turning point for my country. Soldiers planted nine wooden posts in the sandy ground and tied one man on each post. The victims were government ministers and cabinet members from Tolbert's administration. These men faced the end of their lives in their underwear and without being blindfolded, while bystanders cheered on their deaths. Thousands of civilians, soldiers, and journalists stood and watched precious lives being snatched away in a blink of an eye. Just imagine what that might have felt to them, seeing the very people you once knew and talked with, standing there with fingers on their triggers, ready to take away your life. The one question that remained in my mind was how people could commit such evil in the name of "good"?

When the first group of people had been shot, their bodies were taken down and laid at the base of the posts on which they were killed. Next, four more victims faced the assassination through such a painful and disgraceful death. In total, there were thirteen men killed on the beach that day. Meanwhile, the bodies of former government officials and the mutilated bodies of Tolbert and his personal guards were taken in an open cart through the city streets of Monrovia. They were later dumped into a mass grave in a swampy area next to the Palm Grove Cemetery.

In addition to Tolbert and his top government officials, there were other politicians arrested as well. These officials faced a tribunal set up by the People's Redemption Council, which consisted of military personnel. The tribunal investigated them on charges of corruption, for which they failed to provide any proof. The officials were denied any legal counsel. If found guilty, they were to be sent to Belle Yella, a renowned prison in the bush of Lofa County, from which most prisoners did not come out alive. Their sentences ended in death, either quick or very slow.

Chapter 16

SAMUEL DOE, AMERICA'S NEW FRIEND 1980-1989

Green Behind the Ears

The daily events of my life—school, graduation, meeting Tony, getting married, starting my college studies and having a baby—preoccupied me to the point that there was little time for me to recognize that the political climate of Liberia was changing. While the political backdrop of Liberia had little adverse effect on me personally during those years, the instability of my nation's government was never really far from my mind. This was especially true as Tony and I made our home in Monrovia, the capital city, where strict curfews reminded us of the turmoil that swirled around us.

Following the 1980 coup in which Tolbert and his administration were overthrown, the United States immediately stepped in to rescue Liberia. They feared that Samuel Doe and his military administration would bring the country to financial ruin. America also knew that Doe was "green behind the ears," as we say in my country, and could easily be influenced to run into the arms of the wrong country for assistance. The late President Ahmed Sekou Toure of Guinea once said, "A starving child does not ask where his food comes from." Such was the case with President Doe of Liberia.

Chester Crocker, a former U. S. Assistant Secretary of States for African Affairs, said, "An illiterate, low-ranking and highly vulnerable

28-year-old who became president of Liberia should feel insecure" (Huband, page 29).

As we normally say in my native land of Liberia, "An evil doer is an evil thinker." Crocker also correctly stated that Doe was only twenty-eight years old when the 1980 coup took place. However, he backdated his birth certificate to meet the required age of thirty-five years and older that qualified one to run as president in Liberia. Yet, this was never a problem to the United States government. He was still favored as their ideal candidate for President. Rumor had it that Doe was so concerned or afraid of someone killing him that he never slept in one location twice in a row.

Doe had one desire only: to create a name for himself. He had no plan of learning how to lead his country that had endured so much oppression from its previous leaders. Each year of his regime he would stage a huge festival in Monrovia to celebrate his birthday. With the ignorance of youth, Doe touted soccer matches as major achievements and spent more money than the country could afford to support soccer in Liberia. On the sixth anniversary of the coup, Doe opened a multi-million dollar sports complex in Monrovia. He also built a million-dollar marketplace in honor of his wife, Nancy Doe, who it is believed was illiterate and once sold vegetables and charred coals in the local market place in Monrovia. The price tags for these extravagances came out of the pockets of financially struggling taxpayers and severely crippled our beautiful country of Liberia.

The United States did not look through the same lens as that used by the Liberian people to see Doe and know who he was. They turned a blind eye to the horrendous murders committed by Doe and his fellow coup leaders during his regime. Crocker again had this to say about President Doe of Liberia:

"Had we been candid about the standard of government in Liberia, it would have been very damaging to U.S. interests. Great powers don't reject their partners just because they smell" (Huband, page 27).

It appeared to Liberians that America was protecting its interests and during this time, Doe and his soldiers committed some of the most horrendous abuses of human rights imaginable. Killings were frequent and gruesome. Anyone of any age who publically opposed his government was murdered. American policy makers had failed to recognize these abhorrent crimes against humanity and were able to attribute them "to the people." They washed their hands of any personal responsibility.

On the first anniversary of the 1980 coup, the United States provided special Green Beret training for six thousand Liberian soldiers, as well as investing heavily in building new barracks and equipping the Liberian military. According to Mark Huband,

"The United States granted Liberia, its new West African partner, $60 million in military assistance. While $42 million was paid to improve the living conditions of the Armed Forces, the rest went to military supplies. According to James Bishop, these supplies included 4,000 M-16 assault rifles, light weapons, mortars and light artillery, as well as communications, trucks and the refurbishment of Navy patrol boats" (Huband, page 31).

According to reliable sources within Liberia, the majority of these military supplies went to President Doe himself and he, in turn, supplied them to his tribal Krahn soldiers who were stationed at his Executive Mansion. Aid that was meant to support the infrastructure of Liberia ended up in the hands of Doe's Mansion Guard, which was heavily armed with high tech weaponry and military equipment secured from the U.S. government. The equipment was used by his soldiers to commit atrocities against the entire population of Liberia.

In 1982, America gave more financial aid to Liberia in the sum of 62.3 million dollars, making Liberia the top financial aid recipient from the United States government. Along with their projection that Liberia would recover, the United States hoped that Liberia would re-establish diplomatic ties with the State of Israel. They also hoped that Liberia would adopt a strong stance in both domestic and international areas against Soviet policy and against countries such as Ethiopia and Libya, who were friends of the Soviets. The United States desired for Liberia to condemn all Soviet expansion in Africa, especially in Chad. The U.S. further encouraged Doe's administration to adopt the Western-based form of capitalism. To facilitate this request, they asked Doe to acquire a new Foreign Minister who would put American interests first and dissipate all domestic opposition through strategy or force.

As I was growing up, it was reiterated that we Liberians and our country were the most beloved among nations to the United States. We had convinced ourselves that if any political unrest fell upon Liberia, we would swiftly be rescued by our Uncle Sam. Liberians, who had always looked to America as their greatest ally, began to realize that they had been left alone to fry by their longtime friend and founder, the United States of America. How deceived we were by our own hopes! The United States was looking out for its own interests, and concern for Liberia only extended to how much our nation assisted the U.S. when they needed us.

During the Cold War, the U. S. used Liberia to enhance its military capabilities. The Robertsfield International Airport in Monrovia, which was built by the United States government, has the longest runway of all other airports in Africa. It was constructed mainly to facilitate the landing and refueling of B-47 bombers. They built some U.S. military installations, along with a sophisticated intelligence relay station called the voice of America (VOA) outside of Monrovia which transmitted all diplomatic communications throughout Africa to Washington. The Omega Tower, the tallest structure in Africa built outside of Monrovia, also allowed ships in the Atlantic Ocean and aircraft to navigate safely due to its geographical position in the country. By agreement, "the entire Liberian-registered merchant fleet-the biggest in the world-could be called upon to assist American forces in time of war or national emergency" (Huband, page 30-31).

The U.S. had the strongest influence over this tiny West African nation and controlled it economically, politically and strategically. Both the Omega Tower and the Voice of America relay station served America's interests well during the Cold War.

Samuel Doe seduced most of the opposition leaders into joining his corrupt political party. If they did not listen to his threats or receive his bribes, they were harassed and tortured. An example of this is Liberia's current president, Ellen Johnson Sirleaf, who was charged with sedition, convicted by a secret military tribunal, and sentenced to ten years of hard labor in Belle Yalla. Due to her connections with the World Bank and her influence beyond Liberia, she was eventually granted clemency - otherwise, I believe she would have met the same fate as many of our other leaders: snuffed out by Doe's bloodthirsty soldiers before the world even heard a whisper of them.

When the next elections were held in October, 1985, Emmet Harmon, Chairman of the Elections Commission, personally took pleasure in counting more votes for Doe than even existed in the Liberian population. During these elections, ballot boxes mysteriously became full of ballots even before the actual voting began. Children between the ages of six to eleven, mostly children of military families, evidently turned out to vote for Doe. Doe had banned two political parties from participating in the elections. He even went so far as to put these opposition leaders in prison. Doe's administration failed to bring democracy that was so dearly needed in Liberia, yet American politicians did not see anything wrong with his regime.

America, whose representation was greatly welcomed in the country by its leaders, refused to intervene, despite the obvious corruption of Doe's administration. With no objection or interference from the Unites States, or any other outside nations for that matter, Doe was declared President of the Second Republic of Liberia. In addition, Doe did everything in his power to please the American politicians.

"We are getting fabulous support from him (Doe) on international issues. He never wavered in his support for us against Libya and Iran. He was somebody we have to live with. We didn't feel that he was such a monster that we couldn't deal with him. All of our interests were being impeccably protected by Doe. We weren't paying a penny for the U.S. installations," said Crocker, a key American policy maker (Huband, page 36).

Evil Begins to Boil

The United States may have stood by President Doe even in the face of such a farcical election, but behind the scenes, U. S. operatives were making plans to get rid of him. In 1984, the United States finally realized that Doe was no longer the right leader for Liberia. They decided to find a Liberian organization that would remove him from office. Thomas Quiwonkpa, a member of the Gio ethnic group and one of the original People's Redemption Council members who had staged the coup in 1980, became an obvious candidate.

Quiwonkpa had distanced himself from Doe and his fancy lifestyle, seeing himself first and foremost as a soldier. In an effort to remove Quiwonkpa, who was highly regarded by the people of Liberia, President Doe accused him of corruption in 1983 and removed him from political power. Quiwonkpa was forced into exile in the United States, where he earned both a high school and college education. Quiwonkpa was approved and supported by CIA agents in the Ivory Coast to stage a coup against Doe and his regime. He also received approval from Israel, whose troops were providing intensive training for Doe's Mansion Guard as a part of the defense agreement (Huband, page 38).

Opposition leader Henry Boimah Fahnbulleh now became part of the equation. He was a left-of-center politician and was wary of Israel's participation in the upcoming coup. While the coup was still brewing in the crock pot, a senior U.S. State Department policy maker confirmed that U.S. Embassy officials in Monrovia had already gone to Doe and alerted him to the upcoming coup soon to be staged against him. Before Quiwonkpo could even step foot onto Liberian soil, Doe had begun to gather both arms and the military to stand against him.

In the early morning hours of April 12, 1985, right after the elections, the Liberian radio station, ELBC, announced that the "patriotic forces under the command of General Thomas Quiwonkpo had toppled the Doe regime." This announcement was received with massive jubilation by the Liberian population. Photos of Doe were stripped from the walls of public buildings and replaced with ones of General Quiwonkpo. The streets of Monrovia were filled with demonstrators, singers and dancers, especially those of the Gio and Mino tribes. This announcement, of course, was false and within a few hours of its broadcast, General Quiwonkpo was captured and tortured.

A few days later he was castrated and killed, his body dismembered. Parts of his body were publicly eaten by President Doe's victorious Krahn troops. A mass killing of civilians was then carried out by Doe's Krahn soldiers in parts of Nimba County, where

Quiwonkpo was born. Gio and Mino civilians, government officials, police officers and even soldiers were rounded up by the Executive Mansion Guard and slaughtered. Civilians who had celebrated in the streets and were caught by Doe's soldiers were taken to beaches outside of the city and massacred.

According to eye witnesses, truckloads of bodies were taken from the grounds of the Presidential Mansion to be buried in mass graves outside of the city. Doe personally watched and supervised the slaughter of these human beings.

Charles Julu, a member of the Krahn tribe whose son was killed in 1983 during the Nimba raid by some Nimbians, was permitted by President Doe to avenge his son's death by killing as many Gio and Mano people as he could. Julu collected a large number of Gio and Mano civilians at the LAMCO iron ore mine and allowed his soldiers to beat them. The beaten civilians were then transported to the Sika Valley near Yekepa where they were slaughtered and their remains disposed of in an old mine shaft. Most Liberians who lived in these areas knew what was happening and understood whose soldiers were responsible for the atrocities they were witnessing.

Yet, they remained quiet because they desired to wait for their own time of revenge against Doe and his soldiers. This is what Africans do and as the old saying goes, "A man does not pray for wings like a bird does for feathers in order to fly from its predators. Instead, he prays for a long life in order to get revenge. And as he seeks revenge, the circle of violence continues."

It was announced, by the only government-owned radio station in the country that four hundred people were killed in the coup attempt, but many believe that the death toll was as high as three thousand. This slaughter was just the beginning. It would be repeated in many future Liberian massacres. On paper, the 1985 Liberian elections had returned the country to civilian rule.

This satisfied the United States' hope that democracy had won its day in Liberia. The reality was that Doe, having previously lived in ramshackle military barracks and diamond mines, now discovered that he had become rich overnight. His humility apparently had vanished and he found himself riding in a "Chauffeured Mercedes and living in plush country homes. His men-young, uneducated, and before the coup mostly desperately poor-took everything they could get" (Sirleaf, page 107).

From the beginning of Doe's regime until the 1985 elections, the United States government had given Doe close to 400 million dollars. The more aid Doe received, the greedier he became. Money that had been given to move our country ahead instead ended in Doe's pockets. Leaders of his government who were mostly young, embarrassingly uneducated, and who lived in poverty before the 1980 coup, became outrageously rich. But the corruption and human rights violations went unheeded by the United States government because, after all, their interests were being protected. The aid given to Liberia was a small sum compared to what the U. S. would have paid to relocate their Liberian manufacturing installations. By the outbreak of the Civil War of 1989, that amount had risen to 500 million dollars. Despite all of this aid, "The United States, which had created Liberia, financed Doe, and effectively championed human rights' abuses in the belief that they were for the greater good, did not care what happened to Liberia" (Huband, page 100).

Liberians in these tribal areas waited for an opportunity to exact revenge on Doe and his tribal allies.

Chapter 17

THE GATHERING STORM

Charles Taylor

During General Quiwonkpa's failed attempt to organize a coup against Doe, Charles McArthur Ghankey Taylor arrived on the scene. Taylor claimed he wanted dearly to restore democracy to his long-oppressed and corrupted country of Liberia. His father, who served as a Monrovia judge, was a descendant of Americo-Liberians, and his mother was a native of the Gola ethnic group from the Suwen-Bomi area. In 1972 his father sent him to Chamberlain Junior College in Boston, Massachusetts. He also attended Bentley College, in Massachusetts where he acquired a degree in economics.

Taylor returned to Liberia from America a few days before the coup that destroyed the Tolbert regime. Doe gave Taylor control of the General Services Agency of Liberia (GSA). In this position, he became the most powerful and influential government official in Doe's government. However, Taylor was not so popular with the military and government officials because he, as GSA director, made a number of decisions that affected them negatively. He was forced out of the government and then fled the country in 1983. On December 19, 1983, Doe ordered Taylor's immediate extradition to Liberia. British police arrested Taylor in London and sent him to the United States, where he was imprisoned.

What happened next is the subject of debate. Some say that Taylor escaped from a Boston jail on September 15, 1985. Most Liberians do not believe this story. They believe that Taylor was released from prison for the purpose of getting rid of Doe's regime. Taylor traveled to Ghana, and then to Ivory Coast, where he met with other Liberian dissidents like Moses Duopu, Harry Yuen, Tonia King, Cooper Teah, Alfred Mahn, William Obey, and Major General J. Nicholas Podier.

NPFL Training Base in Libya

In 1987, Taylor connected with the Libyan government to secure training for his rebel group. With the help of the Mano and Gio tribes, who had suffered terribly at the hand of Doe, Taylor quickly assembled his first group of dissidents. Initially, forty rebels managed to cross the Liberian border by telling the Ivory Coast guards that they were participating in a soccer competition. They made their way to Tripoli, Libya, to begin the training required to overthrow the Liberian government. They were soon joined by others. On May 6, 1988, one hundred and sixty-eight men graduated from the training course.

Meanwhile, Taylor traveled to neighboring countries surrounding Liberia to find a place from which he could invade his homeland. His rebels, now called the National Patriotic Front of Liberia (NPFL), began to find their way from Libya to Burkina Faso in July of 1989. Before they left for Liberia, Taylor demanded that his twenty-five commanders from the Mano and Gio tribes swear allegiance to him. Taylor killed a sheep and mixed its blood with a black powder and gin. All present drank this mixture and swore, "If I go against you, I will die in war."

The Invasion

On December 24, 1989, one small group of rebels, led by Prince Johnson, managed to cross into Liberia. They headed straight for the town of Butuo where the Armed Forces of Liberia (AFL) had a barracks containing large amounts of military supplies, arms and ammunition. With the aid of many Gio civilians and villages, the rebels were able to quickly enter into Butuo and capture it.

However, within days of Taylor's rebels crossing the border into Liberia, Prince Johnson and his rebels broke away from Taylor. Taylor decided to send some of his rebels to Monrovia via a different route. These men were arrested by Doe's soldiers, then brought to Monrovia and were forced to publicly confess to their rebellion. They denounced Taylor and his connection to Libya which caused unrest within the city and surrounding areas. It is believed that these rebels were terribly tortured and at last beaten to death by Doe's soldiers but the public were never given clear information of what happened to them.

To this day, they have never been seen. It was later disclosed by insiders from Taylor's organization that these men had been set up by Taylor to be captured by the Liberian government. Taylor suspected their disloyalty to him, so this was a convenient way to be rid of them. Meanwhile, another group of Taylor's rebels were arrested on the border as they attempted to cross. Taylor escaped by the skin of his teeth but not without leaving behind a briefcase of valuable documents, including maps and photographs. He flew to Burkina Faso as he awaited another opportunity to try again.

The unrest in the country was growing by the hour but Liberia's closest ally, the United States, showed no sign of intervening, nor did it appear to Liberians that there was an interest in bringing an end to the killing that was rapidly destroying our nation. To Liberians, it appeared that America had forgotten them.

Taylor's Connection to the Ivory Coast

The Ivory Coast had very strong connections to Liberia especially during former President Tolbert's regime. President Houphouet-Boigny of the Ivory Coast, who was a good friend of Tolbert, was secretly furious at Doe following the assassination of Tolbert along with his son, A. B. Tolbert, who was married to President Houphouet-Boigny's foster daughter, Daisy. Houphouet-Boigny, together with Burkina Faso's president, President Blaise Compaore, assisted Taylor in trying to rid Liberia of Doe. However, Nigeria refused to sit idly by and see this happen; that is, for Liberia to become the favorite and shining star of President Houphouet-Boigny, not to mention of President Qaddafi of Libya.

Taylor's troops crossed the border from the Ivory Coast into Liberia and marched towards Monrovia. Thousands of civilians became victims of the fighting which ensued. In the process of trying to eradicate Taylor and his troops from Liberia, Doe flushed away an entire front line of villages bordering the Ivory Coast and Liberia, killing everyone in sight. During our own escape to the Ivory Coast, Tony and I and our small group of family and friends walked past these places that were once major towns and villages. It was as if nothing had ever been built there. Civilians were gunned down without mercy; entire villages were set on fire; and no one was able to escape.

As a warning to others, Taylor's rebels had a habit of decapitating civilians and leaving their bodies along roads that were frequently traveled. Pregnant women and their unborn babies were viciously killed while young boys of an enemy tribe were unmercifully massacred. This detestable act was common and an assurance to Taylor that these boys would not grow up to take revenge against him.

Many of Taylor's rebels were teenagers between the ages of nine and fifteen. Taylor's rebels, who were mostly Gio and Mano, literally drugged these child soldiers with marijuana, opium and other dangerous drugs that were given to them by their commanders. The drugs helped to promote a euphoric state which freed the young boys to loot, fight, rape and kill, over and over again. On their march to Monrovia they singled out members of the Khran and Mandingo tribes and ruthlessly killed them.

On May 29th, the most shocking and tragic killing took place in the city. A truck filled with Doe's men, Krahn army soldiers, drove to the United Nations compound and forced their way inside of its walls. Seventeen Gio civilians were taken at gunpoint and were loaded into a truck that drove them away from the compound. They were unloaded from the truck, undressed, shot and killed. Finally, international headlines erupted across the globe but nothing happened beyond that; no outside nations cared enough to intervene, not even the United Nations. The only surviving victim was a man named Jimmy, who was treated at the ELWA hospital. The doctor who had treated Jimmy refused to allow the press to interview him. The next day, Jimmy made a statement to the international press and before long, news arrived that Doe's soldiers were planning to attack the entire ELWA compound including the hospital where the interview took place.

Most of Nimbi County was destroyed by the heavy fire of rocket-propelled grenades into its villages and towns as fighting intensified in the region. This caused a large evacuation of Liberians, who fled to the neighboring countries of Guinea, Sierra Leone, the Ivory Coast, Ghana and Nigeria. Those who remained had no money and were stranded with no means of escape.

This was not the case with Tom and June Jackson, who were missionaries in Nimba County. The Jacksons were Bible translators who had worked in Liberia for forty years. During the Liberian Civil War, all American citizens residing in the country were warned by the U.S. Embassy in Monrovia to leave, yet due to their unconditional love of the Liberians, they chose not to leave but to stay and share the burdens of those Christians that were unable to flee to safety. Sadly, Tom and June Jackson were killed in crossfire between government soldiers and the NPFL rebels in Nimba.

My husband first met the Jacksons while attending the African Bible College in Nimba County. According to Tony, Tom once spoke at the college chapel about their project, which was translating the Bible into the Mino and Gio languages. They also had plans to translate the Bible into the Bassa dialect. The Jacksons were devoted to their ministry and their exemplary lives shall forever be remembered in Liberia among Christians and non-Christians alike. The news of their deaths spread like wildfire throughout Liberia. Fear erupted and most embassies began to evacuate their citizens, especially non-essential staff.

The Liberian Civil War knew no frontline; no place was safe within the country so many began to seek refuge in other countries while others got stranded and could not get out. As many Liberians heard of and witnessed Doe's barbaric killing, they joined Taylor's rebel forces in order to protect themselves and their own families from being harassed and killed, as well as fighting for the eradication of Doe's government. Taylor's army increased swiftly to three thousand fighters and the rebels accumulated hundreds of weapons and ammunition from AFL soldiers who had deserted their assigned areas to flee the rebels. It was at this point that the Civil War turned into a tribal conflict. The majority of the Gio and Mano tribes joined Taylor's rebels, while the Mandingos and Krahns sided with Doe's soldiers.

The War Comes Home

By this time, Tony and I were already married and living in the city, away from the violence—for the time being. My hometown of Tahn, was attacked at the early stage of the war. On the day rebels attacked our hometown, my sister Marie had just given birth to a son. Forced to leave immediately, she walked for an entire week right after giving birth, causing her feet to swell. She also suffered from internal hemorrhaging from the recent birth. My parents had to find the nearest town with a medical facility to try to help her as quickly as possible. My aging grandmother, however, could not make the journey on her own. My father and his brother-in-law took turns carrying her on their backs but, exhausted from the long journey, they could no longer carry her up the hills and narrow paths in the bushes.

Therefore, my parents decided to separate into two groups. My father, his two sisters, his mother, his brother-in-law, and their large families stayed in the village where they had stopped for the evening. The other group consisted of my mother, her mother, and my siblings, who took refuge in the town of Bong Mines. My sister and her family then headed for the Ganta hospital in Nimba County so that she could get some immediate medical assistance. This separation which was the direct result of the painful reality of our brutal civil crisis was to last for the next two years with no communication between my mother and father. As Marie's health improved, her family traveled further into Nimba country to join her husband's family.

Two years later, news finally reached my father about the location of my mother and the rest of my family. He visited them in Bong Mines, but while there another rebel group entered Bomi Hills, where he had been staying with the rest of his family after escaping the village where they all got separated, and captured the city. Every able-bodied person fled for dear life, but because my uncle could not carry my grandmother alone to safety, she remained in the house and it was set on fire by the rebels.

When the news of my grandmother's death reached my father, he was devastated and heartbroken. As the only surviving male in his family, he regretted not being there to protect his mother from such a miserable and painful death. His misery was compounded by the fact that he was unable to rejoin the rest of his family soon after hearing the news of his mother passing. This was due to the closure of the road leading to Bomi by another rebel group who had captured the area, refusing to allow civilians to return to their homes. When I heard of my precious grandmother's death, I was very troubled and greatly saddened. It reaffirmed how cruel Liberians had become to one another under the watchful eyes of superpower nations that were only in Liberia to exploit our vast natural resources for their own gain.

Chapter 18

ANNIVERSARY NIGHTMARE

Caught in the Crossfire

Tony and I woke up with hugs and kisses on July 2, 1990, congratulating each other for surviving our second year together as a married couple. I kissed Tony goodbye and he walked out into the cool, rainy morning to the SIM headquarters, a three to five mile walk from the ELWA compound, the same place we had earlier taken refuge. We knew that the rebels were very close to the city's Capitol, yet we were trusting in God to protect us from danger. Perhaps we were too naive to realize the wisdom of getting out of the city before the rebels came.

Tony and I had invited a few friends over for dinner to celebrate our anniversary. By mid-morning, Abigail had eaten breakfast and was playing until her afternoon nap. As I prepared the food for our anniversary celebration meal, some local friends stopped by and warned me about the close proximity of the rebels. They congratulated me on my anniversary and encouraged me to keep my eyes and ears open.

Tony's day at work began as any other, but as the day progressed, the SIM staff began to hear sounds of gunfire in the neighborhood surrounding the campus. It was not long before the SIM staff including Tony, were caught in crossfire between government soldiers and

Taylor's rebel forces, which had secretly crept into the city overnight. As the sun burst through the dark clouds hanging over the Atlantic Ocean, local residents tried to make sense of the terrifying sounds coming from outside of the city. The different patterns of gunfire suggested mortars, artillery, machine guns, and AK-47s.

Some of our friends who live across the ELWA compound, not those we had invited for the evening dinner, knew of our special day and had stopped by in the morning to wish me a happy anniversary. They also warned me of the danger that was now visible on every street corner in the city. Two hours after their visit I received a phone call from Tony. Speaking in firm, hurried words, he cautioned me to stay inside. The tone in his voice made my blood run cold. He told me of the shooting around the SIM compound. Nationals and missionaries alike were lying flat on the floors of their offices, praying for safety from the stray bullets that were passing through the compound. Tony told me that the shooting had continued off and on all morning. Nobody was brave enough to venture outside.

I was a nervous wreck by the time Tony got home. I was worried about my baby, my husband, and myself. I recalled during the early stage of the Civil War conflict in early May, 1990, when another rebel group had captured Bomi Hills. I had been separated from my dear family during this conflict. My brother-in-law had arranged for me to travel back to my hometown of Tahn with his own brother, Benjamin Sehkar, but we knew that Doe's soldiers were headhunting all Gio and Mano ethnic groups. Though I was from the Gola tribe, even associating with these other tribes could cost me my life. The rebels had set up many checkpoints on the road to Tahn. They were beating to death and gang-raping women and girls in the presence of their loved ones. They took others as permanent sex slaves. Based on this information, Tony and I had decided that it would not be wise to make the trip.

Later, we found out that my brother-in-law's name was indeed on a government list of those who were being sought to be killed. Ben had worked as a journalist for the ELWA radio station, broadcasting the local news to Liberians in his native Gio language. As an educated man from the Gio ethnic group, this meant that his life was in great danger, even though he worked for a Christian organization that was neutral in the conflict. Tragically, he did not survive the war, but thankfully his wife and children were saved.

In the end, God protected us from these dangers, and we were thankful that we had not made that trip to Tahn. But now my own family was caught in crossfire. I began to imagine worst-case scenarios of what would happen to me if Tony was killed or if the rebels came and captured all of us at the ELWA compound. My thoughts focused on my husband, who was caught in crossfire on the other side of the city, away from me and our baby.

After I hung up the phone, my body began to shake uncontrollably. I was paralyzed by fear. I sat in a chair close to the phone and tried to take slow, deep breaths to calm my heart and my mind. I felt nauseous, and my stomach began to churn. I was weak and at the same time terrified. No matter how hard I tried, I was unable to relax. I began to cry out to God in a loud voice for His mercy.

Eventually I managed to get up from the chair and wobble my way to Abigail's room. I woke her up from her sweet dreams and gave her some water to drink. I reasoned that if Abigail were asleep when the rebels entered the compound, I might not have a chance to take my precious baby with me. Everyone understood that when the rebels ordered you to leave quickly, you obeyed or were killed. We had heard horrible stories of this very kind, and I was now afraid of losing my baby in the same manner.

I sat on the floor by the bed with Abigail in my arms, trying to somehow shake off the confusion that continued to possess me. As her wondering eyes stared up at me, I began to think more clearly. I started to relax, but I could not forget the danger outside. I decided to carry Abigail on my back, which is called "backing a baby" in Liberia. This is like a piggyback ride except the child is secured to your body with a six-inch wide strip of cloth called a "lappa," which keeps the child from falling. Knowing that Abigail was strapped securely to my own body gave my heart the precious consolation it needed.

I began to wonder what I would do if Tony did not return. Once again, I cried out to God for mercy. Only He, and He alone, could bring Tony back to us. I could do nothing but continue to make plans and preparations for our escape in case the rebels should come. I went into the kitchen and turned off the stove. I did not know what I would do with the rest of the frozen food that I had stockpiled. As a precaution, we had filled both the freezer and refrigerator in our home while the rebels were still some distance from the city. A group of us Liberian staff wives had rented two Land Cruisers from the mission so that we could shop and get enough food stored up for our families. For our small size of family, we had enough food to last us for months! Because we had been told that the ELWA compound would be the safest place in the entire city, we felt prepared for the toughest of times ahead. We had gone so far as to hide some of our worldly possessions in the attic of our home across the street from the ELWA compound so that we could stay put if the conflict should come our way.

The house where we were staying on the ELWA compound was only a temporary accommodation, but it had become a second home to us. This home had once belonged to Ron and Pauline Sonius, Tony's spiritual parents. It was at Pauline's Bible study that Tony first believed in the Gospel message given to us by Jesus Christ. We had spent many precious hours in this house before we actually lived in it. Besides what was hidden in our own attic, we had brought most of our important items, such as our wedding presents, with us to our temporary home. The sentimental value of these earthly possessions was beyond human appraisal.

By early afternoon, the shooting finally subsided on the Old Road outside the compound. Soon I heard a knock on the door and my mind went blank. I stood paralyzed and began to shake, wondering whether I should answer the door. I frantically called out to Kemah, my little aunt, and firmly instructed her not to open the door or to speak. Much to my relief, the voice coming from the other side of that door was Tony's, asking, "Beth, where are you?" I immediately flung open the door and rushed into his comforting arms. All of the frantic thoughts that had built up in my mind quickly vanished. A flood of relief and joy settled into my heart. Tony was home.

Tony and the other staff members somehow managed to drive to their respective families, but not without being stopped by government soldiers at makeshift checkpoints set up on the Old Road and at the ELWA junction. According to Tony, the streets were completely empty. The fear of death cast an eerie atmosphere along the route home.

Tent City

Tony sat down and began to tell me all that had happened while he was gone. He said that hundreds of people were taking refuge on the ELWA campus, which was a privately owned piece of property. As the fighting intensified, hundreds turned into thousands as the campus became a camp for displaced Liberians, who thought the campus would be a safe refuge. Everyone believed that because these twenty-five acres of land with a beautiful beach front campus located in Paynesville was a property owned by an American religious organization, it would not be destroyed or bothered.

I walked outside with Tony and could hardly believe my eyes. We were surrounded by an innumerable crowd of people who were carrying bundles on their heads, which is the African way of transporting possessions from one point to another. Most people arrived on foot because cars are a luxury in Liberia. Among the people entering the campus were a vast number of women carrying babies on their backs, along with a few men who carried children who were too young for such a long journey. From the compound housing area to the radio station, from the International Church building to the hospital, there was a steady procession of beat-up, old cars filled with destitute and homeless people trying to get to safety. The sight was heartbreaking and desperate.

This was the moment when all Liberians became equal. There were no longer any rich or poor among us, no greater or smaller. Every person wanted one thing only: to survive. Some came with only necessities; others came with a few of their worldly possessions like TVs, radios, mattresses, and cooking utensils, which had been smuggled through many checkpoints. The only possessions they had left were the ones they had carried into the compound. Everything else had been, or would be, confiscated by the rebels or government soldiers.

As I watched the newly displaced people wander aimlessly through the compound, I was reminded of the many homeless people we used to see in the streets of Monrovia. This was long before our Civil War. These were very thin and strange-looking women who wore many earrings with different styles of clothing than those worn by West African women. They moved hopelessly around the city with their babies on their backs while their older children walked beside them. These women went from private homes to businesses begging for food. Some slept along major streets until they were shooed away, while others sat at entrances of stores waiting for shoppers to exit so that they could ask for handouts.

Most Liberians despised these people and considered them lazy. They believed that they had come from East Africa to make a living in our country, but the reality was that the very events that were now happening in Liberia had probably occurred in their own home countries. War! Now, these same Liberians who had scorned these homeless people were as desperate, homeless and powerless as the very people they had once ridiculed. We as Liberians were now on the receiving end.

Tony and I watched as a parade of displaced people began to settle on our front porch, the palaver hut, and every area surrounding our home. The ELWA campus had spacious, wide-open fields, and most of them were already completely occupied by people. Some were building makeshift homes and shacks out of palm thatches, while others slept out in the open fields. There was no room left on the campus to accommodate any more people. Every facility—the guest house, the church, the school building, and more—were packed to capacity. For the protection of the displaced people, ELWA increased campus security, and guards began to patrol around the clock. As the scene changed minute by minute before my eyes, I could not help but ask God why this was happening.

Later, after the fighting ended, I learned that all twenty thousand of us civilians who took refuge on the ELWA compound had put our lives directly in harm's way. The compound was literally sandwiched between two major military barracks, camp Schefflein and the Barclay Training Center, along with the government broadcasting radio station in the eastern part of Monrovia. Government soldiers and rebel groups alike were headed for these facilities, looking for supplies and the means to promote their propaganda as they fought. They were headed towards us.

Chapter 19

REBELS ON HOLY GROUND

From Our Living Room Window

On the 22nd of July, 1990, Taylor's rebels set foot on the ELWA compound. When the rebels were not fighting the government soldiers, they were harassing and killing powerless civilians, looting civilian property, and raping women and girls. When they entered the compound, we knew it could only mean that the fighting had ended or that the fighters were getting bored. From that day forward, the fate of our lives was in the hands of bloodthirsty youths and illiterate young men dressed in bizarre outfits: women's wigs, choir gowns, skirts, dress coats, and filthy shorts. Some even wore bright red lipstick!

Many of these young boys had ropes tied around their heads as amulets or voodoos talismans. As frontline fighters, they knew they could be killed at any moment, and it was common for them to use talismans for protection. It gave them a strong confidence that they would be protected from gunshots and weapons. They clutched AK-47s and Beretta handguns in their hands, their fingers resting on the triggers so that they could kill anyone, especially a member of an enemy tribe, in an instant. They moved confidently among the twenty-two thousands of helpless, displaced people who now feared for their lives. Other rebels went across the major road in front of the campus into Kpelle town and its surrounding neighborhoods. They frequently made their presence known to government troops by randomly shooting into the air.

One afternoon we peeked through the huge bay window in our living room and saw a large crowd of panicked civilians running and shouting that they had seen government troops fleeing for their lives. They had seen rebels shooting at soldiers at Vice President Harry Maniba's house. This news sent a new wave of panic and terror through the already traumatized people, who feared that the fighting would soon erupt on our own compound. Those who had gone to the coastal side of the ELWA compound next to its beach gathering food from coconut trees abandoned everything and ran to their families on the compound.

In normal days, no Liberian would have considered the coconut trees a necessity. But these trees—planted to beautify our campus and represented in the campus logo—helped saved thousands of lives during the Civil War. The displaced people on the compound used their branches for shelter. They ate the coconuts and the palm cabbage that is found at the very top of the tree. Soon they had cut down and stripped all the coconut trees on the campus.

This day proved to be the beginning of our own tragedy. The rebels intercepted a communication from a major general of the Liberian Army who had disguised himself and was taking refuge among the displaced on our campus. Evidently, he was in communication with the heavily armed troops stationed at President Doe's Executive Mansion and was conveying information regarding the proper time to attack the ELWA compound. The rebels arrested him, put him in a pick-up, and took him away to be killed. They also arrested others on false accusations. A renewed flood of fear swept over the people watching. Our freedom of movement was severely limited, and everyone was walking on eggshells, always fearing the worst.

According to a report that quickly circulated around the city, Doe had enlisted trained Israeli soldiers in his antiterrorist unit. They were allegedly residing in the grounds of his Mansion, ready to take action at any time. We also heard that Doe had rockets and mortars, which he planned to use to protect his troops from the rebels. They had a twelve to fifteen mile range, which meant they could easily reach the ELWA facility from the Executive Mansion.

Fighting intensified in the Buchanan and Firestone areas of Liberia where the rebels had closed in on government troops. Several civilians were injured by stray bullets. Some government soldiers who had been stationed on the Robertsfield highway and in other towns along the road began fleeing into the city. Others decided to stop in the Paynesville area across the road from the ELWA compound. A few even took refuge on the compound among the thousands of civilians who were already there. The soldiers who had gone into Kpelle Town began to harass the few civilians who had bravely stayed in their homes. They took whatever they wanted from these homes, and no one dared to raise any objection.

Adding to our fear and discomfort, a heavy downpour of rain drenched the compound on that same evening. Those who were living in ramshackle, makeshift palm thatch huts were heavily affected by the dreadful weather. They were soaking wet in no time and there was no place to run to escape the pouring rain. We managed to squeeze a few more into the gym and the school. Tony and I decided to take a few of them into our home, especially those with children. Making the selection of whom to take into our home was not easy because everyone needed help. An air of depression settled over the entire compound.

Next door to us in a three-bedroom house an Americo-Liberian family had taken up residence. They had been some of the first people to arrive at the compound when the fighting started.

The older man, who must have been in his sixties, was a former government official, and one could tell that he was financially well-off. Sadly, he met an untimely death on the compound. The rebels ordered him to give up his car. When he refused, they shot him on the spot.

Day after day, we continued to wait out the storm, always wondering what would happen next. Though the Freedom Fighters were now in our compound, we still hoped and prayed to be spared from the outrageous violence that had settled in around us. We believed that the compound was the safest place to be. History tells us that Doe had already planned to attack the facility. Meanwhile, his former Minister Bowier and other top government officials had asked him to resign and leave the country.

When his own Krahn soldiers heard of this plan, they held Doe hostage so that he would not escape and leave them to be killed by the rebels, realizing that if he left the country and flew into exile, they would automatically face their own deaths at the hands of the rebel soldiers. They decided to use Doe as a human shield. They gathered at the Mansion, refusing to let Doe be seen by anyone. While Doe was being held hostage by his own soldiers, Prince Johnson and his rebel forces, along with Taylor and his Freedom Fighters, were building up the fire underneath him in the Paynesville area as well. There was heavy fighting in most suburbs in and around Monrovia. Many innocent civilians had already perished at the hands of the fighters.

At this stage of the war, all businesses in the city had been shut down. In early June, the Roberts International Airport had been closed and had cancelled all commercial flights in and out of the country. Liberians were stranded in their homeland and caught in the outbursts of violence with no escape available. The only means of leaving the country was through Sprigs Field, a small airstrip located on the Old Road in Monrovia. As the means of transport and escape dwindled, the prices of tickets for charter flights out of Sprigs Field increased exponentially. Middle-class Liberians could no longer afford a ticket; only businessmen and women along with expatriates could afford this luxury.

July 24 was my birthday. On this day, many more NPFL rebels made their way into the compound than usual. The thought of a birthday celebration did not even cross my mind. All that mattered was staying alive and trying to figure out how our family could survive the gruesome killings of Charles Taylor's rebels and the government troops of Samuel Doe. Soon we learned that many of the Gio and Mano tribal members who were on staff at the ELWA compound had contacted the rebels when they had first arrived. They had disclosed the locations of the Krahn and Mandingo "enemy tribe" members in the compound so that the rebels were able to map out the locations of their enemies. These staff members even took the ELWA compound phone directory, which contained a map of the compound, and used it to point out the locations of Krahn and Mandingo tribal members who worked for ELWA and were taking refuge within its walls. Instead of trying to save their lives, they were sending them to their graves.

The rebels began to search homes on the campus and other possible hiding places for government officials, former soldiers, and others from so called enemy tribes. They searched from house to house, collecting people and taking them away to be executed. They collected Mandingo tribal members who had chosen to side with the government troops during the Civil War. They had joined the Krahns, President Doe's own tribal group, and worked hand in hand with them against the other tribes, thus making them one of the targeted enemy groups for the rebels. After they were rounded up and arrested, they were taken to the beach or across the road to be killed.

Ironically, as the rebels patrolled among the twenty-two thousands of displaced people on the compound, many cheered and clapped their hands, believing that the rebels had come to save them from the hands of Doe's soldiers. What the majority of these civilians did not know was that many of these rebels had come into the compound on a reconnaissance mission, while others had come only to rescue their Gio and Mano families, knowing that the heaviest battles would take place in the city.

I struggled with the severe challenge this posed to my Christian faith. How could Christians who worked for a Christian organization commit such cruel acts against other human beings? Unfortunately, the small American missionary staff that was left in charge of the compound, along with its Liberian leaders, had no inkling about the evil that was taking place right under their noses.

The rebels were wicked and unmerciful. Before the end of the day, Tony and I got a call from a friend of ours who was from the Mano tribe, warning us to slow down our activities and movement among the displaced people. Rebels were now on the ground and civilian lives were in grave danger. We also received disheartening news from members of the Liberian team working closely with the ELWA missionaries who were doing everything they could to meet a few of the desperate needs of these thousands of displaced Liberians. The compound immediately became a center for displaced people where food had to be allocated by the missionaries in order to feed the large number of people gathered there. A message was received from the U.S. embassy instructing all American missionaries and citizens to leave the country as soon as possible as it was believed that an attack on the compound by government troops was imminent. The compound was no longer safe.

Thousands of people had come to the ELWA campus because of the protection they presumed the Americans could offer Liberians, so this news was frightening to us. We believed that there was a safety net of protection wherever Americans were present. In fact, based on our history, we thought of ourselves as Americans at heart. Our close ties to America, though this made other African countries suspicious, gave us confidence. Every Liberian on that campus believed that neither the rebels nor government soldiers would do us any harm as long as U.S. citizens were in our midst.

The Storm of Violence

Tony and I woke up on the morning of July 25, 1990. We ate breakfast and went outside in our yard to greet those who were taking refuge around our home. By this time, these people felt like family to us, and we did our best to share food, our few possessions and whatever we had with them. John Shea, an American missionary who served as SIM's West Africa area director, saw Tony and came to speak with him. He had previously been caught in the crossfire outside ELWA with Tony at SIM Headquarters and had been told to join the rest of the missionaries inside the compound.

On this same day the search and mapping of the compound intensified. People were picked out from among their neighbors and families. Even though innocent, they were taken to the beach or placed along the roadside, then shot to death. Unexpected gunfire was also erupting outside of the compound, and we found ourselves in more dangerous crossfire. Civilians who were in the open fields lay low on the ground as missiles landed on fields of dry grass. Fires broke out across the open fields, and people sought shelter behind anything they could find. After a while, the shooting quieted down and everyone began to move freely again.

Tony and Mr. Shea continued to talk, while I went into the house to do some chores. In less than thirty minutes I heard some more gunshots from nearby. Soon the shooting seemed to be coming from inside of our campus. Immediately, everyone was on the ground once again, lying flat and hoping to survive. Some ran to the few banana bushes that were in our yard, while others lay close to the house for protection from bullets. Tony and Mr. Shea were also lying flat on the ground. A few brave people were running to get babies out of the crossfire, screaming for family members to help.

I stood with Abigail in one arm and held our front door open with my other, urgently calling people to come into my home for shelter from the flying bullets. This time, unlike the 2nd of July, I was fearless. I wanted to assist as many people as I could. I did not consider the danger to myself or Abigail.

The shooting went on for about thirty minutes and then stopped. Tony at last parted from Mr. Shea and returned to our home, while Mr. Shea also left for his home which was only a couple of houses away from us. After a little while the shooting again erupted and this time it lasted for hours. At one point, the guns were so loud and frightening that everyone thought the house would cave in and we would all be crushed. Tony kept advising us to lay flat on our stomachs and to speak very quietly, if at all. Abigail, who was only fourteen months old at the time, became restless and hot from the tropical heat and high humidity trapped in our closed doors. There were two other babies with us who were also uncomfortable, crying helplessly for the comfort of their mother's milk, which helped to quiet them for a short time.

The shooting stopped for a second time, and some of the women ventured out of the house to see what was happening. Everyone wondered what had happened to the twenty-two thousand people who had been lying in the open fields of the compound. Tony and I chose to stay inside of the house, but when we looked outside, we were not prepared for what we saw. We saw thick smoke coming from two directions on the campus. We saw two groups of rebels running on the beach, weapons and ammunition hanging on their bodies as if for decoration. This renewed our fear. While we were trying to figure out what was going on, more shooting began. This time it lasted for almost four hours.

Those four hours became the most intense and desperate hours I have ever spent, praying and crying out to God for the safety of my family and the others around me. As the shooting continued, it became crystal clear to me that we were now in a war zone and our lives were in great danger.

The fighting had left four people dead, eight injured, and thousands scrambling for their lives. Some of the wounded bled to death right where they had been shot. Others were taken to the ELWA hospital. The hospital was in chaos. Later, Dr. Bill Ardill, SIM's medical doctor, would report:

"During the fighting, while we were lying on the ground, we received a call from the U.S. Embassy saying that they expected 'heavy activity' in our area later in the day. They urged us strongly to leave. We asked if they could help us leave and advise us where to go. They could not help us leave and did not know where we could go. I asked our U.S. HAM radio contact person to stay on standby because of the urgency of the situation. I then drove to the hospital and began to sort out the chaos there. I worked on a lady who had been shot in the shoulder. The bullet had blown away the middle third of her clavicle, the middle of her first rib and the top of her scapula. Amazingly, she had no major vessel injury and no pneumothorax. Because there was no electricity, we couldn't do X-rays on any of these people. We turned on the Honda generator to give us some light in the OR and to help the lab do a few quick tests."

People began to flee the area. Some took their loved ones out of the hospital to join them on a dangerous and treacherous journey to nowhere. The ELWA missionaries transported the rest of the patients to the Bong Mines hospital. These missionaries risked their lives helping these people. The patients would have died without their aid.

Hope was officially gone for all Liberians, as ethnicity became the cause for barbarism. A country that had proclaimed to be a Christian nation was being overrun by its own citizens, some of whom had returned to the worship of voodoos and to the drinking of human blood. Christian brothers and sisters had turned against one another. They used ethnicity as their number one reason for such barbaric behavior. Bible College students who had sat together at the same table, who had read the Word of God together, took up guns against one another. Friends identified friends to the rebels to be killed. Neighbors killed neighbors they had known for years, including neighbors with whom they had shared wells and a cup of water simply because they were from different tribes. Spouses and children of inter-tribal marriages were killed by members of their in-laws' tribe solely because they belonged to the so-called enemy tribe. These were people who had once cooked meals together and shared the same firewood place, lived under the same roof, and most importantly, "eaten from the same bowl or pan," as we say in Liberia.

Our tradition teaches us that when we share food with another person at the same table or from the same bowl, we vow never to betray that person. If a problem or argument arises between us, we would say, "For the sake of the salt between us, I will not do you any harm." In the older days of Liberia, and in most parts of Africa, when a guest arrived at your home, your first was to offer them a kola nut and salt, which you both ate. This represented friendship and a pure heart. Then you shared a meal. If this guest ever committed a crime or brought harm to this home or any of its family members, the food they had eaten would become harmful to the guest's body. This was called "kafu," a curse that could extend to the guest's offspring.

That was how Liberians once lived, but this was no longer the case. My fellow Liberians had turned completely away from their duty and traditions. Many chose to live by the sword and had forgotten the teaching from the Bible, which clearly says, "Whoever sheds the blood of man, by man shall his blood be shed; for in the image of God has God made man (Genesis 9:6).

As I watched these atrocities take place before my very eyes, I struggled in my mind, wondering if God had left us alone to fend for ourselves and die by the hands of the wicked. We had heard continual reports of what the rebels had done to the civilians they caught. They were torturing them and brutally killing them, and I was terrified beyond words. Fear of the rebels' brutality encircled my heart with a heavy cloud, leaving no way of escape. Liberians became so desperately wicked to one another that I began to wonder if God was allowing an entire nation to perish, a nation that had always proclaimed the need and the duty to know and to fear God. Where was God as Liberia tore herself apart? I am sure, if I were to see Him, He would have answered and said, "The same place I was when I saw my son Jesus Christ crucified on the cross for your sake!"

As I pondered this, instead of asking how a loving God could allow my nation to perish, I began to ask where we had gone wrong to bring such bloodshed on the heads of our own people. The decline of my nation was so tragic that even foreign nationals who had once sought refuge in Liberia, considering it to be their home, could not comprehend what was happening. They wondered in despair what had happened to such a beautiful and stable country and its people. Every other country around us had experienced some sort of political instabilities but Liberia had remained peaceful. This stability drew many Africans from other countries into Liberia, who wanted to settle there for the rest of their lives. But now this was no longer the case. My beautiful country had become a killing field with no hope in sight. Everyone was doing all they could to flee from Liberia as quickly as they could.

The Escape to Nowhere

While we were still in the house, we heard a bang on the door that almost took my breath away. A command followed: "Open the door and come outside!" Before Tony could get to the door, a second call came in a louder voice, "Everybody get outside!" When Tony opened the door, two NPFL rebels ordered us outside, and we quickly complied. More rebels came forward and began to search our group and our home. We had no idea what they were looking for at the time, but it soon became obvious to us that they were searching for government soldiers and Krahn or Mandingo people.

I instantly became numb and my stomach began to spasm. The urge to vomit came upon me, but there was nowhere to go. I held my stomach and squeezed every muscle within me to calm myself down. My stomach continued to hurt until later when I was finally able to throw up.

When the rebels had finished searching, they ordered us to leave the house and go to the rebel-controlled areas where they had gathered other displaced Liberians. The men looked at each other, filled with fear and uncertainty about what to do or say. From the barbaric stories we had heard about the rebels, however, we knew not to argue with them. Rather, wisdom advised us to do everything they told us to do.

With more courage than I knew I possessed, I pleaded with the rebels to allow me to go inside our house and grab a few things for my toddler and me. Thankfully they allowed me to enter the house, but not the men. I took Kemah with me, while Tony held Abigail tightly against his chest.

Because of my great fear of the rebels who were high on drugs with bloodshot eyes, I was totally confused and did not know what to take with me. I forgot to grab any of my daughter's necessities, even her diapers or food. I took with me her diaper bag, which contained her feeding bottles, a Sippy cup, and some photos. I also took two of Tony's dress suit coats and put them under my arms as I went to the kitchen. Knowing that the rebels had only given me ten minutes to gather a few items, I now panicked, fearing they would harm me for taking too long. I put some uncooked rice in a bag, grabbed Tony's set of Francis Schaeffer books, and ran outside with Kemah ahead of me.

Why the books? I have no idea. Besides the dress I was wearing, I was only able to take for myself one skirt and a top that had been left lying on our bed. Within ten minutes, my family and I were out of the comfort of a nice modern home with running tap water and electricity, though we were rationing for the lack of fuel in the country. I was out of the house and headed to the unknown. In the blink of an eye, our lives had changed for the worse. We were no longer free people—we were under the control of these savages who had no regard for human life.

We knew that these boys were drugged by their commanders into doing the unthinkable. We also knew they were convinced that voodoo made their bodies bulletproof. As we made our way out of the compound, we saw evidence of the falsehood of this belief which was intended to empower these young men. This belief had allowed them to commit the horrendous crimes requested by their commanders, yet along the roadsides, countless rebel bodies lay in bushes where they had been caught in the battle with government forces.

The sight of these dead rebels was our first appalling experience within the rebel-controlled area. The smell of decomposing bodies was thick in the air. We literally had to step on corpses as we walked because it was impossible to avoid them. I felt sick to my stomach, and once again the urge to throw up came over me. This time it was not fear alone but the stinking smell of rotting flesh which filled me with nausea. As the crowd of other refugees surged towards us, there was no time to stand and compose myself. We were on the run.

Dr. Ardill described the scene as the ELWA compound emptied:

> We continued on and just before the Duport Road we encountered the twenty-two thousand displaced who had run from ELWA. It was very disturbing and sad to see so many of our staff running for their lives. It reminded me of Moses leading the children of Israel. The crowd was huge and we could barely make it along the road with the cars. Many begged for a ride and we felt badly we could not help them. We saw more bodies along the road and smelled the sickening odor of decomposing bodies left to rot on the ground (Ardill, page 203).

My family and I were hidden within the masses of humanity walking on the Duport Road on that day which Dr. Ardill so accurately described. We were among the thousands of others whose fears were as great as our own, whose hearts were as terrified as ours. We were headed into the unknown with no understanding of what lay ahead. There was no transport for civilians except for the rebels and the handful of expatriates like the missionaries from ELWA compound who were fleeing for their lives. Many people walked for hundreds of miles before reaching their destinations. Others were killed while fleeing ELWA and Monrovia in a desperate and unsuccessful attempt to save their lives.

When the rebels had captured the compound and waved us towards their controlled area, most people did not know the specific location or direction in which to run. We did not know which areas or villages were safe. As we headed toward the public radio station, ELBC, which was located on the other side of the city from the ELWA compound, people flew in many directions and everywhere in the surrounding bushes. It was a stampede.

Tony, Kemah, Abigail, and I joined our friends Frank, John, and Moses, and started to walk together as a group. Moses and Frank were college classmates of Tony's at the African Bible College in Liberia, while John was a friend of Frank. The size of the crowd made it impossible for families to stay together with their walking companions. The tall grass, which had once been at waist level, had been trampled completely down to the ground. After a while, Tony and his friends got separated from me, and I was left alone with Kemah and Abigail.

As we approached a long swamp, I saw children crying and parents trying as hard as they could to keep their little ones in sight. I had Abigail on my back while clutching her diaper bag close to my chest, fearing that people would knock it off of my shoulder. With my other hand, I held tightly onto Kemah's dress, pulling her along for fear of losing her in the crowd. As God would have it, we were able to get through the crowd and cross the swamp, only to find that there was another one and another one.

As we approached the second body of water, people slowed down to remove their shoes and flip-flops so they could cross more easily to the other side. Some, with young ones and the elderly, found it difficult to cross. On the other side of the dark, muddy swamp, we found dry land.

There is one scene, in particular, that I shall never forget. We had just arrived at the first swamp. An old woman, who was surrounded by her young grandchildren, was conversing with her daughter. This elderly woman was in her mid-seventies or early eighties. Her daughter and young grandsons had taken turns carrying her in a wheelbarrow. When they arrived at the swamp, they took a closer look and realized that they could not take the wheelbarrow across.

The family stood on the bank of the creek in fear and confusion, wondering how they would get their precious mother and grandmother across the creek in the wheelbarrow. The old woman looked sternly into her daughter's eyes and asked her to leave her alone in the field and go on. Not wanting to abandon her dear mother, the daughter objected, but once again the old woman looked her daughter straight in the face, this time with her eyes wide open. In a commanding voice she said, "Leave me alone and go. I have lived my life. I don't want you and your children to get killed. Go, and let God go with you!"

With this abrupt goodbye between mother and daughter, everyone in the family began to cry. As I stood there and listened to their conversation, I felt my own tears rolling down my cheeks. I was overwhelmed with sorrow, and my heart broke for this family. I thought of my own dear grandmother, who would have been in a similar situation if she had been with me. I could not help but walk away from them devastated. This senseless war was taking a massive toll on precious human lives. I knew that my own battle was nothing compared to what this family was facing at that moment.

My thoughts began to return to my own crisis. I needed to figure out a way to get my little Aunt Kemah, Abigail, and myself safely across the swollen creek. I knew that I could get myself across the creek with Abigail strapped on my back, but as I looked at the huge number of people struggling through the water, I was afraid that Kemah would not make it across the water. I looked for Tony, but he was nowhere to be found. At this time, I did not know if he was in the crowd ahead of me or behind. With my flip-flops in my hands and standing in bare feet, I took Kemah's hand and we both stepped into the water. By the grace and mercy of God, the three of us were able to cross safely.

Chapter 20

BY THE CREEK OF SOUL CLINIC

In Darkness and Mud

As we stepped out of the water of the creek, miraculously, we reconnected with Tony and our friends, Moses, Joseph, and Frank, who had left the ELWA campus with us. We had no time to explain how we had become separated; rather, we continued our journey to the rebel controlled area. With each step, more and more shooting erupted around us, bullets constantly flying over our heads. People were being hit by random, stray bullets as they tried to walk their way to safety. There was no time to stop and give assistance to anyone, even if they had been hit by gunfire. As our journey continued, darkness fell upon us, making it more difficult to see where we were going.

Darkness in Africa, especially in a city that is without electricity, has a much greater impact than it does in the western world. When it is dark, it is indeed pitch black. There was no sign of light anywhere except for the fire shooting up into the sky from the constant blast of machine guns and heavy artillery.

As the sounds of missiles and artillery shells went up into the air, so went my prayers up to God. I continued to plead with God for deliverance from the hands of our captors. In the same breath, I was also praying for the turmoil in my stomach to subside because I was

197

still feeling very ill. The constant gunfire was terrifying. It would literally light up the entire area for seconds at a time.

After crossing the mud-filled swamp, I was covered in mud up to my waist and felt like a filthy rag. We watched as the so-called Freedom Fighters took pleasure in beating civilians and using dried cow tails as whips to keep us in line. They were pushing and shoving everyone, young and old alike. I was frightened of these ruthless creatures and could not bring myself to look into their eyes. As far as I could tell, the rebels on Duport Road wore the same attire as those who had come onto the ELWA campus.

It was still pitch dark when we finally arrived at a river. Those who had come earlier were able to cross to the other side of it, where the Soul Clinic Mission was located. The Soul Clinic Mission compound was a nonprofit organization owned and run by Uncle Ralth Lampkins, a Liberian, and his African-American wife, Justine. The rebels had set up a checkpoint in front of the creek leading to the compound. They had closed every road leading from the city to the Monrovia-Kakata highway, compelling all civilians to struggle across the many creeks and rivers and into Soul Clinic.

As the group ahead of us came to a standstill, we began to wonder what was going to take place. We were then told that those of us who remained on the side of the creek coming from the city would not be allowed to cross and enter Soul Clinic until the rebels screened us the following day. We would be spending the night in the field. This was one of the many tactics they used in getting rid of their enemies from among us civilians.

Sleeping in an open field on a cold July night, with nothing to eat or to sleep on, unsettled our hearts. We had left a warm home at the compound that had electricity from the ample supply of generators, running water, beds, warm clothes, and everything we needed. Now we were cold, dirty, and destitute, and we certainly did not know what our fate might be.

Throughout the evening we heard loud shooting coming from the city and the ELWA area, but especially from the open field where the rebels had detained us for the night. We constantly ducked in fear, dropping to the ground to protect ourselves from stray bullets. This went on for an entire night and into the next morning.

Early in the evening I opened the diaper bag, and to my surprise I did not find what I needed. I had not realized that I had failed to bring food and diapers for Abigail, assuming there were some already inside of the diaper bag. I had also failed to remember to bring water for her to drink. We had left the ELWA compound at three o'clock that afternoon, and Abigail had not had a drop of water or a morsel of food from noon to the early morning hours the next day. She was soaking wet and extremely hungry. The thought that Abigail might starve to death or die of thirst suddenly crossed my mind, and I immediately became anxious. As I started to panic, she wiggled on my back and started to cry. I stood up and untied the lappa, the material that I had used to secure Abigail tightly to my back.

By this time, she began to cry loudly, and nothing I could do would console her. Her father took her from me and tried to calm her down, but to no avail. My fear began to escalate as I realized that her continued crying might be heard by the rebels. I took Abigail from Tony's arms and tried to console her, but even the tender touch of a devoted mother could not stop her screams. Her precious, bare little feet were very cold, and I had no socks or shoes for her. Because there was no clean diaper to soothe her wet bottom, I decided to put Abigail on my back again, hoping that my body warmth would soothe her. As God would have it, she quickly fell asleep the moment I put her on my back.

The tree that the men had secured earlier for shelter allowed me to lean against its strength in order to support Abigail's weight. As I leaned my head against the tree, I closed my eyes and prayed that I would somehow fall asleep and forget the horrors we had experienced that day. I prayed that I would wake up the next day and everything I had seen would have been a dream. Regrettably, my wish did not come true. The shooting continued, and tension in the group of wearied travelers was growing. At two o'clock in the morning a group of rebels came to our area of the field and took away all the men, including my beloved Tony. We were not told why they had been taken, but we had learned at the ELWA campus that men who were taken away were usually either taken to the battle front to fight for the rebels' cause or taken to a killing field to be slaughtered.

My whole world turned upside down with the stark realization that my dearest husband was in grave danger. I could not help but join in with the other women who were sobbing for their husbands. I cried and begged God to bring Tony back to me alive. This time, unlike previous times, I doubted that I would see Tony alive again. The thought of raising our baby alone without my husband overwhelmed my heart and my mind. The painful realization of this possible and probable outcome was almost more than I could bear. I remembered the words of David in Psalm 42:3: My tears have been my food day and night, while men say to me all day long, 'Where is your God?'

I cried silently to God within my heart so that I would not arouse the suspicion of the raging rebels. At any moment, they could hear my voice and come to take me to my death as well. I wondered what I would tell Abigail about her beloved father when she grew up. What memory would she have of him? What would I be able to teach my daughter about forgiveness? How could I ever forgive the ones who were persecuting us? I had no answers for any of these questions.

From the moment they took Tony away until dawn, I sat with Abigail on my back. Sitting in this position for so long caused me severe pain in my lower back. I still suffer to this day from severe backaches from the many months of walking we did during the war.

These challenges were not the only ones we faced. Little activities that we do every day, like attending to calls to nature which we often take for granted, suddenly became a great task. For instance, trying to find a place to privately urinate among thousands of scattered people was a battle of its own. There were no restrooms or outhouses in the open field. We dared not go far into the bushes because rebels were constantly moving all around us. In some areas, the rebels would sit and wait to ambush government soldiers. They might automatically consider us an enemy if they caught us in the bush. The best we could do was to try to find a place that was not overly crowded and attempt to attend to the call of nature. Most women squatted down as low as they could, but I was reluctant to go down that low for fear that a snake or some crawling creature would attack me. With few men left among us, except for small boys and children, nobody took notice of a woman's naked body. After all, we were all fighting for our survival.

At the first sign of daylight, most people began to move around in search of their family members. Others were sobbing for loved ones who had been killed. As for me, I did not have one ounce of energy left to leave the tree I now called home. I believed that this tree was God's good provision for me. I did not have any sheets or blankets to lie down on, so the trunk of this tree had given my weary back a few moments of relief from the excruciating pain of carrying a child for such a long time.

When I took Abigail off my back, I noticed again how miserably wet and hungry she had become. Her tiny stomach was totally empty and folded into several rolls. Her belly button, which was normally large and sticking out, had completely sunk inside and could hardly be seen. Suddenly, I remembered something that my mother used to do to my younger siblings when they were babies.

Without any diaper pins, my mother would tie a string or thread around the baby's waist. Then she would take a piece of cloth and pass it through the string from both the front and the back. I decided to use one of Abigail's dresses to create a makeshift diaper for her. I folded it in half and placed it between her legs. With the help of the only pair of rubber pants I had in the diaper bag, I was able to keep the dress in place, which kept her warm for a while.

After I attended to Abigail's needs, I noticed that my back was soaking wet. The wet diaper could not contain all of her urine and it had leaked out, running down my back all the way to my underwear, then to my feet. There was mud covering the lower half of my body, clinging to my skin like black clay. I looked pathetic, as if I had been rescued from a pit latrine.

At that point, though, nobody cared about how we looked. The facts were clear—we were caught in the middle of a nasty, brutal, and senseless civil war, and only the grace of God could get us through it.

The River of Leeches

July 26, 1990, was the one hundred and forty-third anniversary of our country's independence. To those of us who were displaced, it did not feel like a day to be celebrated. Rather, it was a day of judgment for the thousands of us who had yet to know our fate. Our lives were in the hands of renegades and the bloodthirsty cannibals of Taylor's rebel troops. We knew that in order to survive, we had to cross the wide, muddy river in front of us. The river was full of leeches, filth and corpses, some of which that have just been killed and dumped there.

While I was deeply engaged in my own personal sorrow and pain, I heard a voice from the crowd behind me. "Beth, how are you doing?" Oh! It was such a surprise and a huge relief to see Tony standing so close to me. Before I could answer, he took my hand and said, "Let's get the diaper bag and get out of here!" Tony immediately grabbed our daughter, and with command and urgency he told Kemah to pick up her little bundle and follow us. As we forced our way through the huge crowd, we felt our bodies being pushed from one side to the other. Everyone was pushing and shoving each other. We slowly moved to the middle of the field, where we thought our exit would begin. We did not know at that moment we would spend twelve more hours in that same spot.

From seven o'clock until noon, we watched as the rebels shot and killed scores of people and beheaded many others in the presence of their loved ones. Our dear friend Frank Gibson, who had been one of our travel companions, was singled out from our midst by one of the rebels and was taken away to be killed. As Frank walked out toward the rebels, he was asked about his occupation. Frank said that he was a counselor for a Christian radio station, ELWA. The rebel questioning him obviously could not read or write and had no clue what type of counseling Frank did at ELWA. He immediately interrupted Frank and said, "Oh, are you one of those who were advising Doe and his bad government?" Without allowing Frank to explain the duties of his job, he ordered another rebel to take Frank away to be killed.

When I saw Frank being led to his death, I screamed out loud and slumped to the ground. Everything around me felt dark and I could not think straight. Tony became terribly afraid and begged me to stop crying. If the rebels considered us sympathizers, they might take us away, too.

We were unaware that Mark Dahn, one of our ELWA hospital staff members' husband, was present as Frank was being escorted to his death. From the middle of the crowd, Mark quickly ran to intervene on Frank's behalf, along with another ELWA employee, Nathaniel Gaye who is also Mano. They both spoke in either Gio or Mano, one of the two "heavenly" languages endorsed by the rebels for the release of Frank. In no time at all, Frank was sent back to us healthy on the outside but empty and vulnerable on the inside. Just as I was not able to cry out when they led Frank away to be killed, so was I not able to rejoice when he was released and returned to us. Any reaction on our part could be seen as a threat to the rebel cause. Even though Mark and I were unable to communicate with each other, the tears running down both of our cheeks spoke volumes to us. We both knew how grateful we were to God for sparing Frank's life through the words of Mark.

We remained quiet for the next hour. I finally got the nerve to ask Frank about his thoughts. He still could not express his thoughts and feelings at the moment. All he said was, "When that guy called me out, my spirit immediately died within me." Frank's rescue was a miracle that took place right before our eyes, but there were many who were not rescued on that day. I found myself asking God why, if he had set Frank free, he could not have set the others free, as well? I may never know the answer to this question. God's ways are not our own.

While we were still being held in this field, a few of the Freedom Fighters came and introduced a song for the captives to sing. The words of the song were nothing but curses. The rebels walked through the crowd, making sure that everyone sang. Deep in my heart, I refused to sing such a song. I tried very hard not to be seen by the rebels that I was not singing. Otherwise I would be killed immediately for not obeying their order. Once again, I was reminded that I was not the only one who had suffered such atrocities and harassment. I remembered when the Israelites were asked by their tormentors to sing the Lord's song while they were in captivity in Babylon.

By the rivers of Babylon we sat and wept when we remembered Zion. There on the poplars we hung our harps, for there our captors asked us for songs, our tormentors demanded songs of joy; they said, "Sing us one of the songs of Zion" (Psalm 137:1-4)!

Our captors continued to have their fun with us. They instructed us to lie down flat on our stomachs, to stand up, and then to sit down once more. They shot their guns with each command, and it did not matter to them who they shot. They called out random people to lie flat on the ground and "swim" from one end of the field to the other. Meanwhile, they were still taking people away and shooting them to death. None of us dared to disobey their requests. Any defiance at all was rewarded with a short walk to the shooting field.

While the rebels toyed with us, gunshots were flying over our heads and randomly killing people in the crowd. The worst and saddest thing about it all was that those still living were not allowed to mourn their dead. There was no mention of burial. Whenever a person was hit by a stray bullet and fell among the crowd, the rebels would order us to move along. No one, not even a family member, was allowed to assist the wounded. The rebels allowed no simple acts of decency because they had no respect for human life. Killing had become a sport to them. Instead of killing animals to eat as food in order to survive, they were killing human beings, just for the fun of it.

Near-Death Experience

At seven o'clock, the rebels instructed us to form a single line in order to cross the wide, muddy water. For three hours we stood in line. While we waited, Tony decided to go towards the city to try to find some drinking water for us as we had not had anything to eat and drink from the day before. Abigail became very restless and was crying hysterically from hunger and thirst. She had not eaten for almost twenty-four hours. As I stood there, an older lady behind me tapped me on the shoulder and asked that I take Abigail off of my back so that she could try to help keep her quiet. I quickly complied, but Abigail was inconsolable and continued to scream.

After an extended period of crying, Abigail suddenly stopped and looked faint. Her eyes began to roll into the back of her head. I took one look at my baby and screamed out loud for someone to help. The woman who had previously offered her help came to my rescue. She quickly grabbed Abigail from my arms and poured some water on her head, which poured down over her entire body. The water was in a small bottle provided by a young man standing next in line with me. Just as for everyone, this water I believe was the only source of fluid or food for that young man, yet he gave it to save my daughter's life. Amazingly, he was no stranger to me as I came to realize later. He was a childhood friend of mine from Tahn, my home town. As God would have it, Abigail responded with a loud scream and her eyes returned to normal. While this angel woman lovingly cradled Abigail in her arms, she asked me, "Have you given this baby some food to eat today?"

"No," I answered. Without further questioning, she placed her hand on Abigail's mouth and gave her two handfuls of water taken from the young man next to us. His name was Junior Boakai. I was amazed and grateful that he was willing to share his precious water with my baby, considering how difficult it was to find drinkable water. The muddy river in front of us was filled with hundreds of fresh and decaying corpses and everyone was scavenging in all directions to find clean drinking water. There were not enough words to thank this kind woman who had come out of nowhere and rescued my baby.

A few minutes after Abigail had consumed the water, she started to cry again. A woman who had been watching told me to take Abigail out of the line and sit with her on the grass. I followed her advice. Abigail quieted a little bit, but she still had not had any food to eat. I began to hope and pray that Tony would be able to find some food and water for my baby to eat and drink.

As I sat, I saw Eunice Dahn, whose husband, Mark, had rescued Frank a few hours earlier. She walked towards me and asked, "What is happening to Abigail"? In a choking voice, I explained about Abigail's near-death experience and her lack of food and water. I watched as pain spread across Eunice's face. She told me to remain where I was. In less than fifteen minutes, Sis Eunice returned with a bowl of cream of wheat that she had prepared earlier for her son, T. Mark, who was about the same age as Abigail. I gratefully received the spoon and the cream of wheat from Eunice, as well as some cool, clean drinking water. Abigail ate the cream of wheat as if she had not eaten in an entire week. When she was finished eating, warm sweat poured down her little face as if her head had been immersed in water. I was filled with so much gratitude and joy for Eunice's kindness toward my daughter that I began to shed tears.

Tony returned with only one small bottle of water. The water in the bottle consisted of rain water which had been taken from an unfinished septic tank. In normal days, nobody in their right mind would have drunk water from such a source, but this was not a normal day. Every person around us was fighting just to make it through this one day and, hopefully, the next one would follow. We ate and drank whatever would come our way in order to sustain our lives. It was either septic tank water or water from the infested river with leeches and corpses whose stomachs had blown up into giant balls, about to burst open at any time.

In no time at all, my beautiful baby girl returned to her usual self. When I looked at Tony staring down at his daughter, I saw that tears filled his eyes. He had not realized how close he had come to losing his precious baby girl to thirst and starvation. Together we thanked God for sending Eunice to us to save our beloved Abigail.

Crossing Our Jordan River to Soul Clinic

By noon, we were still crawling in line like snails, waiting to cross the river to Soul Clinic. While we waited, people continued to be killed by the rebels, some just a few feet from us. Now the rebels had made a new game of it. When they took one person away, they would randomly ask two other people to follow him. After they shot their first captive, they would ask the other two to pick up the body and throw it in the bush. When they complied, the rebels would say, "You can't leave him alone in the bush! One of you will have to stay with him."

Suddenly, one of them would be fired upon and drop dead. The brutality seemed unending. Life became hopeless to me and my fight for survival began to dim. I had been standing so long that I was physically and emotionally exhausted. I prayed to God for relief. Even though I had not eaten for almost twenty-four hours, I did not feel one bit of hunger. I had witnessed so much killing and seen so much human blood that my mind would not allow the thought of any food passing through my lips.

As we continued to stand in line, we saw a dear friend of ours, Patrick Nuah, who was also from Nimba County. He was a former classmate of Tony's from the African Bible College in Yekepa. As Patrick walked through the middle of the field with his family, he saw us and instantly motioned for us to leave the line and follow him. Patrick was from the Mano tribal group, the same as the Gios who made up the majority of Taylor's rebels. He could go where ever he pleased in Taylor's territory, and he became our ticket to cross the river and enter the Soul Clinic Mission compound. Patrick walked us safely out of that place of torture. All of those who came to our aid during that time were either Mano or Gio. They had more freedom of movement and suffered less than other tribal groups. When we at last placed our feet in the dark brown, leech-infested river, it was chest high.

The River Bath

We finally made it to the Soul Clinic Mission. The compound reminded me of a prison cell of desperate people awaiting their death sentences. My little Aunt Kemah and I soon joined a group of women going to bathe our weary, mud-caked bodies and to wash our filthy clothes while Abigail remained under the watchful eyes of her dad as he searched for a safe place to rest our exhausted heads for the night. I had no other clothes to wear; however, I got into the light brown chocolate water and washed my clothes that were still on me as modestly as possible. While I watched other women walked around with absolutely nothing on. A few others had wrapped some materials around their waists, which only covered the lower parts of their bodies, leaving their upper bodies totally exposed. There were men walking around the proximity of the river, while others were in the river taking their evening baths. Thankfully, before finishing my bath, most of these men had moved offshore in little groups away from us women. I swiftly squeezed the excess water from my skirt and crawled to the edge of the river and walked out.

This experience was the biggest risk to my modesty that I had ever taken. It surprised me to see the majority of women walking around the area naked while men watched. It is very unusual for an African woman to do such. It is a common practice for some women in Africa to expose the upper parts of their bodies, especially when they are breast-feeding their babies or working on the farm, but a woman would never uncover the lower parts of her body in a public area. When I noticed the "I don't care" attitude of these women, I sensed the negative impact that the war had already taken on our lives, even in this short period of time. The value of human life, which we had once proclaimed as important and honorable in our society, had quickly evaporated from us. After all, if people do not respect or care enough for the very life of a human being, why then care for the body that carries that life? This was now the attitude of many of my fellow Liberians. The body, which God had fearfully and wonderfully made, was no longer considered precious to most of my fellow Liberians.

Meanwhile, Kemah had taken her bath and was sitting on the grass waiting for me. We headed back to Tony and the rest of our group. With the tremendous assistance of Patrick, we were able to take shelter in an unfinished house with only a roof on it, but no doors or windows. The beautiful four-bedroom frame, abandoned by its owners when the fighting began, was patched up with cardboard boxes and packed to capacity with destitute people, including my family. Our room alone was occupied by twelve people.

When we arrived at the house, Tony and I began to look for some cardboard boxes to sleep on. A lady who had already been there for about a week gave me a small amount of cooked rice for Abigail to eat. The rice, which only had some salt and palm oil on it, was enough to sustain her until the next day.

When darkness fell upon us, everyone spread out on the floors of their rooms for the night. A few of us had the luxury of sleeping on cardboard boxes, while others lay on cold cement floors. The majority of us displaced civilians at the Soul Clinic compound had not eaten or drunk anything except for the river's unclean water. Looking at the river once again during my bath I briefly paused and took a deep breath, remembering all that my family and I had endured there, but hoping that what lay ahead would be better.

Many people had tried to fight their way through the river without making it to the other side. While thousands were still trying to make it across the river at the upper end of the compound, another large group was at the lower side of it. Some were washing clothes in the river, while others were hauling the same water to the compound and the make-shift homes they had created to be used for drinking and cooking. The most unpleasant thought that came into my mind was when I remembered that the upper part of the river contained hundreds of dead bodies that would be floating downstream. Many had been decapitated; many had lost other body parts, as well. The bodies of pregnant women were in the upper part of the river who have also been violently killed. The rebels did not want any of these enemy children to survive simply because they did not see these unborn children as innocent, but as vermin from another tribe.

Both children and the elderly died in the river that day and watching those horrors take place was heart-wrenching. It was at this very river where my precious baby, Abigail, nearly died and where our friend, Frank, almost lost his life. However, it was also at this river that God sent His angels not once but twice to rescue and deliver my family and me from the hands of our persecutors. Tony and I both praised God for sparing our lives even though we knew the tremendous danger that still lay ahead of us. Through God's deliverance, He allowed us as a family to dance through the flames to safety at the Soul Clinic mission and onward.

Chapter 21

A JOURNEY FOR LIFE

Our Long Walk to the Fendell Campus

We had hoped that Soul Clinic would be a safe sanctuary after the horrors of our journey, but we were disappointed. What we saw at first glance was far more unexpected. The compound was overcrowded, chaotic, and more and more shootings were taking place there. Rebel soldiers continued to falsely accuse and kill people from other ethnic groups or "enemy tribes." No one was safe, and we feared that we might be placed among those who were falsely accused. So, bright and early the next morning we again started our journey into the unknown.

We did not know where we were headed or how far we would have to travel to reach safety. However, there was this little sense of calm among the hundreds of us traveling displaced people. Taylor's rebels could still be seen but not in a large number as they were close to the city of Monrovia where the heaviest battle was still to be fought. We were free for a while from the crowds and the cruel harassment of the rebels. We continued to walk along the Monrovia-Kakata Highway, which is the main road that heads towards the Fendell campus of the University of Liberia, located northeast of Monrovia. There was debris everywhere. Smashed vehicles belonging to the rebels littered the way. We also saw human remains, both civilians and soldiers. Scattered on the road next to some of these decapitated bodies were what seemed to be empty army uniforms devoid of human life. Many of those who had worn the uniforms had been killed by cars and left by the roadside. They were unrecognizable as human beings, leaving behind their uniforms to testify to the horror that had been committed.

The devastation we encountered along this route was horrific. Our eyes were now fully open to the reality of the effects of war and violence upon the lives of humans. After walking for five more hours, we came across another creek and I saw a gruesome scene that almost took my breath away. The creek was filled with dead bodies. Nestled among the decaying bodies was a dead woman, whose baby was still fastened to her back. I tried very hard not to look at those decomposing bodies, especially the woman and her child. Deep down, I realized that this could have been my body floating in the water. This could have been my baby floating in the filthy water with me.

The thought that such a crime could have been committed against me or any of my own family members caused me to say a quick prayer to God for His continued protection. This horrendous sight was seen by everyone who passed by; yet, nobody dared to whisper a word about it. Every one of us passed by their remains as though they had never existed. Their lifeless bodies were left alone to rot without being buried.

We continued to go deeper into Taylor's territory, where his rebels had become self-proclaimed lords and masters of all human fate. Doubt and fear built in my heart as we walked past villages and farms which had once been filled with life and happiness. Now they were completely deserted. Most of these villages had the appearance of empty ghost towns, while others still reeked of the offensive odor of decomposing bodies. With each step, I continued to believe that our chances for survival in this violent storm were slim. The further we went away from Soul Clinic, the more teenage rebels we encountered who took pleasure in harassing and killing innocent civilians, randomly shooting into groups of people who were simply trying to make their way to safety. There was no law and order; there was no civil justice.

The rebels had established many checkpoints along our route. At every checkpoint they singled out people whom they considered government employees in Doe's administration or members of enemy tribes. Next to the checkpoints, the piles of dead bodies continued to grow. The rebels stripped the dead bodies of their possessions, but also took valuables from those they allowed to pass through their gates. They piled the confiscated personal belongings beside the checkpoint gates.

As we waited at one of these checkpoints, we watched as one male civilian was pulled out of line and shot only a few feet away from us. He was killed simply because his ID card identified him as a government employee. After watching this horrible scene, I immediately turned around to look for Tony. Thankfully, he was standing right behind me. In a whisper, I asked him if he had his employment ID with him. He told me that he did have it in his wallet. I asked him to give it to me and I managed to shove it beneath the lappa which held Abigail against my body, hoping that they would not ask me to take her off of my back.

Tony's ID card described him as a Coordinator for Muslim Ministry Outreach. This was a grave concern to us because Taylor's rebels were killing Mandingos, most of who belonged to the Muslim religion. We knew that the illiterate rebels could have chosen to kill Tony simply for having an ID with the word Muslim written on it. At these checkpoints, rebels also asked every civilian about his or her tribe of origin. For the first time during our escape, I began to hope that my tribal identity would play a role in the survival of my family.

We knew our fate would be determined when we got to the head of the line. The rebel at the gate asked me what tribe I belonged to and then proceeded to ask Tony for his ID card. I quickly interrupted him as soon as the word ID came out of his mouth. I said that Tony was my husband, and with this assurance the rebel soldier waved Tony and our group through the gate. We walked as quickly as we could out of their sight. My tribal identification had likely saved Tony's life.

The reality of hunger began to settle into our stomachs, but we had no time to think about it. We needed to walk further until we could find a safe place to rest. As we walked, the rumbling noise in my stomach kept reminding me of its emptiness. We soon arrived at a village where a huge sugarcane farm was located. It was evident that many people had entered the village and had taken its food. During the war, sugarcane became one of the most sustaining foods available for the people walking along treacherous roads. I was able to restore my strength on one sweet shoot, devouring it like a starving child.

The closer we came to Fendell, the more the harassment of the rebel forces grew. We watched scores of people lose their lives at the hands of these bloodshot-eyed rebels. The intimidation and killing of civilians at the checkpoint closest to Fendell was so severe that people referred to it as the "God bless you" gate. Indeed, those that survived the brutality and the unmerciful tortures at this gate were truly blessed by God and His angels who protected them from the hands of those savages. The rebels were especially thorough at this gate, checking every personal belonging. They commanded me to take Abigail off my back so they could search me. Thankfully, along the way I had destroyed Tony's ID card, tearing it with my teeth into tiny pieces before we arrived. God did bless us on that day. We had survived up to that point, and we had God to thank for it.

Fendell: A Story of a Death Camp

We arrived at the Fendell University campus on the afternoon of July 27th. The Fendell campus was jam-packed when we arrived. Tony decided right away that we should continue about ten minutes farther to reach the village of Gaynah's Town, where he had done some evangelism work in the past. Tony had developed a close relationship with the village pastor, Dickson, and his wife, Ma Musu. Because of this friendship, Tony felt comfortable going to Gaynah's Town at such a difficult time in our lives. When we arrived, we were grateful to discover that this family was still in Gaynah's Town and that their little mud house was still intact. Dickson and Ma Musu warmly received us into their home even though they were faced with the same devastating circumstances as everyone else in the country. We had brought seven people with us, and Dickson's family graciously lodged all of us.

Immediately upon our arrival, Dickson asked Tony to take a leadership role at the village church, and he began preaching twice a day, every day. Each time the church bell rang, many people gathered at Dickson's home to hear the Word of God. The uncertainty of survival from one day to the next caused everyone grave concern. We never knew if we would be able to hold the next service. As a result, Tony ended each worship service with an altar call, giving people the opportunity to trust and believe in the Lord Jesus Christ. This continued for about a month, and there was still no end in sight for the violence of the Civil War.

It was difficult and risky to travel from the village to the Fendell campus, but Ma Musu and I went there every day, hoping to rescue friends or family members who might have arrived and might be in need of help. Life on the campus was deplorable and pathetic. There were around 75,000 displaced people living in the huge university buildings. Before the distribution of food commenced on campus, hundreds of people died from starvation and simple ailments such as diarrhea. There was no water and no bathroom facilities available anywhere on campus.

These masses of people lived in darkness, with no electricity. They used the books in the university library as firewood for cooking and as toilet paper. The sanitary conditions became so poor that a cholera epidemic broke out and took the lives of many people, especially the elderly and children who were more susceptible to diseases and bacteria due to their low or weak immune systems. As the food shortage continued, more and more people lost their loved ones. Families had no place to bury the dead, so they began to dump the bodies in a designated area.

Between the Fendell campus and Gaynah's Town was Adam and Eve Creek. This creek had large numbers of leeches swimming in its waters, but because it was the largest creek close to the campus it became a gathering ground for attending to toiletry needs, the laundering of clothes, bathing, and cooking. It was given the name Adam and Eve Creek because both men and women used it for bathing, and standing around naked without shame. It also became a burial and meeting place for family members. Life in the tiny village of Gaynah's Town was difficult, but it was nothing compared to living on the Fendell university campus each day. Though I only had one skirt and two blouses as my wardrobe, I was at least able to keep my body clean. My clothes became threadbare and ragged until Ma Musu gave me some clothing of her own to use, some of which were so huge on my tiny frame that I had to take them in with a needle and thread.

Though I had refused to eat palm cabbage on the ELWA campus, I could no longer hang on to my personal preferences if I wanted to survive. I ate whatever we could get. As time went by and Tony continued to preach at the village church, life became a little easier. Some of the local rebels who became regular attendees of our little church began to give us rice from the supplies they frequently received from their rebel leader, Charles Taylor. They would bring rice and fish to Tony and say, "Pastor, here is your food. You need to continue to preach to us."

When Tony's beard grew too long and he wanted to shave it, he asked two of the rebels attending our church if he could shave his beard. The rebels replied, "Pastor, today we know you with a beard, but tomorrow, if you do shave, we will not know you without a beard." The rebels had spoken. As long as Tony kept his beard, they would continue to be his friend. If he shaved, he would become their enemy and they would treat him as one. This might be surprising. During the war, the rebels thought of clean-shaven men as new government recruits so they killed them. With such response from both rebels, Tony sported a long beard for several months. There came a time when if Tony stood far from me, I could barely recognize him because of his beard. His overgrown beard made him look so different from the well-groomed Tony that I had married a year and a half ago. In order to have him survive, we both vowed not to have any razor touch his head and his beard till we escaped from Liberia. I would much rather have him with his long beard than not have him at all.

Chapter 22

THE HIDING PLACE

Friends and "Friends"

After staying in Gaynah's Town which was around the Fendell area for about two months, a good friend of ours (who was also an employee of the ELWA radio station), Daniel McGee, heard from a source that we had survived the battle at the ELWA compound. Daniel, who was now residing at the Bouake Washington Institute (BWI) campus located in Kakata with his family, wasted no time searching for our family. But, before he could commence the risky search to find us, he, along with the other staff from the radio station, was arrested by Taylor and ordered to turn on the radio station.

Taylor had demanded that the radio station be put back on the air by Thursday of the following week after the mass exodus of the 20,000 displaced people from the ELWA campus. With guns pointed to their heads, our friends had no choice but to comply with the bloodthirsty rebels' demands. The staff tried to get the radio station back on the air, but failed. Our friend, Frank, was one of those asked to turn on the generators, as the batteries had no energy left in them to run the station. Taylor then sent some of his top commanders to various displaced camps to find some of the other ELWA missionaries who could help get the radio station working again. By this time, however, two of the missionaries who had escaped from the compound had already gone to the police station to get passes which would allow them to travel safely through Liberia to the Ivory Coast.

According to Dr. Ardill, these missionaries had only been gone for about ten to fifteen minutes on the dusty road to Bong Mines when one of the ELWA vans whizzed by them towards Kakata, a town located in Mount Margibi County. Thinking that the van contained ELWA missionaries, they frantically waved it to a stop only to discover a rebel driver. Stan, Jon and Dave, all missionaries from the ELWA campus, were sitting in the back. They were now in the hands of rebels, who took them all back to the ELWA compound to meet Taylor's demand for media coverage.

The ELWA radio station was re-opened and became operational which allowed us to reconnect with Daniel and his family in Kakata. As Daniel often traveled to Monrovia from Kakata to work with the station, he began searching for us, asking people who knew us where we were. Through God's intervention, he finally found and rescued us from Gaynah's town on September 20th after the death of President Samuel Doe. We decided to travel to Kakata and when we arrived, Daniel provided us with a bedroom where Tony, Kemah, Abigail and I stayed. Our friends, Frank, Moses and John, who later traveled to Kakata on their own, went to another building where most of the single men of the ELWA staff were hosted. Our stay in Kakata was a little more peaceful than our stay in Gaynah's Town because Taylor's rebels were stationed at various workplaces in the city. However, the rebels in Gaynah's Town were often bored and frequently walked through the streets harassing innocent citizens.

Upon our arrival at the BWI campus, I found that most of our wedding dishes and clothes were being used by people we knew very well. They had looted them from the house in which we had taken refuge at ELWA and carried them along for their own use just like other civilians who were now in the habit of taking others personal properties. Not only did these people know us, they were also good friends of Lee and Michelle Sonius, into whose house we had moved on the ELWA campus for our safety before the war entered Monrovia.

One would have thought they would think twice of taking things that belonged to us. However, this was not the case. Most of my dishes that they had taken had not even been removed from their original boxes since our wedding day. I was heartbroken to see my property being used by people who claimed to be our friends while I was in desperate need of them. And, shockingly, not one was ever returned to us as a goodwill gesture. As people fled to safety, neighbors who managed to stay in their homes had gone from house to house, taking whatever items they wanted with no thought of returning them to their rightful owners.

The family that had taken my dishes refused to return them; it hurt me that they were so insensitive to the needs of my family. They did not care how I felt losing my personal belongings. Daniel's wife, Laurinda McGee, had compassion on me and supplied me with a few things to use for cooking and eating. We did everything together when it came to housekeeping. Their daughter, Ida D., was only a year older than Abigail and they played happily together. The girls became very close friends and were inseparable.

During our two-month-long stay in Kakata, Tony found out that Francis, one of his college classmates, was exceedingly fearful of being seen by Taylor's rebels. As a Ghanaian, his life was in great danger. All Ghanaians and Nigerians were being actively sought by Taylor's regime to be killed. Taylor believed the peacekeeping forces from these two West African countries had a hidden agenda against him. He also believed that these countries, especially Nigeria, planned to get rid of him in order to rescue Doe. At this point, Doe was already dead, but Taylor continued to target citizens of these countries who were stranded in Liberia.

Realizing the dilemma of our friend, Tony and I decided to allow him to stay with us after getting permission from Daniel and Laurinda. We secretly moved him into our building and kept him closed up in our bedroom for the two months we stayed in Kakata. He did not step outside of that room from the moment he stepped into it. Our lives were put in immediate jeopardy the moment we took him under our roof and if Francis were to be discovered by the rebels, we would have also been killed because we had hidden him.

According to Francis (whose nickname was Bongoma), no one, not even his good friends, would take him into their homes. After one week of staying with us, we could tell that he was still very worried so I decided to talk to him. I reassured him that Tony and I would do everything possible to keep him out of the hands of the rebels, even to the point of allowing him to eat all of his meals in our bedroom.

The building in which we lived had once had indoor plumbing, so there were two toilets that were being used by both families. We did not have the luxury of flushing them automatically, but they were still usable by pouring a full bucket of water through them as quickly as possible, which then created the pressure necessary to cause them to flush.

Laurinda and I got up early each morning to prepare breakfast. We chose to prepare our food for the day in the early hours of the morning because of the uncertainty of our lives at that time. We were still in a war zone. Fighting could erupt at any time and the necessity of fleeing from our home at a moment's notice was a very real possibility. This kind of unforeseen event could cause parents to lose their children and the elderly could pass out from starvation as a result of not having enough food prepared for the coming day.

To try and ensure against this we always made enough food so that we would have leftovers for the next day, just in case.

During our stay in Kakata, Laurinda and I made friends with a few of the rebels who resided near the campus. Their job consisted of guarding the military equipment of the resistance movement. We often asked them to escort us to nearby villages where most of the women went in search for food. We returned their kindness by sharing our cooked food with them and by this action, we established somewhat of a relationship with them. Our relationship with them helped to curb any harassment to our families as well.

One of these young men was known as Sergeant Quick-Quick. He was given this name because of his quick instinct to kill, both at the battlefront and among civilians. Sergeant Quick-Quick was greatly feared because of his aggressive behavior among his fellow rebels. Nevertheless, he was always willing to help us. He went with us to villages to purchase fish and other food items. We were grateful for his presence because our own husbands could not go with us. The lives of men were in much greater danger than women during this time. Many who tried to venture on the outdoors were captured by the rebel group and taken to the battlefront to fight against their will.

On the Run Again

As time went by, we began to hear rumors that an attack was about to take place in Kakata, mainly on the BWI campus, which had become an operational base for Taylor's troops. This information caused great distress among us and many around us began to flee Kakata. Our family, along with Francis, the McGees, and the family of Uncle Joe, formerly called Joe Mulbah, who later became the Information Minister for Charles Taylor, decided to leave for the city of Gbarnga. In a state of panic and confusion, we began another long journey. At least this time we had chosen a destination, unlike our first exodus from Monrovia.

By this time, Francis had become a part of our family and we continued to be concerned about his safety. We could not leave him, but the danger of traveling together with him was terribly high. My dearest husband and I decided to ask God for discernment in the matter. If God wanted us to take Francis with us, He would have to give us peace and wisdom about the situation, just as He had done in previous months.

When the day of our departure arrived, Tony and I looked at each other with troubled hearts. Tony asked tentatively, "What shall we do?" He was looking for an answer from me. I looked at my husband and said, "Let's do it!" Tony hurriedly went into the bedroom and told Francis to get ready to leave for Gbarnga. Everyone was frantic and there was a lot of pushing and shoving going on all around us as we prepared to go. I took a moment to be quiet and prayed for the safety of everyone on our journey, especially for Francis, whose life was at risk. Thankfully, no one in our group objected to bringing Francis with us. We departed from Kakata on the twenty-fourth of November and arrived in Gbarnga late at night on the same day.

Our trip seemed to last forever, but we finally arrived at a new home in Gbarnga which had been previously secured by Daniel for us. The house had four bedrooms and a good-sized living room. The kitchen was an outdoor kitchen, which is typical of a rural Liberian home. This home became our little safety nest. It was secluded from the other houses by several fruit trees. During our two-month stay there, we spent most of our days outside under the trees to rest from the raging hot, tropical sun. We played many games of UNO because it was our only means of passing the long, boring days. In

Gbarnga, Francis was no longer forced to be confined in hiding since we lived in an area off the beaten track. He often came outside and sat on the front porch with us while we visited with our neighbors. He was also able to eat his meals with us.

After a few weeks, Francis informed Tony and me of wanting to travel further to cross the border into the Ivory Coast, where he would travel to his home country of Ghana. We knew the journey would be risky for him but we did not stop him from leaving because his life was more at risk than we were. Gbarnga was like a time bomb, where fighting could erupt at any time. Taylor had a contingent force housed in Gbarnga and the peacekeepers in Monrovia were looking for ways to overrun his forces. This meant that the possibility of attack was very high. With many prayers and tears, we gave Francis our blessing to leave. We asked Uncle Joe and Daniel to give him a pass for exit from the country. Without the pass, Francis would have had a tough time getting to the border because every feature of him spoke loudly of being Ghanaian. There were multiple gates on the road from Gbarnga to the border town of Legato, Ivory Coast. It was only by God's grace that he made it out safely home to Ghana.

Our stay in Gbarnga was somewhat peaceful for the first month but our little time of tranquility soon ended in violence and more chaos. When we first arrived in Gbarnga, we had been amazed to see the local Liberians going about their business with little harassment from the rebels. We discovered that Taylor had just given a strong mandate to punish any rebels caught disturbing the public or harassing innocent civilians. This law made life for locals more bearable in places like Gbarnga. We continued to play UNO and Ludoo, a game which is played with two to four persons. The goal of the game is to capture your opponents' seeds in order to safely bring all of yours home. We enjoyed the comfort of our cool, breezy yard until mid-December, 1990, when Nigerian peacekeeping air bombers flew over Gbarnga.

As God would have it, Tony and Daniel were home with us on one hot and sultry afternoon when we heard the loud engine of a plane flying much lower than normal. We saw our neighbors running into the bushes and gardens within our neighborhood, attempting to escape the shelling which followed. Thankfully, Abigail and Ida D. were with us, and their fathers quickly grabbed them, laid them on the ground and shielded them with their own bodies from the bombs that were expected. Fortunately the plane disappeared without dropping any bombs but people were afraid to come out of their hiding places for fear that the plane would return. After waiting indoors for a while, people came out from cover and began trying to figure out what had just happened.

The next day, as the sun was trying to shoot its rays out from beneath the early morning sky, we once again heard the sound of the bomber coming in the distance. Laurinda and I were making breakfast for our families when we heard our husbands call out in terrified voices, telling us to get out of the kitchen quickly. We ran from the house and hid in the grass with some of our neighbors. This time, the plane damaged several homes and properties and caused an awful lot of destruction on human lives. The peacekeepers' plane had not only targeted Taylor's military base but had also bombed the common market area and surrounding neighborhoods, killing hundreds of people. The cruelty and senseless killing by the Nigerian peacekeepers angered Liberians so much that Taylor's rebels began to kill and harass Nigerian and Ghanaian civilians once again. When the killing became more rampant in Gbarnga, all we could do was to give thanks to God for allowing Francis to get out of the area safely.

Now that Gbarnga was no longer safe, civilians began to desert the city. People, once again, became fearful of Taylor's army rebels.

Evidently, Taylor was convinced that enemy forces were moving among the thousands of civilians taking refuge in Gbarnga, so Tony decided that we needed to leave Liberia completely. We decided to flee to the Ivory Coast. Our plan was to leave Gbarnga, and when we told Daniel and Laurinda about our plans, we discovered that they were also contemplating leaving Liberia. This made our plans more comforting, knowing that our families could escape together.

By the end of the third week of December, Tony and Daniel informed Uncle Joe about our plan to leave for the Ivory Coast. Uncle Joe, who had been very helpful to us during our stays both in Kakata and Gbarnga, was saddened to hear the news. However, we could not afford to stay in Gbarnga any longer, knowing that fighting could erupt at any moment. The town was like a ticking time bomb that would explode at any time.

The next section of my book is about the United States marines who had earlier anchored off the coast of Monrovia aboard their heavily fortified war ships. The "hands-off-policy" of the U.S. government in regard to Liberia required that they remain on board their ships and watch as thousands of Liberians were massacred around and within the city of Monrovia by President Doe and his soldiers. Without the aid that many expected from the United States the rebellion against Doe and the violent upheaval that followed were unstoppable. I have already described the effects of the "hands off" policy on the lives of my family and the lives of many of our friends, as we struggled to escape the violence and bloodshed of the Civil War. The suffering of many other Liberians, as well as that of my extended family, was intense and as will be seen in the next chapter. It was not until countries from the West African region came to the aid of the Liberians that the outrageous bloodshed came to an end.

Chapter 23

MARINES ABOARD THEIR SHIPS

When All Hope Seems Lost

On June 19, 1990, the Secretary of State for African affairs, Herman J. Cohen, informed Congress that "the resolution of this Civil War is a Liberian responsibility." He continued, saying, "There is no intention of using these forces for any political end. They are there to preserve American lives. United States forces will not intervene to stop the fighting or to influence the outcome of this crisis in any way" (Sirleaf, page 178).

Liberians were sorely disappointed in the American response because they believed that the American government had helped to create the situation that caused the civil war.

As fighting intensified in Monrovia, many civilians were stranded with no means of escape. Most decided to hide within their own homes out of the roving eyes of the militant killers in order to avoid possible beatings and torture, including the possibility of execution by Doe's bloodthirsty soldiers. Doe's forces were not the only threat at this time. Prince Johnson's rebels, who now occupied the center of Monrovia, were also threatening citizens.

Liberians shut themselves inside of their homes, trying as much as possible to avoid showing any signs of their presence to the outside world. Unfortunately, this decision created another desperate situation, as the civilians experienced real difficulty in obtaining food. While trying to avoid physical harm, Liberians had condemned themselves to extreme hunger which eventually drove them out into the streets again to search for food. As they searched in vain for nourishment, these starving Liberians began to eat the dogs and cats that roamed the streets of Monrovia. The dogs, themselves had already feasted on decayed human bodies to survive.

When there were no more dogs and cats to eat, people began to eat grass, weeds and anything they could find on the streets of Monrovia. "People hid, expecting the terror to end soon. But the days became weeks and then months, and after eating the dogs and cats which roamed the rubbish-tops, or sending their children to dig up the grass and the weeds for soup or to eat raw, they began to starve to death" (Huband, page 140).

The rebels cut off all routes of escape from the city. No one was allowed to enter or leave the city. Civilians from Bomi Hills also experienced a severe shortage of food and more people died at the merciless hand of forced starvation, adults and children alike. My uncle, whom we commonly referred to as Da Armah, was the only man in the home at the time the rebels arrived in Bomi Hills. In order to feed our family, Da Armah would go out into the bush to search for food. One of the most common foods which now could scarcely be found was cassava, a tubal starchy root that grows in the ground. One day he went out into the bush and was never seen again.

By this time, according to my family, they had not eaten any food for three days. The only thing they could put into their aching bellies was water which was not safe to drink. Later, the body of my uncle was claimed to have been found by a man who was also searching for food for his own family. This fact was never proven because no one in our family was strong enough, due to the lack of food, to go out into the bush to search for him.

A couple of months after the death of my uncle, the situation in Bomi Hills became so acute that the United Nations and other relief agencies from other countries began to send supplies to our starving people. The starvation in this area of Liberia made international headlines, which referred to its victims as "walking human skeletons." One of those human skeletons was my aunt, Hawa Forgoo, the wife of my uncle who died in the bush. Many of those people who suffered from malnourishment due to starvation were taken to Monrovia to be hospitalized and fortunately, Ma Hawa was one of those who were blessed to be alive after she had been treated at John F. Kennedy hospital.

St. Peter's Lutheran Church Massacre

One of the most devastating and barbaric group killings that took place on Liberian soil during the Civil War occurred at St. Peter's Lutheran Church in Sinkor, Monrovia. As fighting became fierce and dangerous, many civilians, especially those from Nimba County, went in search of safe havens of shelters.

The Red Cross, having seen the severity of the crisis for the Gio and Mano people, decided to secure St. Peter's Lutheran Church as a displaced shelter. They draped huge Red Cross banners and flags on the walls of the church building to signify that the church was indeed a bona fide Red Cross facility. This, however, did not stop Doe and his troops. President Doe's Krahn soldiers were always anxious to fight against their enemy tribal members. "The soldiers have come around here every night for the past few days just before the curfew. They drive around here to make sure that nobody can go out on the streets. They drive around; sometimes they shoot in the air and rattle the gate and yell things at us," (Huband, page 153).

On the night of July 29, 1990, the unthinkable happened. President Doe's Executive Mansion Guard murdered hundreds of displaced Liberians at St. Peter's Lutheran Church. A place which had been regarded by the world as holy and sacred had become a place of massacre. Harry Maniba, former Vice-President, told Mark Huband, "Some people said they saw Doe at the Lutheran Church. Doe's cousin, Jackson E. Doe, was there, as was Colonel Goah of the Executive Mansion Guard" (Huband, page 173). Huband continues to explain that "Mike Adams, the administrative counselor at the Embassy said that the United States could not protect the church. We knew they were sitting ducks and the AFL was going to them. The United States had a figure of 186 dead but this did not include bodies in the outlying buildings, said an official who was at the American embassy in Monrovia that night" (Huband, page 174).

A man by the name of Tahseen, a Palestinian whom I believe had lived in Liberia during its peaceful days, was a part of Prince Johnson's rebel group who was organizing to overthrow Doe's government. When the massacre took place, Tahseen went to the church to see for himself the gruesome deaths of civilians. He told Huband, "They made me strip off my clothes to let me inside. I saw women with their heads smashed to pieces with babies still tied to their backs. I saw the bodies of people draped over the altar; they had been butchered with knives and shot with machine guns. The floor was thick with blood and there were bodies huddled together underneath the pews where people had tried to hide."

"The crucifix had been thrown to the ground and the ceiling was riddled with bullet-holes. And then, outside in the school buildings, where there had been people sleeping, everybody was dead. People had been killed where they lay on their mattresses.

Everywhere, dead people. There must have been hundreds. Six hundred, I counted; around six hundred or maybe more. And there were people who survived and jumped over the wall and went to houses across the road. And I talked to people who said they saw the soldiers going into the houses finding these people and then taking them down to the road to the beach. I don't know what happened to them then. Then they made me leave the area" (Huband, page 174).

Huband gave another eyewitness account. "There were more than 200 AFL who came that night. They came just before the curfew, just after 7 p.m. They had come before at the same time to shoot outside, to threaten us, but they didn't come in. You see, we had a Red Cross flag on the wall and they wouldn't come in because we had the flag on the wall," said Jonny, one of St. Peter's Lutheran Church victims to Huband.

Jonny survived by the grace of God. He also chronicled many events which transpired on that night of evil. "The soldiers shot the door open and took all the food they could see inside, and they killed the woman who had the key to the warehouse after raping her. And we saw the AFL soldiers arguing over the food, and then they left...and they left guards on the gate and said that nobody could leave. The guards stood on the gate and we stayed inside. Nobody could leave and then it got dark, and then they came back again the same night. The soldiers came back. They broke in again through the door on the side of the church. There were around 200 of them; they came in, all speaking Krahn. And they began cutting a boy with a knife, and they cut and cut and came inside the church, and cut everybody with their knives and machetes. And then I heard one of them say: 'Boss, I'm tired,' so they shot. And one of my friends, Saye Dolo, he saw President Doe there. He saw Doe take off his mask. And then the next day, the death squad came back at around 5 a.m. to see if anybody was alive. They killed a person then.

But I lay there with my eyes closed and then I escaped" (Huband, pages 174-175).

According to Huband, Jonny stopped talking because he was unable to talk about the brutal ordeal he witnessed anymore. There were at least a thousand people taking refuge inside of the church. About six hundred people were killed and around one hundred and fifty were wounded. Another forty of these survivors bravely walked through the streets of the AFL-controlled territory to the hospital to receive medical care. The survivors of this tragedy had no way of knowing that this was only the beginning of more evil yet to come.

The day after the massacre, Tilly, the appointed commander of Doe's death-squad, came to the Catholic hospital. Tilly and his group checked the identity cards of all patients and staff in the hospital. They separated the Liberians from the remaining expatriate doctors, and threatened to kill all the Liberians present. The same government soldiers had busted into JFK hospital a week before, where the doctors and staff had extended their facilities because there were so many injured people. At the JFK hospital, soldiers had forced the gate opened and entered, looking for rebels. They killed many of the patients that were hospitalized.

In the midst of these atrocities, the U.S. government sent three war ships to the coast of Monrovia with 2,300 Marines aboard. Every Liberian, including me, was hoping and praying for some sort of intervention, particularly from the United States, considering the close historical ties between us. We were jubilant at the news of the Marines' arrival in our country that was about to be torn apart. We believed that at long last the United States was coming to our aid. We finally felt cared for and no longer ignored by the rest of the world, which we believed had turned a blind eye to our suffering, including the United Nations.

On the morning of August 5, 1990 U. S. Navy helicopters finally landed with only 235 Marines from the 2,300 who were already on Liberia's soil, along with vehicles, razor wire, and fresh vegetables for their skeleton staff that remained at the U. S. embassy. They had sat offshore on their enormous ship since their arrival in May, waiting for a command to take action.

To the great surprise of every Liberian and the entire West African region, the Marines did nothing but care for their embassy staff and increased security around all of their installations within the country. When those had been put in place, the USS Saipan, the enormous amphibious assault helicopter-carrier which is also a Navy ship stationed on the sea coast of Liberia, began to sail to other parts of the country evacuating foreigners that had been stranded. When these marines did what was needed to be done, they returned onboard their ship and sat and watched President Doe and his soldiers massacred hundreds of civilians in St. Peter's Lutheran Church and around the city. I am sure some of these Marines must have even wondered what their mission to Liberia was all about as they watched precious lives being brutally taken away without any intervention on their part for the sake of human rights.

This military action spoke loudly of America's "hands-off policy" for countries like Liberia whom they had once worked with but were no longer needed as "friends" unlike the Philippines, Grenada, Panama and the Gulf where the United States quickly intervened and rescued them from their crisis. Sadly, Liberia's geo-economic position was no longer considered important to America's foreign policy. With this disappointment, the African region was left with no other alternative but to immediately send in peacekeeping forces to Liberia.

This action was clearly an eye-opener and indicated to Liberians and all other African countries that America was going to stand behind its "hands-off" policy in Liberia. Herman Cohen, former U.S. Assistant Secretary of State for African Affairs (1981-88) had this to say: "I believe that Liberians had a perfectly legitimate reason to believe that we had a responsibility to take a role in the war." A similar statement was also made by Warren Clarke, former U.S. Deputy Assistant Secretary of State for African Affairs: "We are very concerned about the Liberian situation. We have a strong historical relationship." (Huband, pg. 27) Yet, American policy makers refused to intervene and rescue Liberia in its crisis.

Liberians were angry because they understood that America had initially financed Doe and enabled him to be the president of Liberia when in fact they knew he was not sufficiently qualified to run the military of Liberia, let alone the country. Later, it became apparent to the Liberian people that the U.S. Marines had come to secure the U.S. Embassy because Prince Johnson had threatened to take hostages "if there was no response from Washington of sending peacekeepers" (Huband, pages 179-181).

Not only did Prince Johnson threaten to take foreigners as hostages, but he had also come to Mamba Point where the U.S. Embassy is located. We heard later that "the United States discouraged contact with him. He was a murderer and we were very leery of him right from the beginning. We knew that Prince was not the kind of guy we were going to do business with" (Huband, page 181).

Liberians became even more outraged, very disappointed and confused about America's role in the country's Civil War. Was Prince Johnson any more of a charlatan than Samuel Doe? Did the United States not understand that Doe was a competent murderer and they had supported him all these years even though he "smelled"?

Formation of ECOMOG

The West African region immediately formed a peacekeeping force to send to my destitute country of Liberia. "Although the conflict is an internal matter, the wanton killings now going on in Liberia have made that country a slaughterhouse," said the Gambian President, Sir Dawdo Jawara, at a meeting in Banjul that established the formation of the peacekeeping force. Finally, the African neighbors surrounding Liberia stepped up to the plate.

This force was to be formed out of an already existing group of nations called the Economic Committee of West African States, (ECOWAS), which comprised fifteen African countries. It was formed in Lagos, Nigeria in 1974 and included the countries of Ghana, Guinea, Togo, Benin, Gambia, Nigeria, Niger, Burkina Faso, Mali, Liberia, Senegal, Sierra Leone, Mauritania, Cote d'Ivoire and Guinea. From this group, the region managed to establish a ceasefire monitoring group known as the Economic Community of West African States Monitoring Group, or ECOMOG. Following the ceasefire, an interim government was to be formed that would lead the country for about a year until elections could be held.

Meanwhile, unknown to the entire population of Liberia, including the group led by Prince Johnson, who had captured the western part of Monrovia, there was another motive behind the formation of the peacekeeping force that was involving the interests of Nigeria. The President of Nigeria, Ibrahim Babangida, was no stranger to President Doe. Everyone throughout West Africa knew that he had been a friend to Doe during his administration of oppression over the Liberian people. Doe, in return, named a Political Science Department at the University of Liberia after Babangida. In 1990, when Charles Taylor first invaded the country, Doe asked Babangida to assist him with arms and 2,000 troops to flush out Taylor's army.

This friendship angered Taylor and caused him to start arresting Nigerian citizens in territories under his control. In retaliation against Taylor, even before the ceasefire group was established on August 6, 1990, Nigeria, which was a member of the ceasefire group, had already sent troops to Liberia by way of the sea. Nigeria was determined to stop the war in Liberia whether any other African countries agreed to join the struggle or not.

Babangida had planned to rescue the 3,000 Nigerian citizens who were being held hostage by Taylor's forces. Unfortunately, his plan was not known to most of his African counterparts, at least, not until after they had already sent in the peacekeepers, which were believed by the people to be 'neutral' in the conflict.

President Doe refused to accept the ceasefire that had been agreed upon, which required him to resign his presidency. Prince Johnson, whose troops were already at the center of the city, could not wait for Doe to leave Monrovia and embraced the coming of ECOMOG to Liberia.

On August 24, 1990, a combined military team of 3,000 African soldiers set foot on Liberian soil to put an end to the destruction of human lives. By this time, Taylor, who had the largest rebel group in the country, had threatened to attack any foreign troops that got involved in the conflict. His target groups were mainly Nigerian and Guinean soldiers, whom he believed were allies of Doe. On the other hand, Burkina Faso and the Ivory Coast, who had offered tremendous support to Taylor during his invasion of Liberia, were also a part of ECOMOG and had also sent troops to help restore peace.

On August 30, the interim government, which had been set in place by Amos Sawyer, a political science professor at the University of Liberia, officially came into power. Other interim groups were also formed from the two major rebel groups: Prince Johnson's INPFL and Charles Taylor's NPFL rebels. ECOMOG troops, along with

Johnson's troops, were able to push Taylor out of Monrovia, which allowed ECOMOG to establish a base for troops in the city.

All of Taylor's claims regarding the fact that ECOMOG could not be trusted were proven to the rest of the region. Not only did they side with Doe's soldiers to fight against Taylor, but they also supplied arms and assistance to their troops. Their double-dealing was confirmed by the U.S. State Department (Sirleaf, page. 192).

Some Nigerian peacekeepers did not only come to keep peace, but they openly took pleasure in looting cars, metal, generators, railings materials, hospital equipment, car parts, and other valuables. Nigerian peacekeeping forces were smooth talkers who robbed Liberians when they were not looking. Because of this, they were nicknamed by Liberians as "Oga"-- which means 'chief' or 'boss' in the Nigerian Yoruba language. Many of these Nigerian peacekeepers stayed in Liberia even after the war ended.

A Dictator's Last Hours

On September 9, 1990, when Doe realized that Taylor had been driven from the city and that the peacekeepers were in control of most parts of Monrovia, he decided to leave his well-fortified Mansion to meet with ECOMOG's commander. This move would cost President Doe his life. When Doe arrived at ECOMOG's headquarters, Johnson's troops opened fire on Doe. In the end, Doe and sixty-four of his bodyguards were captured and taken to Prince Johnson's base in Caldwell. However, most Liberians and those observing the situation from other nations felt that there were some serious questions to be asked. Why was Johnson at ECOMOG headquarters? Where were the ECOMOG "peacekeepers?"

ECOMOG's entire Nigerian continent, that is soldiers who came from Nigeria for the peacekeeping, supported Doe, so why were they not protecting him? Liberians continue to wait for the truth to be revealed one day by all those that were involved.

At Johnson's headquarters, the events that occurred after Doe's capture were recorded on film for all to see. Doe, bruised and bloodied, asked to speak. "I want to say something, if you will just listen to me," he told his captors. "I never ordered anybody's execution." In response, Johnson, who sat behind a desk responded, "I'm a humanitarian," and in the same breath, he ordered the inhumane and painful torture of president Doe.

The television audience who watched this cruelty live sat in silence as Johnson gave the order to begin Doe's torture. Doe was forced by Johnson's rebels to lie down and the audience heard the loud screams as the last inflecting torture on his body was being carried out. The questions continued, followed by additional torture by Johnson's bloodthirsty rebels. Finally, Doe was asked to declare that his regime or government had been overthrown; therefore the Armed Forces should surrender to Field Marshal Prince Johnson.

Doe was captured exactly three weeks after Prince Johnson had signed the ceasefire agreement with the AFL government soldiers. There were many who believed that Doe was tricked by Prince Johnson; that is, by promising Doe that if he complied and left his fortified mansion, he would be safe. Many also speculated that Prince Johnson was working with the United States to eliminate Doe. He was heard and seen by eyewitnesses multiple times on a radio message, saying, "I have Doe," which he kept repeating, but all Prince got was silence from the U.S. embassy side.

Doe was not safe and was brutally tortured at the hands of Prince Johnson and his men. He was then locked in a bathroom in Prince Caldwell's home and guarded so that no rescue was possible. While Doe was in the bathroom, he quickly bled to death as a result of a gunshot wound he had already received, as well as from hitting his head against the bathtub.

When Johnson got the news of Doe's death, he was disappointed because he had wanted Doe to go to trial for all of the atrocities that he had committed against the Liberian people. Most Liberians desired this, as well. Finally, Doe's regime, which had begun in bloodshed, had come to an end in bloodshed. There is wisdom in the Bible passage which says, "He that lives by the sword shall die by the sword." A regime which had been joyfully received by the Liberian people had ended in destructive and painful violence. The hope of the Liberian Second Republic to bring peace, equality and tranquility to all citizens had shamefully and sadly ended in a shamble.

Evidence of Death

The legacy of Samuel Doe is a story filled with massacres, tragedies, self-ambition, greed and hatred. Dogongaro, a close friend of Nigeria's then military leader, General Babangida, a member of the Nigerian junta's Armed Forces Ruling Council (AFRC), strode purposefully along the runway of the Spriggs Payne's airfield in Monrovia, explained Mark Huband. What he saw was shocking. White bones of decayed corpses sprawled down the slope and across the mud into the swamp. Legs lay tangled together beneath falling ribs, as though these skeletal puppets were performing a medieval dance of death. Skulls lay everywhere in the cool shade of the undergrowth.

Further from the branches of the mangrove was a swamp filled with bones that had been picked clean by insects. Doe knew about this particular place, just as he knew about the Lutheran Church massacre. Did he die just as he deserved?

It is believed that the AFL held trials at Sprigg's Payne airfield during the summer. Those found guilty were taken to the end of the runway and shot to death. As they drove back from the airfield, Chris Otulan, the Nigerian major assigned to keep watch on the press, told the driver of the personnel carrier to stop as they came across another site. Old clothes from corpses lay in the mud, which was surrounded by a wall, railings and an iron gate that has been left open, as if it was welcoming its visitors to entry. The floor of St. Peter's Lutheran Church was covered with maggots. Bodies had washed away, leaving only piles of rotting clothes of the dead on the floors. Human skeletons lay huddled underneath the church pews while others were piled up next to the altar in a dark corner. On top of the stairs also lay entangled bodies on the choir balcony which testified to their vain attempts to escape their killers. Bodies hung from the broken windows, showing that the victims were killed while trying to flee. In the classrooms the bodies of adults and children were found rotting in their mattresses (Huband, page 201-202).

What a tragic history of massacre for a President of an entire nation to leave behind for his people! Was this the leader that the United States of America found fit for my country, Liberia? What did we do to deserve such a punishment from the hands of our founding fathers? One cannot fathom that President Doe of Liberia, a 'statesman', would have such a wicked mind to commit these atrocities against his own people and humankind.

Chapter 24

UNEXPECTED JOURNEYS

Ivory Coast: The First Leg of Our Journey Begins

The day of our departure for the Ivory Coast finally arrived on the twenty-first of December. Our husbands had prepared well for the journey, including securing travel passes which would allow us to safely and easily travel through every checkpoint along the way—at least, that is what we *supposed* would happen. We climbed up in the back of a huge trader truck, which was full of desperate and destitute men, women, and children who were all running away from the war. The reality of our situation was that our lives were still uncertain and our future remained unknown.

Before our departure, Laurinda and I made rice and sauce to take with us for our little ones to eat. Our journey should have only taken one day, but it ended up taking much longer. At every checkpoint, the rebels stopped our truck and commanded us to get out and walk to the guardroom. They took us in one at a time and interrogated us about our whereabouts since the war began. They also questioned us about the reasons we were leaving Liberia. Because there were over forty passengers on board the truck, this procedure took a very long time each time we stopped.

The journey was painfully tedious, but we had no choice but to continue forward. If we had chosen to stay in Liberia, our lives would have been at risk. The entire journey was plagued with harassment and insults from Taylor's rebel forces, which were in complete control of the border areas leading to the Ivory Coast. Most of these rebels did not value human lives anymore; many were even practicing cannibalism. One of these was Charles Taylor's top general, General "Butt-Naked", who is believed to have been in the habit of eating children's hearts every morning before going to the battlefront to fight. He received his nickname because he performed his voodoo rituals with no clothes on. Some days he even went to the battlefronts in the same manner. This, he believed, gave him strength and victory.

Taylor's rebels were not the only ones practicing cannibalism; it was practiced by every warring faction in Liberia. Before the war—mainly at the beginning of President Doe's regime—people, especially children, were found dead with body parts missing. Fingernails, hearts, eyes, genitals, and other body parts were used for sorcery to bring wealth and power. Others practiced cannibalism in order to acquire governmental positions. Instead of turning to God, these politicians turned to the forces of supernatural evil believing that this would help them.

When we arrived in Sanniquille, Nimba County, a rebel commander stopped us and refused to allow us to continue our journey through the night. The men asked the commander if he could show us a place to spend the night since they would not allow us to continue our journey. Unfortunately for us, he said that the only place available was one huge room in a building next to the road by their checkpoint. I believe this building was once a store that had long since been deserted. We welcomed the shelter and were grateful to rest our tired bodies for the night.

The next morning, the twenty-second of December, having slept on the floor with only a few rags between our bodies and the dirty floor, we fed the children with the food we had brought from Gbarnga and resumed our journey. As we stepped outside and saw the town of Sanniquellie in the distance beneath the early morning light, we realized even more the tragedy of the depth of damage and destruction that war creates, both on people and their surroundings. This single observation hit me very hard. Beautiful Sanniquellie, a town that was the birthplace of the Organization of the African Unity (OAU) in 1963, was no longer the same. The Civil War had completely destroyed the town. Most of its structures were burned to the ground, and the town was deserted because of the intensive fighting that took place between Taylor's rebels and government forces. Nothing was left but crumbled buildings and overgrown weeds. The few houses that had escaped destruction were covered with makeshift roofs made of sheets of zinc and palm thatches taken from palm trees.

When Taylor's rebels looted homes, they stripped them from top to bottom of anything valuable; they took doorknobs, ceilings, window frames and doors which were taken to Sanniquellie and other parts of Nimba County. The gigantic arch that once welcomed African leaders at the OAU Conference Center outside of town was faded and discolored by the hot tropical sun.

Sanniquellie was once inhabited by a good number of Mandingo people. The town fell into the hands of both government soldiers and the NPFL rebels several times before finally being captured by the NPFL troops. Before relinquishing the city, however, the government troops set it on fire so that the rebels and town citizens would not be able to make any use of it.

After the commander of Sanniquellie had checked our travel documents, our journey resumed. The ritual of getting off and on the truck was also repeated. By this time, I was able to jump in and out of that big old truck with renewed hope, knowing that at the end of the day, God willing, we would be out of Liberia, where the stain of killing and bloodshed colored the landscape like a surreal canvas. The closer we came to the border, the fewer people we saw in the villages along the road.

At last, our tedious journey came to an end when we set our feet on the soil of the last village on the road to the Ivory Coast. We stood along the Cavalla River, which divides the two countries. We could now see the border with our own eyes. We dragged ourselves out of the truck and stood on the Liberian side of the border with our children and the few plastic bags that contained our only handful of earthly possessions. The rebels sifted through everything methodically and took anything they wanted from our meager possessions. This "checking" was really just a form of looting. Rebel troops did not hesitate to steal anything and everything from the destitute civilians who had been forced to flee from the land of their birth to an unknown land just over the horizon.

My Jordan River

As I stood there, waiting for my turn to be inspected, I remained in constant prayer that these rebels would not do a thorough body check on me for fear that they would confiscate the only U.S. dollars we had. They were hidden in a scarf that I had tied around my waist and covered with my skirt. The skirt had become my uniform since our departure from Monrovia. It was the only decent clothing that I had taken from our home when we left.

As I watched these undisciplined rebels ransack our plastic bags, I quickly remembered to tie Abigail on my back, as I was in the habit of doing. I purposely stood a little further away from the rest of the crowd so that if fighting were to break out, I would be able to escape with my baby. After some pushing and shoving for household items and clothing which had been taken from other groups, they finally allowed us to cross the river.

For me, this was my Jordan River. My Jordan River was as frightening as the one that the children of Israel had crossed after coming out of Egypt to escape the clutches of their oppressor, the Pharaoh of Egypt. As we crossed the river, my heart began to cry out loud for my beloved country of Liberia and its people, especially my family whose futures seemed bleak and desolate. In the blink of an eye, my people could face execution by the wicked men who now governed the country.

When we finally set foot on the Ivorian soil, we immediately felt uncomfortable, and a deep uncertainty came upon me. None of us could speak French or any of the tribal dialects that were common to the Ivory Coast. Surprisingly, though, the Ivorian soldiers whom we met were more disciplined and orderly than our own people. We were treated kindly and nothing was taken away from us. Their only concern was making sure that we were not carrying any weapons or ammunition into their country. In no time at all, we were waved across the border.

As my dearest husband walked out of the Ivorian immigration office, he came to a complete stop, turned around, and looked back at the Cavalla River dividing us in our land of exile from our home country. He said, "I will never step foot back onto that land again." Daniel and I laughed a little when we heard Tony's statement, but he was completely serious.

Danane, the Gathering Place

Our swift and calm departure from the Ivorian checkpoint did not prepare us for what we would encounter as we walked deeper into the interior of the Ivory Coast. We traveled from the immigration checkpoint to the large border town of Danane, and ended up meeting some Liberians whom Tony had known in Liberia. There was a young lady by the name of Nako in the group, who was originally from Nimba County but was presently residing in exile in the Ivory Coast.

Nako was an angel, a godsend from above to strangers in an unknown land. When she found out that we had just arrived from Liberia, she immediately took charge of us. In no time at all, she took us to her home, which she shared with many other relatives. As late as it was, Nako went out of her way to make us some rice and soup, enough to feed our entire group. Not only did she fill our stomachs that evening with delicious food, she also gave us some warm water for our baths. Most of all, she gave up her own bedroom to me, Kemah, Laurinda, and our two daughters so that we could rest soundly after such a hard journey.

Although there was no bed in the room, there was a thin sponge mattress that she had spread out on the cement floor. She placed sheets over the thin mattress, and our grateful bodies rested in gratitude for her sacrifice. After suffering for months, I could hardly believe that God had led us to a home where we could once again sleep on a mattress. We were utterly exhausted so we went to bed early.

The next morning, Tony and Daniel decided to go into town to see if they could find anyone else they knew. They also hoped to secure some money for our families to travel to Abidjan, the capital city of the Ivory Coast. We had heard that the majority of the ELWA/SIM employees were in Abidjan, and were to be given their severance pay for the years they had worked with the mission if they travelled to Abidjan.

When they got into town, they met up with a black American married to a Liberian lady, who had worked in Monrovia for years before the outbreak of the Civil War. The man was very excited to see Daniel, whom he had known very well in Liberia. Daniel and Tony informed him of their dire situation and their need of transportation to Abidjan. He immediately promised Tony and Daniel to return the next day with some money for travel. When our husbands returned and delivered the good news to us, we were very excited and could not wait for the next day.

Though Nako had happily received us into her home, we did not want to put a great burden on her by overstaying our welcome at her already full house. As refugees, most Liberians were finding it difficult to make ends meet, so we decided to do all that we could to get on our own feet. Though the trip into town was a long way, Laurinda and I decided to go with the men the following day. We were used to walking by now, and in Liberia that meant walking while bullets had sung songs above our heads. We were excited to see the town of Danane because it was the second largest port of entry in the country for Liberian refugees. At least in Danane, we did not have to worry about being hit by stray gunfire.

After we arrived at the designated location, the man who had given Tony and Daniel a specific meeting time was nowhere to be found. We waited for two hours but he still did not show. The following day we met up with Tony's brother-in-law, George Roberts, who was on his way back to Yekepa, Liberia, where he had worked for LAMCO as an assistant accountant for payroll. We told George that we had just arrived in Danane and were trying to travel to Abidjan but did not have sufficient funds to transport all of us. He gave us $150.00 and wished us well on our journey. In return, we profusely thanked George for his kindness and said our goodbyes.

The money we had received was enough for our journey to Abidjan. However, we continued to search for our friend who had promised to secure funds for us. He was nowhere to be found.

With some frustration and disappointment, Daniel finally asked his neighbors whether the man was still living in the house. To our surprise, they told us that he did still live in that home, so we finally came to the conclusion that this man had no intention of assisting us. He must have made the promise to save face. By five o'clock in the afternoon of the next day, we were at the bus stop with our tickets for Abidjan, ready to roll. Nako had warned us about the long night bus ride to Abidjan, so we had prepared some food for the children and brought it with us.

The bus, which was almost as large as a Greyhound bus, was full to maximum capacity. When we first boarded the bus and took our seats, there was commotion everywhere. Some spoke French while others spoke tribal dialects. We had no clue what was being said around us, but no one bothered us.

By nine o'clock, the majority of the passengers had fallen asleep, including my own travel companions, with the exception of Daniel. We had a pleasant conversation in my native language of Gola, and after a while he also fell asleep. I was left sitting by myself, wide awake in a tall, towering bus. I do not like to ride in a car for a very long time, and I have a fear of heights. To me, this bus was high enough to make every flat surface on the road appear to be mountainous, which made me nervous and very aware of my surroundings. The bus made stops in every major town that we passed through so that the passengers could relieve themselves. It was a big culture shock for me to see the ease with which both men and women relieved themselves in public.

At the end of every bathroom break, everyone went to purchase food, which was sold by the side of the road. Without washing their hands, they collected their food and jumped back on the bus. Once on the bus, they ate their meal and fell asleep.

The Library Hold Up

We arrived in Abidjan at the crack of dawn. The bus slowly rolled into the station at Ajameh, which was the major open-door market in Abidjan. From there we took a taxicab to Cocody, a suburb where SIM's main Ivory Coast office was located. With the help of other Liberians, we were directed to some of SIM's missionaries who lived on the compound.

Around ten o'clock a.m., we finally found one of the missionaries we had known very well in Liberia. He took us into one of the office buildings and offered us some seats in the library, telling us, "I'll see you when I return from church." Before we had time to ask any questions, he was out of the door as quickly as our eyes could see. With our eyes wide open, we looked at each other in silence and dismay. We were surprised to be treated so insensitively by this missionary, especially given the fact that we had known him for many years in Liberia.

We were left waiting in the library with our hungry, dirty, tired and soaking-wet toddlers not knowing where we would go when night fell upon us. We were indeed shocked and disappointed by this man's cold attitude to toward us. In our hearts, we hoped that Tony would be able to continue to work for them in Abidjan, given the fact that his work had not been confined to Liberia, but had included travels for the mission to other parts of West Africa, including the Ivory Coast. Unfortunately, our reception on the SIM campus gave us no hope that Tony would be able to continue his work there.

We had no alternative but to wait in the tiny library with no fresh or clean diapers for our children. We waited for two and a half hours for the missionary leader to return. Meanwhile, Tony and Daniel took the few Ivorian francs we had and went out in search of food and water for our children while Laurinda and I continued to wait in the library. As God would have it, our husbands ran into one of Tony's college classmates, Yender Wantee, who later became the brother in-law of Nako, our hostess in Danane. Yender and his wife, Alice, were very excited to see us and could not wait for us to visit.

During this time, the missionary had returned from church and had given us $150 that had been sent to the office for Tony and me from my missionary friend and mentor, Barb Hartwig, who had served in my hometown in Liberia. I am sure Barb knew that one way or the other Tony and I would show up or connect with the office in Abidjan in that most Liberians were fleeing in that direction for refuge. Barb, who flew to her own home along with other missionaries in Liberia, knew the vast difficulties and hardship we were now faced with. So her gift was very timely and highly appreciated. After she had fled Liberia Barb later served in Ghana, West Africa and the Sudan, East Africa. She has now returned to the US after her long committed years of service and ministry in Africa.

At last the missionary told Tony and Daniel there was nothing he could do to get us settled in Abidjan. For Tony's severance pay, he would need to meet with SIM's Abidjan leadership first. We wondered why he had not given us this information upon our arrival. If he had, we could have left and found a place to rest our tired bodies.

We were saddened and disappointed by the way we had been treated by this fellow Christian, and such an attitude made us wonder whether Tony would ever receive his severance pay. Indeed, he did not receive it during our entire three-and-a-half-year stay in the Ivory Coast. And up to this day, we have not received it, and I am sure it will never be given to him.

The Wantees worked tirelessly to find us a place in the apartment building where they lived. When we combined the $150.00 dollars from Barb with the money we had carried from Liberia, we were able to rent a two-bedroom apartment for our families. The apartment was located in a decent area with indoor plumbing and electricity. During the first night at our apartment, we slept on the cement floor, but this time we had mats that had been given to us by Alice. Though the mats were not luxurious, it was better than sleeping on the bare cement floors like we did in Liberia.

The next morning, Tony and Daniel went to town and returned with two full-sized sponge mattresses for each couple and two single ones for Kemah and Boyed, Daniel and Laurinda's teenage son. With the little money that we had left, Laurinda and I went to the small open-door market and purchased some rice and ingredients to make our first Liberian food since our arrival in the Ivory Coast. I could not wait to prepare my own meals because there is nothing more special than eating your own favorite dishes. During this first week, we did not have enough money to purchase cooking pots, pans and other cooking utensils, so we borrowed a few of those and other dishes from our gracious friend, Alice.

It was difficult during those days to live with the few possessions that we were able to gather, however we were able to manage, one day at a time.

Reunions

The next week, which was the first week of January, 1991, Tony and Daniel were able to contact a few of the missionaries on the SIM Abidjan campus who had been in Liberia, but who had also been evacuated to the Ivory Coast before Monrovia came under siege. One of these missionaries was Dr. Larry Tiedje, who had worked as a dentist on the ELWA campus in Liberia. His goal was to minister to the nationals through dentistry. He assisted hundreds of Liberians and expatriates in this endeavor.

I remember a time when my mother had two wisdom teeth which were badly infected, causing her face to become swollen to the point that she could put absolutely nothing in her mouth. We sought the help of Dr. Tiedje, and with the help of my friend, Barb Hartwig, I was able to take my mother to see him in Monrovia. It took him a long time to convince my mother, beyond any reasonable doubt, that it was necessary to extract her wisdom teeth. In our country, there is a superstitious belief that if you remove a molar, it will result in death. However, more and more dental work was being done in our area, and these beliefs began to fade in the minds of the people.

Tony had his first encounter with Dr. Tiedje in Liberia when two of Tony's wisdom teeth needed to be extracted while he was at the African Bible College in Yekepa. He also returned to Dr. Tiedje when the two remaining molars needed to be removed during his vacation from the college.

Meeting Dr. Tiedje this time, Tony was not in any physical pain as he had been on previous occasions, but his emotional pain was deep. The war had devastated him to the point that he did not think he would ever return to Liberia, at least not for a very long time. He had seen that God had allowed so much injustice and violence to take place, and he could not help but wonder why God was silent to the cry of the needy and slow to rescue them from their oppressors.

Tony had seen how God had rescued us, the McGees, and many others—and that God had allowed us to safely travel to the Ivory Coast. However, my husband could not forget the others who were being tortured and murdered as each minute passed. Were we somehow better than those who still remained under affliction in our homeland? Did God fail to hear their cries for help as they continued to suffer?

Tony was not the only one questioning God about the reign of evil which had been poured down on Liberia. Many people from our country struggled to find answers to unanswerable questions, praying that God would execute justice on the evildoers who had decimated our country and massacred our people.

The Tiedjes, who had been evacuated from Monrovia to the United States with the other SIM missionaries, decided to return to Africa and settle in the Ivory Coast so that they could serve the Liberian refugee community that was growing in that country. They not only helped to bring the gospel to the suffering refugees, but they also did what they could to help with their physical needs, as well. The Tiedjes helped with rental assistance, supplied refugees with mattresses, and provided medical care and friendship to all in need. With the help of God and the Tiedjes' supporters in the United States, they were able to raise significant amounts of money to help Liberian refugees who were in transits on their way to neighboring countries like Ghana, Guinea, Nigeria, Sierra Leone, and the Ivory Coast. With their help, Christians among the Liberian community were able to meet together for worship in several locations across Abidjan each week.

By the end of the week, we decided to invite Dr. Tiedje over to our empty apartment for some Liberian food. With the little supply of food that we had, I made some palm butter and rice for us all. Palm butter is a creamy red sauce made from palm nuts, which grow on palm trees in tropical forests. We had no chairs to sit on and we only had a few dishes borrowed from Alice, so I served Dr. Tiedje's food on a plate while the rest of us (Tony, Daniel, Laurinda, and I) ate from a large pan as most Africans are accustomed to do.

Our own apartment was uncomfortably hot, so to accommodate us all, we sat in the long hallway of the apartment building. Everyone sat on the floor except for Dr. Tiedje, who sat on a small stool next to a wall so he could lean against it. We were grateful that Dr. Tiedje cared enough about us to eat this small meal with us, even in uncomfortable circumstances. This demonstration of caring meant the world to us.

With sincere love and humility, Dr. Tiedje listened as we shared our horrific war experiences with him and God's mercy towards us in bringing us to safety. These events were still very fresh in our minds, and we were still having trouble dealing with the atrocities and evil we had witnessed. Yet, it helped to sit and tell our stories to others. Dr. Tiedje graciously listened to us and empathized with us in regard to our plight. After spending several hours with us, he then took public transportation back to his home. This meager meal became the foundation of a lasting and special friendship between us and the Tiedje family.

After our visit with Dr. Tiedje, Tony met another friend from the Cocody SIM compound named Brian Bliss. Brian was the son of Tony's college professors, Bart and Ruth Bliss, from the African Bible College. Ruth sang the closing song at our wedding; she was also Tony's creative writing professor. As a student at ABC, Tony and Brian became good friends, but when the Civil War erupted everyone went their separate ways. Brian had married his wife, Kathy, and had moved to the Ivory Coast to serve in the town of Bouake at a missionary children's boarding school called International Christian Academy (ICA).

In April, after Brian and Kathy understood the extent of the difficulties we had survived, they asked us to visit them in Bouake, where we could rest for a while. I immediately took a liking to Kathy as she openly welcomed us into her home. This was a request we could not refuse. Our state of mind was very fragile at this time. We immediately left with them to go to Bouake. Upon our arrival, we were pleasantly surprised by a visit from another missionary friend,

Bruce Pinke. Bruce had heard that Tony had been killed during the war, so with tears rolling down his cheeks he repeatedly thanked God for being able to see us once again. At the end of our visit with Bruce, we said our goodbyes and went to sleep in a nice, comfy bed. You can only imagine how wonderful this must have felt to our weary bodies! We had not slept in a bed for a very long time.

We went to bed with the expectation of having a good night's sleep. Early the next morning, we awoke to the loud sound of gunfire. I was immediately terrified after all that we had been through in the war zone in Liberia. Tony and I began to wonder if there was an attack taking place on the leadership of the Ivory Coast. We did not want to disturb Brian and Kathy so we decided to pray and ask God for protection in case we were being caught up in another war in this foreign land.

We both tried to suppress our fears as much as possible and stayed in bed until Brian and Kathy got up. We told them about the shooting and they told us that a military barracks was located next to the school campus. The shootings we had heard were regular early morning exercises for the military. They felt terrible for not warning us about the practice shooting before going to bed.

We stayed in Bouake with our dear friends for one week, grateful for the time of relaxation and refreshment that had so generously been shared with us, a small haven of peace in the middle of our storm. With each day, more and more Liberians fled our homeland and came to Ivory Coast and other neighboring countries. A few of these refugees came to Aquado, a tiny village that was only a few miles from our apartment. As the Liberian communities grew, our needs grew. Most people lived on funds sent to them by friends, family members, and overseas relatives, especially those from the United States. Sadly, many of them wasted the little money they had on pleasurable luxuries in the city of Abidjan, such as nightclubs and lavish lifestyles. Liberians became known to the Ivoiriens as "Pettis Americans," meaning "Little Americans", because they believed that Liberians were rich based on their love of pleasure and entertainment.

Abidjan became a city of transit for Liberians who had the opportunity to travel overseas and reunite with their families separated by the war. Many did absolutely nothing to provide or plan for a better future, nor did they plan for their return to Liberia when the war might someday come to an end. Only a few enrolled their children in the Ivorian school system, and very few tried to find jobs. Indeed, it was difficult for refugees to find employment with the Ivorian government or in the private sector.

One of the few occupations available to Liberians and other foreigners was working for Ivorian families in their homes. While most Liberians struggled to make a living, Ivoirians who owned rental homes noticed how some privileged Liberians were able to afford a higher standard of living with the support that was sent to them from their families overseas, mainly from those living in the United States. These homeowners began to increase rental prices on their properties. Somehow, and by the grace of God, many of my fellow Liberians were able to survive in the city of Abidjan.

Chapter 25

AKOUEDO VILLAGE: MINISTRY IN EXILE

The Founding of Akouedo Christian Fellowship

We had only been in our apartment in Abidjan for a few months when the population of Liberians swelled from a handful to a significant number. I began to notice this growing population of Liberians and thought it would be an excellent idea to start a Bible study for our countrymen, with the hope that it might become a church one day. My hope fell on deaf ears. Tony was not interested and said,

"Beth, I do not feel like getting involved in anything presently. With everything that I've gone through and the things I have seen in Liberia, - it is enough for me."

As we had just arrived in Abidjan, Tony and I were doing nothing to occupy our time except for visiting with other refugees who had similar living situations and recounting the stories of horror and terror that we had all experienced in Liberia. This was how all Liberians who had experienced evil face to face during the Civil War sought to cope with it all. As Liberians, relationships for us are all-important, and finding ourselves in a strange land where we could not speak the language (French) even made it more difficult for us. For that reason it was vital to fill our days by sharing food together and simply enjoy one another's company.

I decided to drop the topic from our discussions and not to push it upon Tony. However, I vowed not to completely let go of the idea, but to pursue it gently as I tried to understand what was going on in my husband's mind. I prayed repeatedly that God would reveal the nature of Tony's discouragement, especially those issues which were hindering his relationship with God. I finally realized that Tony was struggling with one of the most common questions asked by mankind: "Why would a good God allow evil to exist?" In Tony's case, the question was a little more specific: "Why would a true and loving God allow so many human lives to be destroyed so violently?"

Tony had become confused and even angered at the injustice of the evildoers that God had allowed to reign over our country. As a result, Tony did not have any motivation to start a church or even a Bible study group among us in the village. I continued to pray for my beloved husband and began to encourage him to get past all of the troubled thoughts that were plaguing him. I reminded him that it was important for him to continue forward if only for the one fact that through all of these injustices, God had seen fit to allow him to survive. Surely, God must have done that for a reason. Surely, God's purpose was for Tony to testify about His love and His power to save, despite what seemed at the time to be an impossible claim for Tony to make with true conviction.

I refused to accept Tony's "no." With the help of my friends Alice and Laurinda, we began to bring up the issue more often to our husbands, hoping and praying that God would move them to start the ministry that was so desperately needed among us. Finally, Tony agreed to start the Bible study on one condition: we must have more than ten people at the meeting, not counting those of us who lived at the apartment building. With this ultimatum placed before us, we set our minds on finding people to attend the Bible study. We told most of the Liberian refugee community that lived in the village with us. On the first night of the Bible study, we managed to find a few more than ten people to attend. The following week, Tony said there would need to at least be fifteen people in attendance. As God would have it, we had over twenty attendees that evening.

Finally, Tony decided he would continue the Bible study, and this is how the Akouedo Christian Fellowship was born. The "Fellowship," as we called it, grew into a church which reached out to Liberian refugees in the area. With the help of Dr. Tiedje, three other Liberian Fellowships were soon established in other parts of Abidjan. Soon we were able to rent a house with five bedrooms for both of our families and another friend with gifts sent to us by friends. We also received some funding from Dr. Tiedje for the work Tony did with him. The house was located outside the city, close to the largest garbage dump in Abidjan. This dump was one of the biggest I have ever seen in my life. It was nasty and smelled horrible; flies and mosquitoes swarmed around the site. Thankfully, we were still able to use our home as the meeting place for the church, despite the smell.

Serving the Liberian Refugees' Community

One day, we received an unexpected visit from Dr. Tiedje. He informed Tony that he had just received news that his father was in critical condition in the United States. Dr. Tiedje would have to leave as soon as possible, and Tony would need to take over the purchasing of food, medicines and other necessary items for the refugees who were in transit. He left the next day, praying that he would arrive in America in time to meet his father alive in the hospital.

Early the next day, Tony went to town and returned with a huge sum of Ivorian money and some American dollars from Dr. Tiedje which he had withdrawn from the bank. When I saw how much money Tony had brought home, I was frightened because we could easily be killed for such a huge amount of money, even if it did not belong to us. As refugees, we barely had enough money of our own to purchase food and necessities.

The money that Tony brought into our home could have easily bought a large amount of land and even built us some decent homes on it back in Liberia. However, I told Tony that we needed to pray to survive the night so that he could take the money to the bank as soon as morning arrived. I made him promise never to bring this amount of money into our home ever again. I did not want to get beaten or killed for possessing so much money that did not belong to us. God answered my prayer and we were safe through the night. Thankfully, Tony honored my request—he never again brought money home with him during our stay in Ivory Coast.

Dr. Tiedje returned to Abidjan a few weeks later, after his father had passed and was laid to rest. Tony reported every transaction to him, and Dr. Tiedje commented in his report to SIM that Tony was a reliable resource and that he would like him to continue his work. Tony took over this part of Dr. Tiedje's job from that day forward. Although Tony continued to help refugees while in exile, he struggled with the thought of giving food to the people who had killed some members of his own family and friends while fighting in Liberia as rebels. A few of these savages had managed to survive the war by fleeing to the Ivory Coast and sought our help once they arrived. These people also depended upon the good grace of Dr. Tiedje and his ministry. We had many questions in our minds about this conflict. Should we give food to people who had destroyed the lives of others? Should we allow them to suffer and die in shame and disgrace in the same manner as they had treated thousands of others?

When Africans are young, they are told by their parents and adult relatives that they are to wait for the right time to take revenge upon those that have hurt them. As the war progressed, this traditional advice resonated in the minds of many people, and many chose to deliberately harm those who had wronged them in Liberia. According to our tradition, this was the perfect time to pay back the killers in a manner that they deserved. Tony was in charge, and he could have refused aid to anyone. Many people came to him and identified the rebels who had gang-raped and killed their sisters or mothers. The intense pain residing in his heart cried out loudly within its confines: revenge, revenge. But Tony chose a path that would not allow the circle of violence to continue its evil journey. He looked into these murderers' eyes and chose to show mercy.

Later, some of these very men came to the Fellowship Church he had started among the refugees. With the help of God, who first forgave us for our own sinful nature, Tony was able to forgive and preach the Word of God to them about the true love of God and the forgiveness He freely offers to His beloved children. This was a very difficult lesson for my husband and me to learn and accept, but through His divine power alone, many who had been unforgiving learned to forgive because of the Great Forgiver who had forgiven them.

Pursue of a Better Future

As the war raged on in Liberia, our stay in Ivory Coast lengthened. Tony continued to work with Dr. Tiedje, but we also decided to seek opportunities to become better educated so that we could better our own lives. Tony discussed our plan with our German friend, Hartmut Stricker, who had returned to Germany after his mission work in Liberia was finished. Hartmut had always wanted my husband to visit Germany and wasted no time finding a school for us, a home for us to live in, and enough support to cover our cost of living for the first school year.

As time for our departure drew closer, my heart grew heavy, uncertain about our plan. At first, I decided not to tell Tony about my fears, but rather to pray. The more I prayed, the more troubled I became. No element of the trip inspired me anymore, and I finally decided to share my fears and apprehension with Tony. He did not receive this news very well and argued that Hartmut had gone to such extraordinary lengths to make this trip possible that we could not possibly change our minds.

The uncertainty I felt about the trip continued to rage in my mind, and within that time I heard on the BBC's World News that some African immigrants had been killed in Germany by a group of "skinheads." According to the news, this group did not just kill these particular Africans; they were also targeting *all* African immigrants who lived in Germany.

I said to Tony, "You see? This is God's way of telling us not to go to Germany. Based on this news, I am not going to Germany."

In some ways, Tony understood my fear, but he struggled with the fact that he had to tell Hartmut about our change in plans. I could see that Tony was saddened by my decision and did not want to disappoint his good friend, one who had helped him in so many ways when we lived in Liberia. He feared our decision might injure our relationship with Hartmut, so he prayed for a couple of weeks, asking God for wisdom to handle the situation with care and grace. Nevertheless, Hartmut was greatly disappointed and even angry about our decision when we finally informed him. His anger was rightly understood, however, we could not put our family's life in danger, knowingly aware of what was happening to immigrants in Germany.

Chapter 26

A NEW COUNTRY ON A NEW CONTINENT

Getting Visas

A couple of months later, Dr. Tiedje asked Tony if he had considered furthering his education. Tony, in response, explained the events that had transpired with our failed trip to Germany. Dr. Tiedje urged Tony to apply to Denver Seminary in Colorado in the United States. After a time of prayer, we applied to the seminary and included an excellent letter of recommendation from Dr. Tiedje. Denver Seminary accepted Tony as a full-time student in their master of divinity (M.Div.) program and he was granted a full tuition scholarship to cover his four years of study.

We had to obtain visas from the U.S. Embassy before we could enter the United States. For refugees in Abidjan at this time, it was very difficult to be issued U.S. visas. As God would have it, our applications were finally accepted after Tony was able to demonstrate to a U.S. Embassy consulate named Lisa that his motive to attend seminary was sincere. As part of our interview questions, Lisa asked Tony to name the first five books of the Old Testament, to which Tony replied correctly, adding the next two for emphasis. "In case you wanted to know those as well," he said with a smile.

Tony passed Lisa's exam, but she then told Tony that she could issue him a visa to travel to the U. S. only if he would leave me and our daughter Abigail in Ivory Coast.

Tony looked Lisa straight in the eyes and asked, "How can I say that I am going to study God's Word and abandon my wife and daughter who are residing in a foreign country as refugees? If you refuse to issue visas to them, then you might as well deny all of us because I will not leave my wife and daughter in Ivory Coast without my protection."

Lisa looked Tony in the eye, and with a hint of shame in her voice said, "You are the very first Liberian that has ever refused a U.S. visa for not allowing your family to accompany you, and for this reason I will grant visas to you and your family." Lisa asked Tony if he had already purchased his airline tickets to travel to Denver.

Tony replied, "How can I invest in something that I have not even received? You have not given me the visas, so then how can I purchase tickets that would cost me thousands of dollars?"

I think Tony was enjoying every minute of his conversation with Lisa. His honest responses reassured her that our motives for coming to America were truthful.

Lisa said, "Go purchase your tickets and come back to me for your visas."

We left the U.S. Embassy praising God for His intervention on our behalf that day. We went directly to SIM's office in Cocody, and informed the West Africa Field Administrator (WAFA) director, John Shea, about the difficult questioning session Tony had experienced at the embassy. The following morning, Mr. Shea visited the U. S. embassy and expressed his concern for us and all other Liberians who must have gone through similar grueling and unusual questioning at the embassy by Lisa. He expressed his concern at what the Liberian government may do if they got to know how Liberians were being treated and belittled when they came for visas at the U. S. embassy. He feared that such condescending treatment might be reciprocated towards American citizens who request visas from the Liberian government to enter Liberia. After his visit, SIM immediately purchased our tickets with funding that had been provided by Dr. Tiedje as we were later informed.

After living in the Ivory Coast for about three and a half years, our departure date was quickly approaching and Tony needed to tie all loose ends involving his leadership role in the refugee church which he had led over the past years. By this time, we were very attached to our congregation. Our small congregation, whom we had come to love, was like family to us. Our daughter, Abigail, who was now about four and a half years old, had known no other family except the members of our refugee congregation. God had opened a door for us, and it was now time for us to step through that door in faith.

On August 5, 1993, we boarded a plane at the Abidjan airport and left for the great United States of America. Fortunately John Shea, SIM'S WAFA director at the time traveled on the plane with us giving us some insights of what to expect on our journey and while in the U S. At this time, I was seven and a half months pregnant with our second baby. My pregnancy made the trip very difficult and tiring for me. I was also afraid of flying, and for this reason I refused to go to the restroom while the plane was in the air. To use the rest room, I waited until the plane landed for refueling before going. Because of the long hours of sitting and being unable to stretch my legs, my feet became extremely swollen, numb and uncomfortable.

En route to Denver, we passed through New York City. Since our flight from Africa was late, we missed our flight to Denver and had no choice but to spend the night at a hotel. With Mr. Shea's assistance, we were able to stay at a hotel which was wonderfully elegant but bewildering at the same time. The shower in our bathroom had both hot and cold indicators on one handle, which was strange to me. I had never seen one like this; instead I was familiar with the kind with two handles, one hot and one cold. After I was completely undressed and in the bathtub, I tried everything but could not get any cold water to come out of the faucet. The water flowing from the faucet was scalding hot, burning my skin as I tested its warmth. I finally gave up and decided to use the washcloth to wipe my body down, but a shower would have felt so glorious at that moment after such a long trip.

As I walked out of the bathroom, Tony headed inside for his shower. For fear of being ridiculed or laughed at, I did not say a word as he went into the bathroom. After a few minutes of trying to get the water going, he asked, "Beth, did you take a shower?"

"Why are you asking?" I responded.

"Because the water is too hot!" he said.

At this response, I began to laugh out loud, clearly indicating to him that I had experienced the same problem with the shower. I continued to shake with laughter, unable to talk for at least five minutes. Neither one of us was able to figure out how to use that shower. This incident, our first cultural encounter in America, continues to make us laugh. Our marriage has stayed strong because we have always been able to laugh together, even in the midst of tremendous hardship, in the good times and in the bad.

The next morning, August 7, 1993, we left JFK Airport in New York City and arrived in Denver, Colorado. When the plane landed, we took Abigail's little hand and made our way through the terminal with our two small bags containing only a handful of clothing. We saw an American woman holding a poster board sign with the names Tony and Elizabeth written on it. While this may seem reassuring to the reader, my response was to grab Abigail's hand even tighter and pull her close to me. The first thing that came into my mind was that this unknown woman might kidnap my child as I had seen in American movies!

Tony immediately rescued me by taking over the conversation. Ed and Sylvia Copps introduced themselves and told us that they would be taking us to the Denver Seminary campus, where the school had provided us a two-bedroom apartment to live in while Tony was a student. This information brought such a great relief to our hearts knowing that these Americans were not here to kidnap us as we have thought earlier. Ed and Sylvia were good friends of Dr. and Mrs. Tiedje and attended the same church, Bear Valley Church. Tony had actually met Ed and Sylvia earlier on their previous trip to visit the Tiedjes in Liberia. They were now opening their arms and hearts to receive us into their own country, and we were grateful.

When we arrived at our new apartment, we saw that Ed and Sylvia, along with a few members from their church, had donated some household items and furniture to us. We stepped into a new home where everything had been set into place for us. We awoke the following morning to a brand new day, with all of its challenges awaiting us. Everything around us was strange, including the food, which made us miss and crave the food of our homeland very much.

We had heard that a college friend of Tony's from the African Bible College, Aleo Jackson, also lived in Denver and attended Denver Seminary. Aleo's wife, Dr. Patricia Devine Jackson, had been one of the top medical doctors in Liberia but was now living in Colorado. The Jacksons who also lived in the seminary housing heard of our arrival from the administrator and quickly came to our aid. They invited us over to their apartment for a delicious Liberian meal. The food immediately brought back memories of our homeland. This wonderful couple continued to look after us as we adjusted to living in the States.

On September 9, 1993, the Jacksons called and told us to come out of our apartment to see something spectacular. We quickly made our way outside of the apartment, not knowing what to expect. Tony and I watched as tiny white powder fell from the Colorado sky.

Tony asked, "Is this what they call snow?"

Pat answered, 'Yes', but not without having a good laugh at us. This was the first time in our lives to see snow, and the experience made the Bible come alive to us. Isaiah 1:18 tells us, "Though our sins are like scarlet, they shall be white as snow." For the first time since we had read this passage, it made sense.

A few days later, we met Dr. Edward Hayes, the seminary's president, who told Tony that he would start his classes in September. He then asked us to follow him for a bag of rice he had kept in his office for us. As we entered his office, I turned to Tony and said,

"Thank God that we are getting a bag of rice. This will carry us a long way." I was very excited.

Dr. Hayes put his hand into the cupboard in his office and pulled out a tiny sack of rice. He handed it to us and said, "I hope you enjoy it."

Right then laughter bubbled up inside me and I fought very hard to keep myself from laughing out loud. The moment we stepped outside the door I did begin to laugh out loud. I could not get over the sight of the "bag of rice". In Liberia, when a person says that they have a bag of rice for you, they are referring to a big bag— fifty or a hundred pounds. Rice is a staple food in Liberia, and this tiny one-pound bag of rice would be easily consumed by our small family in one or two days. On the other hand, we had to recognize his kindness in supplying even a few meals.

Woodman Valley Church

During our second week in Denver, we decided to contact the Woodman Valley Church in Colorado Springs, which had promised to support us while we were attending seminary. We had become connected with this church through Ron and Pauline Sonius, Tony's missionary parents, while we were still in Africa. After the church heard the horror of our struggle in our homeland, they decided to assist us financially while we were in the United States.

We finally contacted the Church and, got the shock of our lives. We were told by one of the church's administrators that they could not support us because the pastor who supposedly had promised this support was no longer with the church. Tony and I were devastated; our hopes were dashed. I was seven and a half months pregnant with no health insurance, so we were totally reliant on this assistance from the church.

At this point, we had no idea how we would handle this new predicament. Although Tony had been awarded a full-ride scholarship at the seminary, we still needed to pay our bills, buy food and pay the rent on our campus apartment. Most of all, we needed to purchase health insurance. Tony and I began to pray for God's intervention to meet our needs.

During our third week in Colorado, we received a letter from Dr. and Mrs. Tiedje with a check enclosed for what we thought was $250. When our friend Patricia Jackson took it to the bank to be cashed, to our pleasant surprise the cashier told her that the check was written for the amount of $2,500! The Tiedjes had already purchased our plane tickets for us; in no way did we expect them to give us such a large amount of money again. To say the least, the money helped us in so many ways. We paid three months of our rent, bought some groceries and put a little away for the rainy days ahead of us.

The following week, Lee and Michelle Sonius, the son and daughter in-law of Ron and Pauline Sonius, came from South Carolina to visit us. It was a joyous reunion of close friends who understood who we were as Liberians. We hoped that they could explain the fast-paced American culture, which felt so unfamiliar to us. In addition, Patricia decided to assist me with my current medical needs. Somebody had told her that Planned Parenthood could assist me. I was now in my eighth month of pregnancy, and I knew I could have my baby at any time. After all, I had given birth to Abigail when I was eight and a half months pregnant. With my second baby, anything could happen.

Tony and I knew nothing about Planned Parenthood. When we told them of our great need for assistance, they gave us a shocking suggestion that was difficult to digest. The administrator at the Planned Parenthood office we visited told us that the only assistance they could give me was to help abort my baby. When Sis Pat and Michelle translated this message for me in plain English, my mouth dropped wide open. I could not believe what she had just told me.

By this time, Michelle was ready to escort me away from this woman and out of her office completely. I could not believe that a woman could look another woman like me in the eye, who was almost at full term in her pregnancy, and suggest terminating her pregnancy. I could not fathom why she would suggest that I should terminate the life of an innocent baby. This suggestion clearly opened my eyes to the little value that some people place on human life, especially an unborn child. It reminded me of the many horrors and evil of the Civil War that I had seen, suffered through, and struggled with in my own country, the very place I had fled for my life and for the life of my child.

The same destruction of unborn babies that I had witnessed with my own eyes was exactly what this lady was offering to do to my child. But worst of all, I was no longer in a war zone. I was in a free country that speaks against the abuse of human rights. Realizing that the killing of babies was actually happening in a safe country and the great United States for that matter, nothing could have prepared me for what I had heard in that office. After I left the office and had some time to myself to reflect on what had been suggested to me about my unborn baby, I began to wonder if America was somewhat the same as Liberia or any other country for that matter, that does not respect life, especially the one in a woman's womb.

At the end of our search for medical care which I did not receive on that day, I became discouraged with increased worry of what would happen to me and my unborn baby. I felt that the only solution to my problem was to return to Ivory Coast to deliver our baby, leaving behind my husband and our four-and-a-half-year-old daughter Abigail, who had already been enrolled in kindergarten.

Meanwhile, Tony had applied for and received a custodian job at the seminary. Our little Abigail went with us to assist with the cleaning, but after a few days Tony suggested that Abigail and I not accompany him for the cleaning. I could tell that he was having a hard time watching me pick up trash and clean toilets with him. He has always been, and continues to be, a loving and caring husband who does not like to see his family suffer.

One day, Ed and Sylvia called to check up on us, and with heavy hearts we explained to them the medical predicament we now faced. Ed and Sylvia asked us to meet with them at the church to try to figure out what to do with the situation. By this time, I was having some difficulties breathing because of the high altitude and thin air of Colorado. It seemed to be getting worse every day.

We arrived at Bear Valley Church for our scheduled appointment and discovered that Ed, who was the mission's pastor at Bear Valley Church, had already arranged for an OB/GYN who attended the church to deliver our baby. This was exciting news for us, and we were very thankful to God for answering our prayers. This doctor, who volunteered his time at the Inner City Health Center in downtown Denver, agreed to perform my weekly checkups for the next three weeks while we awaited my due date. He immediately put me on some prenatal vitamins, which I very much needed. He also instructed me to drink more water, which helped my breathing problem.

In addition, the Tiedjes introduced us to some personal friends of theirs, Gary and Karen Mitchell from Broomfield, Colorado and Ed and Sylvia Copps with whom we were now in contact with. During the Mitchell's first visit to our campus apartment, they observed our difficulties and decided to take us grocery shopping. They bought us groceries, some personal items for us and Abigail, and items for our baby who was soon to arrive. With their help and generosity, we were prepared for the arrival of our baby girl. They bought us a car seat and with everything set in place, we were ready to welcome our new little bundle into the world.

At 12:49 in the morning on November 1, 1993, I gave birth to our second baby girl, Alieya Leechelle. She was six pounds, twelve ounces. Her birth was quick and easy. My contractions started the previous evening, when we had just returned from the home of some friends from our church. Realizing that this was Halloween night, which reminded me of witchcraft activities, I prayed to God that I would not give birth to my baby on such a night. We could see that the decorations of Halloween symbolized satanic worship and demonic activities, and these activities were frightening to us. In Africa, these kinds of practices are very real, and people struggle with them every day. God answered our prayer and Alieya was born in the early morning of November.

When our daughter, Abigail, started school in August of that same year and began celebrating holidays with her friends, Halloween was the only day that we did not allow her to celebrate. In fact, we would keep her home from school for the day. Because of our experience with witchcraft, the general public's acceptance of this holiday was confusing to us.

The Mitchells did more than assist with the birth of our baby; they remained in our lives throughout our studies at the seminary. They helped to secure other sources of financing through their home church, and in particular, through their Sunday school class. Later, while we were on the mission field in Ethiopia, the Mitchells continued to support us. Up to this day they continue to play a huge role in our lives and in the lives of our kids who call them their grandparents.

Another couple, Allen and Mercedes Green, also sacrificially served and supported us. Mercedes helped me with Abigail after I had given birth to Alieya. She took Abigail to her home for weekends, which gave me some time to rest. The Greens have remained faithful supporters of our ministry and we love them so dearly. There are so many others who showered us with continuing love: Calvin and Louise Richards, Terry and Beth O'Malley, Doug and Terry Erlich, Roger and Sheryl Shoop, Jim and Jean Adkins, and the late Willis Mouttet and his wife, Sue. These men and women of God demonstrated to us the principles of brotherly love by accepting us as we were and opening their arms and homes to us when we needed it the most. They became our family when we had none of our own on this continent. With their assistance and Tony's custodial job, we were able to live comfortably while we studied at Denver Seminary. We also began to travel and speak at various churches and mission conferences in the United States.

Death Announcement

Soon after Alieya was born, I began to take some classes in the counseling program at Denver Seminary while Tony continued his theological studies. In the end, I earned a two-year certificate in the program, which later came in handy during our four and a half years of ministry in Ethiopia as missionaries in 1998-2004. God allowed me to be used for His kingdom in reaching out to hurting people in our church, The International Evangelical church of Addis Ababa, and even across the border to Sudan. We had lost contact with our family as the war continued to rage on in Liberia. The news on American television was limited, so we found whatever details we could get on the BBC news. Every night as we listened to the radio, we heard gruesome reports of what was happening in our homeland. We wondered if our families were still alive.

Nothing is more depressing or worrisome than not knowing if your loved ones are still alive, or whether you will ever see them again. I was the only member of my family to escape the horror and terror of the bloodshed that continued in Liberia, and almost every day and night, I cried for my country and my family that was still trapped there. My increased worries and lack of sleep caused me to develop a chronic stomach ulcer. I was also dealing with severe backaches caused by carrying Abigail on my back during our escape from Liberia.

It was a little over two years after we landed in Colorado that we received a letter from one of my brothers informing me that my family was alive. This news was so exciting to me that I could not hold back my tears. They asked us to do all we could to get them out of the village in Bong County where they were taking refuge. Immediately, Tony and I found some money to send to our friends Lee and Michelle, who had returned to Liberia. My family was finally resettled in Monrovia, where we began to communicate on a regular basis with them.

My parents told us the horrific experiences they faced during the heat of the war. In the midst of all of their difficulties, they had received news from people who claimed to had seen us during our escape from Liberia. However, they believed that Tony and I had been killed. In tears and excitement, they described to us how much they had cried and mourned our deaths. My mother's health had been adversely affected by the news that we were lost, and she became despairing. Life seemed hopeless and unfair, and she had no desire to remain alive.

My family did not know of the birth of Alieya. They did not know that we had traveled to the United States. After we had just resettled them in Monrovia, a renewed round of fighting once again broke out in the ELWA area where they were staying. We heard how quickly the fighting was escalating, and were able to send some money to my family to help them escape to Ivory Coast. For several years we rented a home for them and continued to provide financial assistance for them.

As my family settled into their new lives as refugees, the government of Ivory Coast began to experience its own instability. It was not long before another civil war broke out in the Ivory Coast, and my family was forced to flee back into Liberia. Once again, we found the funds to help them escape to safety in our homeland of Liberia. We continued our support for our family, and remained in constant contact with them.

Ministering In America

Our lives continued to be busy with seminary classes, and two children added to the chores of everyday family life. On March 4th,

1996, we were again blessed with another baby girl, Antoinette Pauline, who was cute as a button. She was quiet and very easy to please, a character she still has today. During my pregnancy with Antoinette, I believed I was pregnant with a baby boy, whom I longed to have. I picked the name Anthony as my baby's name. He was to be the junior for his father, Anthony Weedor.

About two months before my delivery, an ultrasound revealed that our baby was a girl. Deep down in my heart I had hoped that the information was not true, that I would have a boy. When my baby was born, the nurse joyfully announced to Tony and me, "It's a girl!" I turned around and looked at my husband's face to see his reaction, but did not see any glimpse of disappointment in his face. Tony, unlike most African men, was never bothered about us having girls. He was always thankful that God had blessed our marriage with beautiful and healthy children, no matter what gender they came in.

My classes at the seminary were held in the evenings so that Tony could take over the children's care after he arrived home from his own busy day. I would prepare our dinner and have it ready to be eaten by the time Tony came home from class. We quickly ate, and off I ran to class. By the time my classes were over and I returned home, Tony had lovingly tucked our kids into bed for the night and was digging into his homework.

As a full-time international student, Tony was not allowed to work more hours than he attended at school. This schedule fit perfectly with his job as a "student window-washer" because the owners of the business were also seminary students who allowed him to work under these restrictions. The problem with this arrangement was that the money he earned was not enough to meet the financial needs of our family and at the same time provide for our extended families in Liberia. We became more dependent on our friends and the little support provided to us by a few local churches, especially our home church, Bear Valley Church. Eventually God opened more doors for us among other churches and individual supporters in the Rocky Mountain region.

One of these individuals was a man named Dr. Bentley Tate, who was also working on his Master of Divinity degree at Denver Seminary. He had already earned his medical degree and was working as an emergency room doctor at one of Colorado's local hospitals. Tony met Bentley in one of his classes and discovered that he was also missions-minded, as we were. Bentley helped us get to know other parts of Colorado. He took us to Colorado Springs to see the Garden of the Gods, one of the most breathtaking and colorful landmarks in the Centennial State. He also gave us a new printer after our old, broken-down printer died one morning, just before Tony had to turn in a long paper. We were touched by his generosity and kindness to us in so many ways. He later became a major donor for our ministry overseas and here in the U.S. Bentley and his family became members of our family, and our kids referred to him as Uncle Bentley.

In our second year at the seminary, the Lord began to mold our minds and hearts towards returning to Africa for the purpose of ministry. We were motivated to return to our own continent, remembering the positive impact of other Christians on our own lives there. At this time, we did not know where we would go. Liberia was still at war, so the possibility of returning to our homeland seemed slim.

Elroy and Debbie Thiezsen, from Nebraska, were among the many that went out of their way to help us attain this goal. They supported us financially and spiritually. Their home church embraced us and asked us often to speak at their mission conferences. At the time, we did not have our own transport to travel to Nebraska from

Colorado, but Elroy would drive from O'Neil, Nebraska, to Colorado to chauffeur us back to his town to speak at Faith Community Church, and later take us back to Colorado. Their home was always open to us. Debbie made us feel at home whenever we were there. We were part of their family.

During this time in seminary we continued to travel to many parts of the United States, especially in the Rocky Mountain region. We spoke in churches during their mission conferences and helped make people aware of the differences between Islam and Christianity. As we shared these differences with others, it was a reminder to our own hearts about our own family members who did not possess the same Christian beliefs as we did. I struggled with this every day, constantly praying that, one day, my family members would accept Christ into their lives as their Lord and Savior, as their only hope in life and in death.

In 1996, a year before Tony was to graduate from seminary, we decided to find an organization that could help us to return to Africa. We prayed that God would lead us to the right place and that he would provide the means to get us there. After several months of praying, we finally made a decision to join SIM, this time as missionaries, not as national employees as Tony was in Liberia, with the hope that we would be sent to Ethiopia (because of its strategic location in the horn of Africa). Ethiopia is surrounded by many Islamic countries, and we knew there would be many opportunities for us to share the gospel as Muslim converts like ourselves.

In July, we traveled with SIM to Charlotte, North Carolina, to go through SIM's membership training and orientation. We were officially approved and given a field assignment to go to Ethiopia. Filled with excitement, we immediately began to raise financial support for our departure, but not without some bumps and trials along the way. In fact, during our time at SIM's headquarters for orientation, a SIM missionary who had once lived in Liberia confronted us with this question:

"How do you think you are going to raise all of this money needed before going to Ethiopia when you were not born in America and do not have any family connections with these churches?"

My dear husband looked straight into this man's eyes and answered, "Exactly the same way other missionaries raise their supports."

The question from this missionary came as a surprise. We decided to take it as a challenge for us to push forward with our plans. Missions, as most people thought of it in Africa and America was not something done by black people. Everyone who came to Africa as a missionary when I was growing up was either American or European. Tony and I were the first Africans to join SIM with the plan of returning to Africa, our own continent, to our own people, with the ability to possibly minister in our own language. Nevertheless, we knew that our journey would be long and difficult.

Based on these factors, we prayed fervently, asking God that if it was His will for us to go to Ethiopia, He would reveal it to us by providing the funds needed for our trip. Once again, God proved Himself to be true in the process. Many people at SIM were greatly surprised when we raised the money for our family of five within a year, but our plans were not all plain sailing. In June of 1997, during an appointment with my OB/GYN and intending to have my "tubes tied," I found out I was pregnant again.

The news was not only shocking to us but also a setback in our support raising. The amount that needed to be raised increased significantly with the addition of another child to our family. When the news was given to me by my doctor, I broke down crying. The doctor, who was also a Christian, became a little saddened for me and sent in his receptionist to console me, a lady whom I have come to love and respect. God used Karen to minister to my heart in my disappointment.

With our support almost complete, I had been ready to conquer Ethiopia for Christ. But God, in His own timing and plan had said, "Slow down Beth. Slow way down! Wait and watch me lead this family." I can tell you that letting go was not easy for me. I cried and questioned God a lot. I did not want to see myself loading another baby into a car seat in our van and heading for those endless U.S. highways and into churches to raise support any longer. But God reminded me of one His promises in scripture which says: My grace is sufficient for you, for my power is made perfect in weakness. (2Corinthians 12: 8) In the end, God used the birth of our son, Anthony Larry Joshua, commonly called T. J., to teach us something great in our lives. He opened doors of opportunity for ministry that never would have been opened for us had we left for Ethiopia that year.

T. J. was born on March 14, 1998. He was long with huge palms and pop eyes like one of my brothers, Ebenezer, commonly called Debah. I was thankful for his birth. In a quiet voice I asked my doctor to go ahead with my tubal ligation. I was done! When our baby entered this world and the nurse announced his sex, I closed my eyes and absorbed every minute of that moment in my life. I shed tears of joy and was once more reminded of God's grace in my life. I could not have asked God for anything more than this wonderful gift of life. As usual, Tony was his normal self, his expression no different than when his girls were born.

Through God's providence, at the end of 1997 right after our graduation, while I was still pregnant with T. J., we had raised the required amount needed for our family of six. We gave praise to God for providing churches and loving individuals who believed in us and our vision for a ministry in Africa. They seemed to grasp the idea that we might be even more effective than previous missionaries because we knew and understood the culture, with the added bonus that we could adapt to most circumstances.

We have seen God's mighty work displayed in our own lives. We believed that God was not only the God of America and Europe, but the God of Africa and the rest of the world, as well. Once again, Dr. and Mrs. Tiedje became incredible partners and supporters for our ministry. They paid for all our outgoing expenses, an amount that needed to be raised before SIM would give us the green light to leave for Ethiopia. Another couple, Dave and Vicky Andrea, provided a great amount of financial support as well. Together, both of these gifts sent us on the road to Ethiopia for the next four to five years.

Meanwhile, a lot had happened in Liberia after we escaped in July, 1989, and the situation there had continued to be volatile. In October 1991, after the death of President Samuel Doe, West African peacekeepers entered Monrovia and the warring factions accepted a cease-fire. But Charles Taylor and his rebels continued to cause trouble. When the interim government imposed an economic blockade on Taylor's territories, he responded by stopping the transportation of all food supplies into the city of Monrovia, which relied heavily on food crops from his Gbarnga, Lofa and Nimba territories.

The food shortage caused the people to turn to Taylor for help, since he controlled eighty per cent of the country and much of the agricultural land. It did not matter that Taylor was exploiting the natural resources of the Liberian people, selling them for thousands of dollars to foreign companies in France, China, and other countries hungry for Liberian resources such as gold, diamonds, iron ore, and timber.

The proceeds of these sales bought more arms for Taylor. As the so-called ceasefire was being observed, Taylor continued to stockpile arms which he put to use in his "Operation Octopus" war in 1992. On November 7, 1992, another cease-fire began, but lasted only a few months. Members of the Krahn and Mandingo tribes formed a new military group to fight against Taylor's forces. They fought a savage war against Taylor, and many suffered, including my own father, whom the Krahns and Mandingos captured and tortured for twenty-four hours.

After years of terrible violence and so-called peace, Taylor finally got what he wanted in July 1997: he was elected President of the Republic of Liberia. Did the Liberian people genuinely love Taylor, or was it out of sheer exhaustion from the constant fighting, suffering, fear, and intimidation that he was elected? The answer may never be known, but Liberia got some relief from the bloodshed when Taylor finally got the power he wanted.

In June 2003 the Prosecutor for the Special Court of Sierra Leone (SCSL) indicted President Charles Taylor of Liberia for creating and supporting the Revolutionary United Front, a rebel group involved in Sierra Leone's Civil War. He was also accused of harboring members of Al-Qaeda, who were believed to be connected with the bombing of the U.S. embassies in Kenya and Tanzania in 1998.

Facing growing international pressure, Taylor appeared on Liberian national television on August 10, 2003, and announced to our people that he would resign the following day, turning over his regime to Vice President Moses Blah. Taylor went into exile in Nigeria. For almost twenty years this man had wreaked havoc in our country, and now Liberia was free of him. Taylor was eventually captured on the border of Cameroon and handed over to the United Nations. On April 26, 2012, the International Criminal Court at The Hague found Taylor guilty of war crimes and crimes against humanity, and sentenced him to a jail term of fifty years.

After more than fourteen years of violent Civil War, Liberia is slowly recovering from its self-inflicted wounds: the huge loss of human lives and the destruction of much of the infrastructure of the country. The disastrous effects of the war and the ensuing problems caused our capital and most parts of the country to be without electricity and running water for over twenty-four years. Ellen Johnson-Sirleaf, who was elected President of Liberia in 2005, is now serving her second term as President. Life is slowly coming back to normal, but sad to say it will take a long time for Liberians to live secure and safe lives as they did before. We have become a nation of people who do not trust one another, least of all our government leaders. Most government officials are only in leadership to enrich themselves rather than to serve the Liberian population.

Former rebel leaders, who took away thousands of innocent lives and sent them to their early graves, still walk freely on the streets of Monrovia. The rest of the Liberian population has been left to suffer pain and anguish as the result of the brutal Civil War. They have to find room in their hearts to forgive their villains in order to live normal lives.

The best example of such forgiveness was displayed by former President Nelson Mandela of South Africa, when he said: "As I walked out the door toward the gate that would lead to my freedom, I knew if I didn't leave my bitterness and hatred behind, I'd still be in prison."

EPILOGUE

A few weeks after we had escaped from Kakata to Gbarnga, I began to struggle with the hardship of the civil war and the toll it had taken on my life and the lives of my family. I felt emptied and bitter at the same time. The more I tried to connect with God, the further He felt from me. Deeply unhappy and with a heavy heart, one day I decided to go into the privacy of my empty bedroom and pray, openly sharing my pain and sorrows with God.

As I knelt down on the dusty floor next to the mat that had become our bed, I remember saying, "God, I need to feel your presence in my life right now and please give me peace from within. I am hurting and all I see around me is pain, evil, and the devastation suffered by so many others."

The next thing I knew, I felt an intensity of sorrow such as I had never felt before and I began to cry, unable to utter one more word of prayer to God.

After a while, as I was still kneeling down on the floor shedding uncontrollable tears, I began to experience an inner peace slowly filling my broken heart, reminding me of the power of God on my life before the war and reassuring me of my future. Instantly I recalled God's faithfulness to my family and me, especially for my precious little one, Abigail. God reminded me of our deathly walk and how He had delivered us from the ELWA compound through Dupo Road to Soul Clinic, where I faced my Jordan River.

The Lord also brought to my memory how He once again rescued my daughter Abigail when she nearly died from thirst and hunger, And how He delivered us from Fendell campus, a death camp, through Gaynah's Town to Kakata, and now Gbarnga.

As I was still on my knees, I heard a word from God telling me to rise up from my pain and self-pity, because He was about to show me great things, though not without some difficult times ahead. Very quietly I said to God in response, "Yes God, use me in whatever way you find pleasing." As I said these words, I slowly rose to my feet and wiped my dust-covered knees, filled with renewed peace such as I had not felt in a long time since the ordeal of the civil war began.

From then onward, my perspective of the hardships we still faced was now seen in a different light. I was constantly reminded of God's power and protection on our lives as a family and as a nation. God began to heal my heart of the anger and the pain of injustices that I had harbored deep down in my heart.

During my destitute life in the midst of my country's civil war, never could I have imagined that the Lord was preparing me for the future ministry He had called me to, or that my ministry would start with my own husband. Tony's personal experience of this brutal war had caused him to become bitter, and resentful of those people who were causing these hardships for us and other Liberians. He felt so rejected by God that he wanted nothing to do with Him, not even to mention or speak of Him. However, God used the encounter I had with Him in my make-shift room in Gbarnga during the civil war to minister and speak out His love and greatness to others, starting with my own husband who was undergoing a similar crisis: the terrible experience of war!

I was also able to console and minister to Sudanese women who found themselves in exile in Ethiopia and reassure them that I understood their struggles because I had been there. I, like them, had gone for days without food to eat, water to drink and bathe, or clothes to wear or bedding to sleep on. I understood how it felt. But throughout my tough journey, God's presence and protection were with me always even when I could not feel Him. He was always there with me. Needless to say, my journey was difficult, but Almighty God rescued me from the ashes and carried me through those tough days, months, and years. I too, like Paul, can truly say,

Praise be to the God and Father of our Lord Jesus Christ, the Father of compassion and the God of all comfort, who comforts us in all our troubles, so that we can comfort those in any trouble with the comfort we ourselves receive from God, (2 Corinthians 1:3-4).

I knew this book would not be easy to write. I knew that I would need God's power and assistance not only for the physical labor and time required for writing the manuscript, but for the immense amount of mental and emotional stress I would undergo reliving each moment of terror my family and I had experienced during the Liberian civil war. It is only because of the encouragement of many people, one of whom is Dr. Kaeden of the University of Northern Colorado who said, "This is a story worth telling," that I have persisted in penning my story of struggles, persecution, survival, and deliverance from God.

Like a movie, memories of scenes I personally witnessed continue to possess my thoughts even today, etched indelibly and permanently within a mind that would prefer to forget rather than to remember. It is the awareness of God's sovereign fingerprint on all aspects of our lives that has given me peace throughout the retelling of my story. The words of the weeping prophet, Jeremiah, encapsulate this message:

Who can speak and have it happen if the Lord has not decreed it? Is it not from the mouth of the Most High that both calamities and good things come (Lamentations 3:37-38)?

Coming Home

In 2010 we took our children to Liberia, the ancestral home they had never known. I had returned twice before our trip in 2010: the first time was to rescue one of my brothers, who found himself in a difficult situation; the second time to say goodbye to my baby brother, Philip Siafa Fahn, who had died unexpectedly at twenty years of age of unexplained causes.

Tony returned to Liberia for the first time in 2004. Only then was he finally able to walk the land he had vowed never to set foot upon again. He and our friend Dr. Bentley Tate visited Liberia to begin a new ministry there, answering God's call to once again minister among Tony's own people. CenterPoint International, the ministry that grew out of this visit, trains Liberian pastors and laymen to bring the gospel to their fellow Liberians.

It took great courage and much prayer to return to Liberia, especially for Tony. Tony's family had disapproved of Tony's conversion from Islam to Christianity. He was a traitor to his religion and his family, according to Islam. If any still harbored ill will toward him, his visit would be the perfect time to punish him. But thank God, He has kept us safe during our travels in Liberia.

Abigail was only fourteen months old when we left Liberia. Our other children were born in the U.S. They thought of Denver as home, though they also held Ethiopia—where we spent about five years—strongly in their hearts. They had never known Liberia. This proved difficult for me. Because our culture holds fast to oral history, I would have loved and treasured having my children sit at the feet or on the laps of their grandparents and hear stories of their past generations. This was the place where African children were told of their family history from one generation to the next.

I also would have loved for my family in Liberia to have known my children on a personal level, but this was never the case.

Neither did my children have a taste for traditional Liberian food. We packed food for our children to eat during our six-week visit in Liberia, but half of our personal items in six of our suitcases were stolen while we waited in the customs line at the airport in Monrovia. This included the food we had brought. I thought we were raising Liberian children, but watching them eat rice all day, and reacting by not wanting to eat it any more, made us realize that our children were Americanized. We were forced to purchase American food, which was very expensive for us.

Regardless, my children enjoyed meeting their grandparents, great-grandmother, aunts and uncles, cousins, and various other family members. I was so thankful to God for finally giving me the desire of my heart: that my children would meet the rest of their family on both sides. A few days before our departure to the U.S., I brought my parents and my grandmother to the guesthouse where we were staying so we could spend our last days together. Those days were filled with tears. When the day to say goodbye finally arrived, my grandmother said to me in a low and sorrowful voice,

"I do not know if I will ever see you again, and if I am not able to see you again, know that I love you. And thank you for bringing your children for me to see them."

I flew into my grandmother's arms with unstoppable tears flowing from my eyes. My grandmother, who I thought was weak and frail from old age, hugged me tightly and placed a strong kiss on my cheek, as if refusing to let go. This was the first time in my entire life that my dearest grandmother had hugged and kissed me—not because she did not love me, but because this kind of showing of affection is a little foreign to our culture. We clung to each other, not wanting to separate.

The memory of that precious, first kiss will stay with me forever, and even till this day it still feels as if it had just happened. Though it warms my heart when I think of it, yet it hurts and pains me when I do remember because of our separation. As we got into the van to leave for the airport, I began to pray that God would spare her life so that I could see her once again. Abigail joined with me in this prayer, hoping that she and her newly-wedded husband would be able to travel to Liberia to see her great -grandmother once again.

On the day of our departure, every member of my family showed up to say goodbye to us. It was both a joyful and a sorrowful moment when we said our goodbyes, knowing that we might not see some of them again.

My Family

As a family, we have seen God work tremendously in our lives, mostly in times of trials. However, God in His good grace has blessed us and has never left us alone. He has proved to us that His grace is sufficient for us. As Tony and I continue to serve in ministry, God continues to lead us in such a way that we never could have imagined. In August of 2013 Tony was appointed desk director for Africa at our new ministry organization, Advancing Native Missions (ANM), located near Charlottesville, Virginia.

We continue to see God's hand moving in our children's lives as they grow into young adulthood. Abigail, who is the joy of our family and keeps everyone going by having fun, is out of college and married to a wonderful young man, Cody Mylander. Cody brings a different perspective into our family. He is soft spoken, very easy going, and down to earth. As a great observer with an excellent mind for business and numbers, he always keeps our family in line, especially when it comes to spending. Tony and I are blessed to have him as our son. Abigail and Cody have moved to Texas, where they both now work.

Leechelle has graduated from high school and is pursuing singing professionally. Antoinette will be finishing high school in Colorado this year and is planning on entering college. T. J., a sophomore in high school, is our basketball player and is working very hard in school.

The Next Project

As I fight to complete the finishing touches of this book, it is my prayer to comply with God's long-time calling on my life. My second book, which is underway, is about violence against women such as sex slave and trafficking, forced marriage, female genital mutilation and their negative effects on the woman's body and life, and lastly, women in Islam and how they are preserved in the religion. God has given me a burden for women and girls in Africa who have been violated and abused physically through these practices. As a victim of one of these barbaric acts to the female's body, I am compelled by God to speak out and help bring an end to these cruel practices. These practices leave not only bodily scars on a woman, but the mental, emotional, and psychological scars that remain with her for life are enormous.

You may say, "Beth, these old age practices are only being done to women in Africa, not in Western countries." No, my friends and sisters—these violent and human rights abuses are being inflicted on women's bodies right here in the U.S., in North America, and in most parts of Europe as I write this book, especially in London. As people from other cultural backgrounds migrate to the U.S., they bring with them their cultural practices, most of which they do behind closed doors. Please help me fight this violence against women. Let us speak out and bring an end to these crimes. Let us be the voice to the voiceless by speaking out to bring an end to these crimes and human rights abuses on women.

"The only thing necessary for the triumph of evil is for good men [and women] to do nothing." - Edmund Burke

ABBREVIATIONS AND IMPORTANT TERMS

ABC	African Bible College(s), located in Yekepa, Liberia
AFRC	Armed Forces Ruling Council
Amulet	Piece of jewelry inscribed with Koranic verses and magic symbols worn for protection from evil or as a good luck charm
Animism	Indigenous religion attributing souls to inanimate objects
BBC	British Broadcasting Corporation, a British government radio service
Cassava	Starchy, edible root crop
Congo	Americo-Liberian or descendants of freed slaves
ECOMOG	Economic Community of Monitoring Group; the West African military peacekeeping force
ELBC	A Liberian Radio Station
ELWA	Eternal Love Winning Africa
Folk Islam	A mixture of traditional religion and Islam
HAM	Amateur radio operators
Hanging heads	When a handful of people separate from a group in order to make a decision
ICA	International Christian Academy
ICM	International Church of Monrovia
Imam	One who holds the leadership position of the Mosque and Islamic community

INPFL	Independent National Patriotic Front of Liberia; Prince Johnson's rebel force
JFK	John F. Kennedy
Jinn	Supernatural spirits mentioned in the Koran
Kafu	A traditional herbal drink that is taken as an Oath
LAMCO	Liberian American Swedish Mineral Company
LAP	Liberian Action Party
Lappa	A six-inch fabric that Liberian women tie around their waist
Lodu	A table game that is played in most parts of Africa
LPN	Liberian National Police
LPP	Liberian People's Party
MOJA	Movement for Justice in Africa
Mortar and pestle	Use for grinding spices
NDPL	National Democratic Party of Liberia
NPFL	National Patriotic Front of Liberia; Charles Taylor's rebel force
OAU	Organization of African Unity, now called African Unity
PAL	Progressive Alliance of Liberia
Palava hut	A hut or shelter built in a town or village where disputes and issues pertaining to its citizens are settled. Traditionally, its roof is made out of palm fronds
Palm butter	A West African red sauce made out of palm-nuts which grow on palm trees in tropical areas
PPP	Progressive People's Party
PRC	People's Redemption Council; Samuel Doe's governing body after the 1980 coup

RUF	*Revolutionary United Front*
Sandcutter	*Similar to a soothsayer, he predicts one's future by claiming to communicate with the dead or spirits*
SIM	*Serving In Mission (formerly Sudan Interior Mission)*
Soothsayer	*One who predicts the future of another person through mystical means*
UN	*United Nations*
VOA	*Voice of America radio station*
WAFA	*SIM's Western Africa Field Area*

FOR FURTHER READING

Ardill, William. *Where Elephants Fight: An Autobiographical Account of the Liberian Civil War.* Miami: 1st Book, 2002

Huband, Mark. *The Liberian Civil War* London: Frank Cass, 1998

Johnson-Sirleaf, Ellen *This Child Will Be Great: Memoir of a Remarkable Life by Africa's First Woman President* New York: Harper, 2009.

Lamb, David. *The Africans* New York: Random House, 1982.

Parshall, Phil. *Bridges to Islam* Ada, MI: Baker, 1983

Thomas, Hugh. *The Slave Trade* New York: Simon & Schuster, 1997.

CPSIA information can be obtained at www.ICGtesting.com
Printed in the USA
LVOW11s1957130115

422667LV00002B/497/P